The Cinderella Monologues

Inspiring true stories from women who overcame adversity to thrive

Collected by Mila Johansen
featuring 22 women authors

The Cinderella Monologues

Published by: Mila Johansen, Emerald Horse Publishing
Design & layout: Mariah Miller Creative Services

First edition: 2022
Paperback ISBN: 978-1-952508-04-2
Hardcover ISBN: 978-1-952508-05-9

This book is dedicated to all women in the world who have struggled and strived to create better lives for themselves, their children and their families.

And to all the women who have dedicated their lives to helping others on our small planet through encouragement, teaching, volunteerism and counseling, giving tirelessly of themselves to any cause that furthers the optimism and hope of humankind.

We are all part of one planet and need to work together to create harmony, acceptance, understanding and encouragement for everyone of all faiths, cultures and hemispheres.

Table of Contents

Mila Johansen is a public speaker, writing and publishing coach, teacher, and writer. She is the best-selling author of five books, including, *From Cowgirl to Congress: Journey of a Suffragist on the Front Lines*. A first-person account from Jessie Haver Butler, Mila's grandmother who was the first woman lobbyist in D.C. and taught public speaking to Eleanor Roosevelt. Mila also has several more books in progress and loves to write and produce short screenplays. She has developed "The Short Book" concept giving people all over the world permission to write their "short book" first.

Email: johansenmila@gmail.com
Website: milajohansen.com

Introduction
by Mila Johansen

Faith consists in believing when it is beyond the power of reason to believe.

-Voltaire

I often speak on podcasts and summits, around the world, about my journey from poverty to abundance as a real-life Cinderella. I am tied to Cinderella through my maiden name—Grimm. There are all sorts of "real" Cinderella stories out there. Almost every woman has one to tell whether it comes from overcoming being bullied in school or at work, abusive family members or partners, life-threating illnesses, and many other adverse situations.

In all my Cinderella travels, I discovered what is thought to be one of the first "real" Cinderella stories in history. Rhodopis was a Greek slave girl who married the Pharaoh of Egypt. In the Egyptian version, the magical animal is an eagle who helps the Pharoah find Rhodopis by dropping her sandal into his lap. Instead of a cruel step-family, Rhodopis is enslaved and owned by cruel masters. The third pyramid at Giza is attributed to her.

There are life circumstances beyond our control, and beyond our imaginings which create hardships that seem insurmountable. Abuses, illnesses, deaths of parents, loved ones, children, and other life challenges that seem extreme, but can make us stronger.

I speak about my experiences to inspire other women that no matter where they came from, or what has happened to them—they can do and be anything! When the idea came to me to invite other women to tell their stories, I had already been working on my memoir over the past eight years with the working title of *The Cinderella Monologues*.

I also wrote a musical entitled *Ella, Cinderella* and produced it on the main stage in our community. In transforming my favorite story into a musical, I wanted it to have some of the depth of the movie *Ever After,* and yet show a lot of humor, to make it entertaining for stage. I worked hard to achieve that and accomplished the humorous parts with two comical fairies who serve the Fairy Godmother.

A woman who attended the production wrote me a touching letter that reached down into my core. It convinced me that *The Cinderella Monologues* needed to be an anthology of several womens' stories, not just my personal memoir. My own memoir is now entitled, *Cinderella Interrupted*.

The woman wrote me that she had been a "real" Cinderella and that my musical touched her deeply; she thanked me profusely. She told me her story, which made my Cinderella story look like a family sitcom from the 60s. She and her father were close, but he remarried the "Wicked Stepmother" who brought two daughters with her. The new mother made her do all the housework and even serve her and her daughters. Then her father died and the woman remarried a man who was even more abusive, in every way.

I cried as I read her story and knew immediately that I needed to help facilitate other women to tell their stories. I have taught writing and publishing for the past few decades and put together and published several anthologies during that time. So, I got excited and started inviting women to participate in this endeavor.

I have always been touched deeply by any Cinderella story no matter how trivial or well done. I always tear up—because of my own experience growing up as a "real" Cinderella. My favorite rendition is the movie, *Ever After*, I find myself watching it several times a year and call it "Cinderella with a bite!"

I now realize everything that happened to me built my character. Many of the events that took place in my life as a child, became the cornerstones of who I have become today. I was the Cinderella in our household. From the age of 10, I did all of the housework and much of the cooking for our family, spending about four hours a day.

I grew up in a very meager, poor home with a single mother. I often went to school without lunch and watched as all the kids who sat in front of me feasted on sack lunches. But I don't want anyone to feel sorry for me, because I later married a farmer and now have all the food I need. We donate 10,000 pounds, or more, per year of our organic citrus to local food banks. Through this story, I want to inspire people to go out and help children they know and see who may not have lunch, or a decent dinner.

Later, I found out that many of my friends had been abused. Back in those days, we didn't have talk shows to expose those kinds of travesties, so many women believed they were the only one, or that it was somehow their fault. As I grew older and heard these stories from women, I found out that 50% of my friends had been molested or raped.

When the "Me Too" movement came out, many more women I know told me they, too had fallen prey to abuse and the number rose to 75%. Shocking! Living with a single mom turned out to be very fortunate, because there were no men around to abuse me by proxy. I call that an abundance. I count my life in abundances.

As a feminist, I encourage women to speak out and report what happened to them, even if it happened long ago, even if it will ruin a family's life. One of the main reasons I tell women to speak out is so the perpetrator won't be able to abuse someone else.

My mother was a third-grade teacher, which is part of the reason I'm a teacher. She would leave at six in the morning and drive forty minutes to set up her classroom. Due to her long hours away from home, she didn't realize she had moved us into an unsavory and dangerous neighborhood. So, at a very young age, I had to get my brother up, make sure he got breakfast, and get us both out the door to walk a mile to school.

Bobby was two and a half years younger and his only chores were to take out the trash and mow the lawn of our tract home. In some ways, I think the lack of responsibility ruined him. He didn't make it out of our gangland upbringing. When we were very young, I remember we would often go to bed without dinner. Now I appreciate every single thing that is given to me.

Okay, I'm not ashamed to admit it—I am also a real-life "Pollyanna." I think the very first movie I saw in a theatre, at the age of seven, was *Pollyanna*. That one movie affected and is still affecting me, in so many ways. For one thing, I came home wishing there was a big screen on my bedroom wall so that I could watch *Pollyanna* any time I wanted. We didn't have a television in our home yet. I hadn't seen any other movie, except every Sunday night, we went across the street to my grandmother's house to watch Disney's *Sunday Night Movies*. Now, I think it's amazing that any of us can watch whatever we want at any time. I often still marvel about that.

So my life has been a lot like the "Pollyanna" attitude in the movie—"The Glad Game." At one point, she tells the story of a time with her father. Pollyanna wanted a doll, so her father said, "Let's go look in the church donation barrel." The only item they found that day was a pair of crutches. So he said, "Let's play the glad game. Let's think on something to be glad for about finding the crutches." Pollyanna thought for a minute and then said, "Well, I guess I can be glad I don't need the crutches."

That has been my attitude in life at so many times. For some reason, I've always thought I could have everything. I just had a feeling that my life was great and nothing seemed to get me down. Maybe I often went hungry, but I always remained positive. I must have been a "glass half-full" kind of girl, even back then. Now I give back in as many ways and in as many places I can. It's almost like a puzzle and is a lot of fun to do.

My famous suffragette grandmother Jessie Haver Butler became my "fairy godmother," providing me with lifelong tools and strategies I still use today. She took me under her fairy wings and encouraged me to find inspiration and fulfillment through my working endeavors. She taught me public speaking, how to write books, and to work hard for my dreams and make them a reality.

Jessie is the inspiration for this book as a real-life Cinderella. She grew up on a Colorado cattle ranch where she suffered horrific tragedies and abuses, including incest and murder. First, her baby sister Francis died, followed by her mother three days later, leaving her with an impossible workload for a ten-year-old girl. Later, her stepmother and younger brother also perished. A teacher discovered how bright Jessie was and helped her get into Smith College. Against her father's will, she escaped her tragic home life and was soon thrust into the center of several worldwide events. She never looked back. She worked on the front lines in 1920 when women won the right to vote, as the first woman lobbyist at the Capitol in Washington D.C. Her story is your story of winning the right to vote.

I include part of her story, in her own words, at the end of this book, since she was the original inspiration. I published her memoir, *From Cowgirl to Congress,* in 2020 for the 100th anniversary of women in the U.S. winning the right to vote on August 18, 1920. I included passages that are not in that book to reveal what really happened to her on that Colorado cattle ranch. In her late 90s, she often shared the podium with Gloria Steinem and Marlo Thomas and took me along.

Each story from this book's amazing authors represents what women have had to go through in centuries past, and what they are still going through now. What I find inspiring is the resilience, fortitude and creativity of each one of the women in this book, and how they overcame often unthinkable obstacles to become the amazing people they are today.

~ *Mila Johansen*

We have to reinvent ourselves until the end.

~ Oprah Winfrey

Olivia Vo is a heart-centered entrepreneur and founder of Savvy Social Enterprises specializing in virtual collaborations, live streaming events and promotions.

Laughter Yoga, as well as Practical Magic, is an integral part of her business persona and lifestyle. She loves to show people how they can experience laughter by choice, apply humor, and see levity in life. Olivia has contributed to other books such as *Heart Notes Anthology of Inspiring Letters to Matters of the Heart* and *The Impact of One Voice.*

Email: Oliviavo.savvysocialpro@gmail.com
Facebook: facebook.com/oliviavo.savvysocialpro
LinkedIn: linkedin.com/in/oliviavo-savvysocialpro
Youtube: tinyurl.com/SavvySocialPro

Chapter 1

Practical Magic: *Wingardium Leviosa*

Olivia Vo

Be so happy that when others look at you,
they become happy too!

~ Harbhajan Singh Yogi

Amidst the bleak rubble, a defiant chin raised to the sky and a severe determination seeped into the creases of her face. Communist society created dire living conditions and my mother resolved to rise above her situation. Willingness to rise above is the first component of the levitation spell, "Wingardium Leviosa," from the *Harry Potter* book series. A clear decision was imprinted in my mother's heart and that's all it took to carry her forward, to embrace me as she snuck away into the dangerous night, and escape from her homeland, Vietnam. That was the moment she would change our entire family tree and disrupt our ancestral roots.

"Whether we survive or die on this journey, at least my daughter and I will be together," she proclaimed already casting a spell of resilience over me.

Wingardium Leviosa is the magic spell of levitation. How can we practice the spell of levitation in life and business? There are five components: rising above, lifting others up, lifting the energy, lightening the load, and lightening the mood.

Growing Up Too Fast

While there was no wicked stepmother in this Cinderella story, there was a Wicked Aunt. My mother, Xuan Chi Nguyen, was tasked with grueling chores from age seven. As the eldest daughter, she took care of her siblings and cousins and tended livestock—mostly pigs. My mother's family raised pigs and butchered them for sale at the market. Xuan Chi was left in charge whenever my grandmother was away running the meat stalls.

My mom's name means "springtime" since she was born on the second day of Tết, the Vietnamese New Year. The New Year date changes yearly according to the lunar calendar, and for any official documents, my mother's birthday is recorded as February 2nd. It could be said that "spring" would be a theme for her life, with the constant renewing of self. She had to learn to transform, morph, and demonstrate these magical elements at various stages of her life. In short, "Xuan Chi" was a poetic name filled with promise.

The Wicked Aunt, the only adult present, took clear advantage of Xuan Chi to care for her children, too. Her chores included: going to the stream and carrying buckets of water, making multiple trips, washing clothes for both households by hand, preparing the meals, and chopping and gathering scraps to feed the pigs, before school. These, and many more burdensome tasks, left Xuan Chi no time for play or to even enjoy a decent childhood. Her one desire was to go to school, study, and do her homework assignments. The adults around her scoffed and dismissed her wishes and were so cruel as to deliberately pour kerosene over her notebooks. The waxy film that coated the pages made it impossible to write out her lessons. Completing chores at home was the first priority as the oldest of seven siblings and however many cousins.

While her classmates had new school uniforms and bicycles, Xuan Chi had none to boast of. Her outfits were sewn and patched together at their ragged seams. Her mother, my grandmother, was shrewd and successful in the marketplace. Yet money seemed to slip through her fingers, and the cunning Wicked Aunt was left to manage all the finances, ensuring her comfort above anyone else's. Her father, my grandfather, could have been a very good tailor, yet he squandered much of his earnings through gambling. He abused and beat Xuan Chi for even her most meager wants for food or attention. They had no intention of being parents, teaching lessons, or even understanding what was required to raise a family. Children were accessories, a necessary nuisance, extra hands, and free help.

Hearing these stories of neglect and mistreatment is painful and hard to reconcile with about my grandparents. I've never been close to them and took on the attitude of "why bother," when all they did was create a lineage of bitterness and resentment. Yet, bound by duty, my mother still cared for both of them throughout their old age.

It wasn't until the springtime of her teen years that Xuan Chi saw a way out and sought opportunities to leave her countryside home, and moved to the major port city of nearby Da Nang. She eventually earned her own money and acquired a bicycle. Her other siblings finally grew up too and did not have to rely on her as much. It seemed she finally broke free of any familial responsibilities.

However, there was one more type of bondage left, and that was the birth ties to her native country. Under Communist rule, Vietnam became a country that she no longer recognized. Living up to her name, she wanted to find the promise of a fulfilling life elsewhere. With the renewing of her mind and strength, she explored secret groups planning escapes and vowed to save and set aside money for this perilous journey.

Eventually, my mother met my father who had the same desire and ambition that matched her own. Although risky to include children, let alone babies, on the escape route, my mother could not bear to leave me behind with my grandmother or have me fall into the hands of the Wicked Aunt. My mother's younger sister, my Aunt Kim Tuyen, would also join this trip.

The Escape

The waves rocked the boat from side to side as if it was a cradle, and only the sea knew of the secret eerie lullaby. For many in their dazed stupor, they questioned if this was a dream, nightmare, or fantasy.

Thirty days at sea with no food or water. My mother is still queasy when she recalls the horrific moments and the things people did out of anguish and desperation. We are one of the countless stories of boat people who searched for a better life. As for me, the sleeping drugs to keep me quiet and numb had tapered. At 2-years-old, there must have been a greater spirit guiding my fate. Fortunately, no pirate ships threatened the boat and eventually, a container ship from Hong Kong rescued everyone. Amnesty was granted and we were safe in the refugee camps, as my parents put in their applications for America and enrolled in skills training and English classes. For two years, we anxiously waited for our turn to be transferred to the Philippines Refugee Camps, the last stop to process our paperwork.

Coming to America

Once we reached America my Father's older brother, my Uncle Nam, welcomed us in Seattle, Washington and helped our family get acclimated. My Aunt Kim headed to California to pursue her dreams, and my parents chose to relocate to Worcester, Massachusetts. Six years old by then, I would soon become a big sister to my brothers, Donald and Jimmy.

I think about all my mother did, to raise three children in a totally foreign land, as magic. Both my parents didn't know anyone and yet were able to transform our lives. Education became the top priority. All my mother's and father's hopes and dreams hinged on education as the only pathway to elevate our future. They based the move to Massachusetts solely on the fact that they had the most well-known schools, Harvard and MIT, among others. My hometown of Worcester has eleven colleges alone!

My parents took on whatever jobs they could manage and saved money to buy their first cars, first house, and other symbols of success. Growing up, we always felt provided for and family Sunday dinners were the best. It was the only time both parents were at the table with us. Throughout the week, my mother and father took turns and worked in shifts because they always wanted one parent at home. Mother would recreate so many wonderful Vietnamese dishes, so we always respected traditional cuisine. And when my brothers and I developed American palates and craved chicken nuggets or spaghetti or french fries, she found a way to adapt those recipes too.

Watching my parents' example, I also wanted to be transformed and school became my personal oasis of learning. I aspired to rise above, advance from my current situation, travel, and break free from my hometown. To that end, my mother made sure to send me off to school with a magical talisman of a single round white and light green jade stone on a gold chain. At the time, I didn't fully grasp the power of the jade stone. As I wore the necklace, the other students teased me that it looked like a "lifesaver candy," and I became embarrassed and hid it underneath my shirt. Then my mother explained to me that she had incanted beautiful blessings and poured all the dreams she had for me into this jade stone. And she promised me that as long as I wore the jade necklace I would be protected and experience serenity, tranquility, and harmony. I still have my magic jade amulet to this day and take care to harness all of its power as a stone of the heart. One day, I hope I can pass the same necklace down to my own daughter.

Meanwhile, at school I looked for Fairy Godmothers and Godfathers everywhere; they helped me explore many scholastic opportunities. Being a first-generation college graduate in my family was a tremendous milestone and I felt proud of my achievement. It stood for something and represented all that my parents had sacrificed by leaving behind the life they had known, to create a new one. Thanks to my many Fairy Godparents, I was awarded scholarships to help with college tuition. One such scholarship was my U.S. Fulbright Award after college, which led me to make a trip back to Vietnam.

Career

Making a return trip to Vietnam was also significant, as I reconnected to a culture and language I thought I had lost. I fell into teaching and discovered I had a knack for it. I would be involved with training, mentoring, and coaching in various aspects throughout my career. I've worked in sales, recruiting, and staffing, and now have created my own business within social media, online collaborations, and video live streaming. I am continuing that lineage of "firsts" as the first self-published best-selling author in my family and am on my way to the first fully established and incorporated business.

More Fairy Godparents would appear on my path and most recently, Braden Daniels has become a Fairy Godfather. He taught me the spell of levitation called *Wingardium Leviosa*. The spell has Latin roots; the English word "wing" compounded with the Latin word "arduus" means elevated and "levo" is Latin for rise. Possible translations include the "rise of the fluttering wings" and to "take flight." Regarding pronunciation, from Hermione of *Harry Potter,* it's "Wingardium LeviOsa" versus "Wingardium LeviosA."

Not only is Braden a Fairy Godfather, but he is also a performance magician and leadership strategist. He helps leaders to transform themselves and their work by uncovering our magician within. As a guest of my live stream show called "Get Your Happy On," Braden was able to demonstrate Wingardium Leviosa and indicate all the ways that I had been practicing magic all along! (The full episode can be viewed here: tinyurl.com/52mknj3e.)

Thanks to Braden, I love casting the spell of *Wingardium Leviosa* in my everyday life, business, and relationships. I share some examples below and invite you to practice this magic for yourself.

Rise Above

The pandemic of 2020 was the bleak rubble I stood upon, and the perfect condition for me to realize that the time had come to rise above the negativity, fear, and paranoia. My recruiting and staffing career had served me well, and I wanted to take advantage of every opportunity for online networking and become a virtual entrepreneur. The rewards of that decision have been miraculous and way beyond my imagination.

I've been able to meet so many heart-centered business leaders all over the world and develop meaningful relationships. One of the relationships that I am eternally grateful for is Cathy Nesbitt who trained me in my Laughter Yoga Certification and introduced me to a whole new community. Teaching Laughter Yoga to others, being a practitioner, and adopting it as a way of life for myself, has helped to release my own magical essence or ripple of influence, "ROI." This is something that I like to teach and create for others too.

Because of my parents' experiences, always playing it safe, I wanted to take bold risks. Being able to develop a business for myself, based on my own bankable skills, is a huge risk: going against the grain, and being willing to infuse my own sociable personality into it too. Just like my mother's defiance that set things in motion, so is my resolve to make this work and fulfill my heart song.

I encourage you to consider and reflect upon: ***What are the moments in your life that you can rise above?***

Lift Up Others

With my teaching background, I've found ways to be an encourager and to be a positive influence on others. I love being able to draw out someone else's potential. This characteristic parlayed well into recruiting, as I examined countless resumes and LinkedIn profiles, advocating for my job candidates and consultants, and matching them with coveted positions in top companies. Beyond the resumes, I held their hands and coached them through the entire application process of interviews, onboarding, and overseeing their assignments at client sites.

I'm currently guiding others on how to utilize live streaming technology to help their businesses soar. I'm creating flow charts and mapping out processes that can be adapted for a variety of live stream show concepts.

In considering your family, friendships, business relationships, and teams: ***What are some things you can do or say to lift them up?***

Lift the Energy

With my Laughter Yoga background, I've become recognized as a Group Energizer, especially during the Sing Your Heart Song virtual summits. I enjoy fostering an open, conducive environment for community and learning. I love utlizing various humor tools and music to raise the group's dynamic and vibrations.

One of my favorite quotes is, "Be so happy that when others look at you, they become happy too!"

Take some time and explore humor tools. I recommend HumorPoint.com, created by Robert Bostick, which curates a variety of tasteful cartoons, memes, gifs, and video clips.

Now, notice when your energy is low and what you do to raise that through movement, writing, song, or play. Then think about: ***What can you do to increase the vibrational energy of others?***

Lighten the Load

As a virtual entrepreneur, I specialize in online collaborations. When I first got started, I learned to barter with coaches and other people whom I wanted to learn from. I also love that I can connect with others across time zones and cultures. When we come together, we can leverage each other's strengths and bridge any gaps.

As I reflect upon my school and work, I have leaned more towards being a team player and have readily offered to take things off my manager's plate. I wanted to be seen as the official point of contact or go-to person and worked behind the scenes to make my manager, team, and company look good.

Social media platforms and live streaming technologies are constantly evolving at a rapid pace. I'm able to absorb and learn this information to act as a resource partner for other business owners who need a co-host, online event facilitator, or community manager.

Practicing magic requires that you know what your unique strengths and talents are. There are many assessments available to help you with this such as CliftonStrengths from Gallup, DISC Profile, Kolbe, Myers-Briggs, and Enneagrams. Once you've identified what you naturally do best, you can begin to include this in your business branding and openly discuss it with others, as well as set boundaries for preferred ways of working and communicating.

I invite you to take inventory of your magical skillsets and think about: ***Where do you best fit in when it comes to activities or projects and where can you share personal resources?***

Lighten the Mood

Finally, your mood is an important aspect of the levitation spell. With Laughter Yoga, humor, and many self-care wellness tools, we can alleviate stress and have better mental health. We can seek levity and the joy of life. We learn to recognize in each other that we are "Humor Beings" and appreciate the humor that is all around us.

If you'd like to learn more about your Humor Persona, here is a free 129-second quiz resource from Andrew Tarvin: humorthatworks.com/assessment

In this digital age of online events and meetings, let us not immediately react to stress or frustration, especially when it comes to technical difficulties or technology overload. We can overcome these temporary setbacks through breathing and humor.

Moreover, be willing to make mistakes and learn from them. Perhaps in your self-reflection, you can acknowledge these lessons with grace and compassion, then reframe and analyze them from a humorous point of view. Elbert Hubbard remarked, "The greatest mistake you can make in life is to be continually fearing you will make one."

I am grateful for the opportunity to connect with AATH (Association for Applied Therapeutic Humor), and I am in the process of further developing my certification and skills for humor application through the Humor Academy studies.

What can you do to view life lightly and blissfully? What are some things you can do to deliver delight to others?

Living a Charmed Life of Flow and Ease

I've solidified my business as a Savvy Social Strategist and am fully stepping out into this persona. Now, in this phase of my entrepreneurship, I have mastered online collaboration and I have embraced the medium of live streaming. I enjoy brainstorming show concepts with others, helping them build their video confidence, and promoting their life-changing programs, courses, and other services.

My top five CliftonStrengths include: Positivity, Empathy, Developer, and WOO (Winning Others Over), and I combine this with humor and Laughter Yoga, along with *Wingardium Leviosa*. I feel that I am practicing magic. It's my turn to be a Fairy Godmother for others!

I didn't realize it at the time, but perhaps I have been in training for this particular role. When I lived in Vietnam as a Fulbright Scholar, I was constantly socializing and making new friends. During a networking event, I decided on a whim to audition for a role in the Cinderella production (Co Be Lo Lem) being produced by a non-profit community theater group called Saigon Players.

Miraculously, I was cast as The Fairy Godmother and had a custom pink gown designed and tailored for me, complete with poofy pink silk sleeves and a golden tinsel wig. I loved every minute of rehearsals and working with the cast and director, Emily Huckson, and truly felt as if I was the star of my life. I look back on that time with fond memories and can appreciate where it's led me today in writing this chapter for *The Cinderella Monologues.*

I feel as if I am floating on my own magical path and golden brick road. Conversations are so much easier because I'm in alignment. I bring my highest and best to every interaction that I have. It feels good and easy and intuitive.

Thank you to another Fairy Godmother, Kate Unger. From Kate, I learned the importance of my core colors and how to apply them to my wardrobe and events. It was as if she waved a magic wand and allowed me to dress in harmony. I'm highly content and satisfied at this moment, and that feeling of gratitude is amazing; I am ready and looking forward to more. I've become a trusted advisor and my reputation has been built on referrals. I have virtual connections that I have been honored to get to meet in person too.

In this state of flow and ease, it's like ether, and I feel divinely guided. I can trust the divine process at work. There's an infinite greater intelligence of life that I can rest in and be at peace with. There's something magical about not solely relying on my own strength or will and surrendering to the breath of life.

I thank my mother deeply for practicing her magic and sharing her methods of transformation, spells, and special talismans with me.

Breath as Magic and Activating Your Soul Essence

There is magic already inside of you. Your breath is magic. Once you become aware of this, there is a feeling of aliveness, and you learn to be present with the breath. Here is one example of a mindful breathing exercise and meditation called, "Connecting Heaven and Earth."

I hope you will practice this meditation to supplement the spell of *Wingardium Leviosa* of rising above, lifting others up, lightening the load, lifting the energy, and lightening the mood.

- *To begin, rub your hands together, then shake them off*
- *Place hands on thighs, take a deep breath into the nose, exhale out through the mouth*

- *Circle arms above your head and hands come down in prayer position*
- *Now in one fluid motion, stretch one arm up and one arm down, be mindful of palms, fingers spread out wide, flatten your hands*
- *Hold your breath and look up*
- *Now let your breath out and look down the other hand*
- *Bring your arms together, hands together in prayer, and relax for a moment*
- *Do this again and reach up on the opposite side*
- *Look up, flatten your hands, hold your breath, LIFTING SPIRIT UP TO HEAVEN*
- *Exhale, release your breath, look down, TOUCHING DOWN TO SOLID EARTH*
- *DEEPLY FEELING THIS CONNECTION BETWEEN HEAVEN AND EARTH*
- *Take a deep breath in, circle arms up, and let breath out*
- *DO IT AGAIN*
- *Reach up all the way*
- *Inhale connecting hand to heaven*
- *Exhale, look down to hand to earth*
- *Take a breath, come into center, release, let go*

- *OTHER SIDE*
- *Reach up, flatten hand, look up, hold breath*
- *Reach down to other side*
- *Take a breath, release*
- *Lastly, bend forward from the hips, allowing your head to hang down between the upper arms*
- *Keep your feet hip-width apart and the knees flexed. Cross the arms and softly grasp each elbow with the opposite hand in rag doll position*
- *Release your elbows, gently hang this way, breathing at your own pace*
- *Begin to roll your hands up your body, stretch all the way up*
- *Then let the arms fall down to your sides*
- *Place your hands at heart center and surrender to the pulse of your magical essence*
- *Feel your breath undulate as it elevates your consciousness*
- *Whisper to yourself, "**Wingardium Leviosa**"*

Use what you've been through as fuel,
believe in yourself and be unstoppable!

~Yvonne Pierre

Dena Silliman Nielson, J.D. is a retired family law attorney who spent 25 years as a litigator focusing a majority of that time exclusively on family law. Dena is now helping professional women with children who are involved in divorce end their marriage, thrive in their new normal afterward, and hopefully never set foot in a courtroom during the process. Dena believes that, much like in her own case, divorce is not the end but can be the beginning of a beautiful new story.

Dena is the author of her first book, *Common Sense Divorce: Ten Steps to Save You Time, Money, and Worry.* She is working on her second book, *Conscious Co-Parenting: How to do it Right*, as well as a novel entitled, *Immoral Justice.* Aside from her writing, Dena has online courses available regarding divorce; a coaching program: Best Case Divorce, for those struggling through the divorce process; and she frequently speaks on the topic of divorce and co-parenting.

Email: denanielson@gmail.com
Website: DenaNielson.com
Facebook: facebook.com/dena.nielson.7
Instagram: instagram.com/denasnielson
Linkedin: linkedin.com/in/denanielson/

Chapter 2

The Unlikely Lawyer

Dena Silliman Nielson

The future belongs to those who believe in the beauty of their dreams.

~ Eleanor Roosevelt

I became a lawyer in 1993 at the age of 41. I'm sure you are wondering why anyone would do such a thing at that age. Going to law school and passing the bar exam is not easy at any age, but some say it gets a little more difficult with each passing year. However, in 1993, at the University of Oklahoma School of Law, there was an entire section of older students. I was not the oldest one there. So really, age is not the issue.

The better question is how did I—a girl from South Arkansas—graduate from the University of Oklahoma School of Law with a passion for Native American Law, and how was I going to launch into a career in that area? It seems unlikely when you think about how I got there. But for some reason, it didn't stop me. Here's a little bit of the back story to help explain.

I was born in South Arkansas and grew up there in the 50s and 60s. I had a good childhood even though I had been in three schools and four different houses by age 9. Maybe that's why moving is, and always has been, an expected part of my life.

The only professionals we knew were the teachers and the doctors we visited. Our town only had two or three lawyers then and we certainly did not know them. My family and our extended family lived simple but comfortable lives. We were for the most part, hard-working, practical, church-going Christians.

I had one sister and one brother, both several years older than me. They both went to college for one year at in-state colleges and then had other obligations. Neither of them got to finish their degrees.

Neither of my parents had been to college or followed any definite career path. During my lifetime, my dad had lots of different jobs. He was a fireman, a cook, and a farmer. He was self-employed for a while selling hot dog machines to convenience stores (that did not go well), and finally, he became an employee of the Federal Department of Agriculture. He worked many other jobs before I was born. My mother worked most of her life and all of my life. She always worked in an office as a clerk or secretary. I loved going to her office and playing secretary or reading my *Nancy Drew* mysteries.

One day in fourth grade, I was called to the principal's office. My teacher said I should take my things with me in case I had to go home. I felt scared because I had never been to the principal's office before, and I knew it would not be good news. My brother-in-law was there and said we needed to get my brother out of class as well. We drove to our house and before we got out of the car, my brother-in-law told us that Daddy had passed away that morning.

I had previously been to two great-uncle's funerals, so I knew what death and funerals looked like. But I struggled to understand how this could happen to my Daddy. He was 45 years old. He went to work on his day off, had a heart attack, and didn't come home. He was always laughing and making jokes, and he read the newspaper to me every night, while I sat on his lap—even the articles on politics. A big man with a large presence, he had lots of friends, and everyone that knew him loved him. I know this because there were lots more people at his funeral than would fit into our church. His death left a big hole in the hearts of his children. We all dealt with his death in different ways, I think.

When Daddy died, my sister was married and pregnant with her first child. So, my mom, a widow at the age of 41, was tasked with raising me and my brother alone. She had a job. That was a good thing. For a lot of years, I think my mom felt very resentful that my daddy died and left her alone. She seemed sad a lot and mad a lot. My brother, unfortunately, did not help. He was 15 when Daddy died. That age is hard enough but add to that losing your dad and you have the perfect storm for lots of problems. When my brother left for college, it was just my mom and me.

I loved school from the start and became very active in various activities in high school. I was in both Junior and Senior plays, on the Annual Staff, and on the planning committee for both the Junior and Senior Banquets. (That is what they called the prom back then.) I also worked in the summers as a retail clerk, or in my mother's office helping out. In the 60s in South Arkansas, girls who wanted to have a career were expected to grow up to be secretaries, nurses, or teachers. Otherwise, you got married right out of high school and started having babies.

The only thing that even slightly appealed to me was working in an office. When I graduated from high school, no one suggested that I pursue a scholarship or even college at all. I graduated 18th in a class of 199 so I could have probably gotten an academic scholarship had I known how to do that. My mother did not have the money for college. So, we made plans for what was within our reach.

In June 1970, I went to business school in Little Rock with two classmates. My mother had gone to this same business school from 1937-38. I don't think much had changed since then. Everything seemed so old—even the faculty! One of my classmates left after two months to go to a "real" college. My other classmate eventually got a job and was married right after we completed the course.

I found a job working in a lawyer's office and really loved it. That was my first experience with lawyers, and the first time I had thought about the possibility of becoming a lawyer. But, the reality was that it was not financially feasible for me to stay in Little Rock without my roommates. So I moved back to my mother's house and started looking for another job. I interviewed with all the lawyers in town, but no one would hire me. I ended up working at a paper plant. They made the paper strips you see on toilets in hotels and the paper on the hangers that come from the cleaners. Not exactly my dream job!

My high school sweetheart, Danny, was in the Air Force by this time, stationed in New York. It might as well have been on the other side of the world as far as I was concerned. I'd never been further than Denver, so New York seemed like another planet! He proposed after mailing me the engagement ring. That was crazy then and seems even more so now. But I accepted and we married on November 13, 1971 at age 19.

We left right after the wedding and started our new life by driving back to New York. I remember being so surprised when we crossed from Pennsylvania into New York and there was no city. In fact, there was no city for many miles. We laughed about that for years. Like many young men in those days, Danny joined the Air Force to stay out of Viet Nam and it worked for him. He was stationed in Syracuse, New York for his entire tour. We were in Syracuse together for about 2-1/2 years. During that time, I worked as a Kelly Girl in various companies. I worked at General Electric for most of the time. I loved it there. The people were so nice, and they all loved my southern accent.

When Danny got out of the Air Force, we moved back home to South Arkansas. Being back home meant that we were expected to attend church services three times a week with my mother. Although baptized when we dated in high school, Danny seemed no longer interested in going to church. So, I went alone for the most part. This probably helped precipitate our divorce. Danny was a drummer and played gigs wherever he could get one while working shifts at the paper mill. He hung out with his old friends who were all single. He smoked marijuana daily while doing who knows what else. That kind of lifestyle just didn't fit with who I was.

I felt that I had to be committed to the marriage, but when I came home from one Wednesday night service and found him standing between the legs of some girl on my kitchen counter—well, I was done. I am a firm believer that everything happens for a reason and that certainly did. Had I stayed with Danny I would never have had children. I knew that when we got married and I didn't think it would matter. But now I know it would have mattered to me.

The divorce was quick, simple, and was paid for by my mother. She seemed happy for him to be gone. After we divorced, I only saw Danny one other time. A couple of years later, he came to see me one night, unexpectedly, to apologize for what he put me through. I was never so shocked in my life. But it felt nice to hear, and I think we were both able to put it in the past after that.

So, at 23 I found myself divorced, living in my little red house on the hill, and working at the local Social Security Office. At about this time, my mother finally remarried. She married someone from the church who she had known for years. He became a super stepdad and I loved him immediately, and he clearly loved my mom. They were perfect together.

Things were good but I really wanted to move back to Little Rock. Most of my high school friends had moved away and I just really wanted a little more freedom. So, I found someone to buy my house and got a transfer to the

Social Security Office in Little Rock. With the help of a high school friend, I immediately found an apartment, and off I went.

I worked at the Social Security office full-time, but as a low-level employee, had a hard time making ends meet. So, I decided to get a second job. I started working in admissions at the nearby hospital on the weekends. Then I added a restaurant job on top of that. This extra employment really cut into my social life. I did these three jobs for about nine months until I got a little money saved and felt like I could cut one out. I quit the restaurant first.

Then I decided I needed to go to a "real" college. Otherwise, I would never have a "real" career. I still thought about the lawyer thing, but not seriously. If nothing else, I have always been a realist. I enrolled for night classes at UALR—University of Arkansas at Little Rock. I only took one class at a time and eventually had 9 hours. Finally, working two jobs and going to school at night for a while, I had the opportunity to take a job that sounded as if it would enable me to live on one salary. However, I would have to quit school because of the travel involved. The job at Social Security was easy and safe. My mother thought I was crazy for wanting to leave. "Think about your retirement," she said. At age 27, I was not thinking about my retirement. And besides, "safe" was never my thing, even then.

The job was with PCA International. Basically they hired me to travel around to various Walmarts and sell parents pictures of their kids. How hard could that be? I quit both of my jobs, did not enroll in school, and started this new adventure. The travel didn't bother me—in fact, I liked it. I had to buy a car with ample room to carry all the photos, and the boxes, along with the setup. This job proved physically demanding, but being young, I thought it was great. After putting 48,000 miles on my new car in 6 months, I began to think, "Maybe there's a better way?" The problem with these kinds of jobs is that you burn out quickly.

The company also operated the photo studios in Dillard's. I could transfer but would have to move to Tulsa. By then, my sister was living in Owasso, just outside of Tulsa. I agreed to the move even though they offered a little less money. Still, it was enough so that I wouldn't have to work two jobs; I was happy. My sister helped me find an apartment and a guy I dated in Little Rock helped me move my furniture. I was thrilled to be close to my sister and her family. I lived in Tulsa for about two years. During that time, I worked at Dillard's and occasionally had to fill in for Oklahoma City studios as well. My social life had been non-existent for quite a while, but I stayed busy with work and helping my sister with her three children and her restaurant. Going to college was a distant thought, but just not doable.

One day while at the Midwest City Dillard's, a guy came in to look at his pictures. While I was putting up the photos for him to see, I noticed his last name was "Dean." I laughed to myself thinking how funny that would be if we got married and my name would be Dena Dean. He chose his portraits, and as he left, he gave me his phone number and asked for mine. I'd never given out my number before. For some reason, I gave it to him. He called and we started dating on a semi-regular basis. He lived in Midwest City, while I still lived in Tulsa, two hours away, so it certainly was not a constant thing or a very serious relationship.

Sometimes things happen in life you just can't explain. During this same time, I had a new roommate whose boyfriend had a personnel agency and wanted to hire me. He promised I would love it. I was always up for any challenge and it sounded great, so I quit my job with PCA and became very excited about the personnel agency.

I hated it the first day. Everyone there seemed so sad, or maybe they were scared of the boss. I thought I should at least give it a week and then re-evaluate. But the second day was worse than the first. On the third day, I stayed until 10:30 a.m. and then told everyone, "thank you, but this is not a good fit for me," and I left. I was so upset that I had quit a perfectly good job for this disaster. On the way home, I cried my eyes out. As I turned into my apartment complex, a lady hit me on the passenger side of my car. Great. Here I was, 29 years old, unemployed, and now my car was probably totaled. I cried even harder. The lady that hit me kept asking if I needed an ambulance. I said, "No, I need a job!"

In the end, I was able to get my car fixed and I called my old boss at PCA to tell him what had happened. He wanted to hire me back, but there was only one catch—I had to move to Midwest City and would be permanently working at the Dillard's there. I took it and of course, that led to a more stable and serious relationship with the guy from the portrait studio—Mr. Dean.

As my 30th birthday approached, I began thinking that I might be single for the rest of my life. I had always promised myself that if I was going to have a baby, I would have that done before age 30. But here it was and there was no possibility of having a baby before age 30. Just as I found myself mildly panicking over this fact, Mr. Dean popped the question! Yes, that question. Would I be Dena Dean for the rest of my life? I laughed, and then after making sure he was serious, I said yes. We had a small wedding a few months later and a short honeymoon. Then we moved on with life. The year was 1982 and I was 30 years old.

My daughter was born in April 1984, the same month that my sister passed away, at 44 years old, from brain cancer. This was a happy and extremely sad time all at once. But it made me realize that if I wanted something I had to make it happen.

Getting my undergraduate degree had been my goal for a long time. So, I decided this was the time to start. I had been working as a legal secretary for a law firm in Oklahoma City for about two years at this point. I worked for an attorney who was about my age. We were talking about my desire to go to school, and he said, "You know, there's no reason you couldn't go to law school once you get that undergrad degree. You're certainly smart enough to do it." He had no idea what those words meant to me. But I decided right then that I would go to law school and I would become an attorney. I just wasn't sure how it would happen.

When I shared this with my mother, she was not so enthusiastic about my ability to go to law school with two kids and a husband. In fact, she said, "Just get your Paralegal Certificate. That's all you really need. You have a family to think of." But I would not be deterred. Even when I got pregnant with my son in 1986, and skipped one semester for the birth, I came right back the next semester. Unfortunately, my mother did not live to see me graduate from Junior College, University, or Law School. But I think she would have been proud anyway.

I got my undergraduate degree in Political Science/Public Service in December 1989. On the night of graduation, my family gathered for the celebration, despite the tornado warnings and sightings of nearby tornados. I remember telling everyone that this was just the first step; the next step would be law school. Their reaction was mixed. My brother, proud of me, said, "Don't give up." My nephew asked if I was sure I wanted to do that much work and what about the babies. He was doubtful that I could do it.

Truthfully, I wasn't sure I could do it either. But I never admitted that out loud. Never. I went back to working at the law firm in Oklahoma City as I went through the admissions process for law school. Finally, in April 1990, I received a letter of admission to The University of Oklahoma School of Law. The dream I'd dreamt of for so long was about to come true. I felt scared, anxious, excited, and truly wondered how I would get everything done.

My kids were six and four at this point. My husband was totally against this decision because it would mean more work for him too, and there was no way I could continue working during the first year of law school. But I had been admitted. I was going to law school. Even when the senior partner at the law firm offered me the position of Office Manager at the firm, a position I would have loved a few years earlier, I politely declined. Nothing was going to derail this opportunity.

During undergrad, I became interested in Oklahoma history and how Native American tribes played into that. But until I got to law school, I had never met a Native American. So, you can imagine my excitement when on that first day of orientation, a representative of the American Indian Law Review came on stage to explain how to join. She said you do not have to be a Native American, and you do not have to grade on or have any certain grade point. I was sold and immediately signed up. And there she was—the very first Native American person I had ever met. She said she was a member of the Creek Nation, and a lot of the people on the Law Review were members of various tribes, but they made me feel welcome. She was so nice; how could I resist? Little did I know how this one decision would have such a profound effect on my career.

By the time classes began, I had read all the books on what to expect, had taken preparatory seminars, and had been warned by my friends—but nothing can prepare you for the real thing. The sheer number of pages that had to be read EVERY night was exhausting. Assignments started even before the classes started. I knew the first year would be the worst, but even so, I felt overwhelmed after only a few weeks. People were quitting regularly and I'm sure everyone thought about quitting. I know I did. But then I would remember how long it had taken for me to get there, which only strengthened my determination.

I made it through that first year somehow. I had made all A's as an undergrad, so I had very high expectations for myself that first semester. Looking back, that was unrealistic. When the first semester grades were posted, it was a wake-up call and made me realize how different this experience was going to be. There was only one A and the rest were, let's say, lower than that. The second semester, I dug in and made my study habits my highest priority. It paid off. My grades were much higher for the second semester, and I had begun to think like a lawyer—which is the goal of law school.

The summer between my first and second years could not have come soon enough. While most others in my class were applying for summer internships, I planned activities to entertain my kids for the summer. I had no intention of working or taking classes during the summer. I needed rest and time with my kids. I also wanted time to reflect on what had just happened, what area of the law interested me most, and how I wanted to go forward. This seemed like the perfect time for all of that.

When the second year rolled around, I was ready to get started. In the second and third years of law school, students can choose many of their classes. I chose Family Law as one of my second-year classes. The professor, a well-known expert, had written the textbook. The class turned out to be much more detailed than I expected, but I loved it! The reading didn't seem like a chore, as some of it had been during the first year, and I looked forward to each class. This class, along with the Indian Law class, changed my perspective on law school and made me realize that I had made the right decision after all. The A+ in Family Law didn't hurt either.

At the beginning of the second year, I decided to look for a part-time clerk position somewhere close to the law school. I didn't want anything too hard and certainly nothing more than 15 hours per week. Coincidentally, my friend from American Indian Law Review mentioned that Browning Pipestem was looking for clerks. His office was nearby, and she suggested that I call for an interview. But, she added, I should not take it personally if he didn't hire me. He generally only hired tribal members. Well, I responded, "He will have to say that to my face." We both had a good laugh from that.

I had the interview with Mr. Pipestem, and he hired me on the spot. He wasn't interested in anything other than whether I was interested in becoming the best lawyer. I definitely was. So, he promised to be my mentor and beyond, and I promised to put in the necessary work. We both kept those promises made that day.

I worked with Mr. Pipestem for eight years—two years while I finished law school and six years following. During this time, I felt out of my comfort zone most of the time. I appeared in tribal courts where I was the only English speaker, administrative courts, state courts, and federal courts, including appearing on briefs for federal circuit courts and the United States Supreme Court. It became an amazing time and the experience I gained there proved invaluable for my career. Unfortunately, in August 1999, Mr. Pipestem passed away, our clerk and secretary quit, and I was left as the sole member of the firm. It became evident quickly that I would not be able to maintain this firm without Browning.

My marriage had been failing for several years. I knew divorce was inevitable, but I wanted the kids to get a little older before making such a transition for them. But I was wrong. I know now that I stayed too long in a very bad marriage. After Browning died, I knew it was time to do something about our situation. In June 2000, I left my husband and moved to Colorado with my children.

I had secured a counsel position with a small firm in Denver. The members of the firm focused on Indian housing, and I had some experience in that area. Unfortunately, this position required much more travel than I could do with two teenagers. It became a difficult four years professionally, but my personal life was looking up. After finalizing my divorce in 2003, and with urging from my then college-age daughter, I started thinking about maybe having a new relationship. After a few months, and some very weird dates, I met my person. I felt instantly drawn to him. He is tall, good-looking, fun, and interesting. We were instantly together all the time. We married four months later and still feel like newlyweds today.

Shortly after our marriage, I had the opportunity to open my own firm, with two officemates who focused on family law. I knew immediately this was a great opportunity. So, at 51 years old I opened a small office in a Denver suburb, and launched into a completely new area of the law, in an unfamiliar court system where I knew only a handful of people. It could have been a very scary situation, but I felt as if I had found what I was meant to do.

It was slow at first, but I put up a website and it immediately started bringing in clients. Many times, solo practitioners have to have a general practice. They have to take whatever comes in to stay in business. That was not my situation. I was a solo practitioner by choice with my focus on family law. I did divorces primarily, but also did stepparent adoptions, collection of delinquent child support and maintenance, Motions to Modify parenting time, restraining orders, and many other types of family law cases. I enjoyed helping my clients by providing a needed service.

As I approached retirement age, 15 years had flown by with my firm. My husband had retired, and we decided that I would close my firm and we would retire to Texas. However, once retirement really set in, I realized I needed to stay busy. I really missed my clients. I missed being able to help them and I knew there were clients out there that desperately needed that help.

I decided to write a book, become a coach, and then a speaker on family law matters. My book, *Common Sense Divorce: Ten Steps to Save You Time, Money, and Worry* is basically a blueprint for those things that you must know as you embark on this divorce journey. Readers have found it helpful and enlightening. An online course became the next project: "Common Sense Divorce: Divorce with Dignity and Reclaim Your Happiness and Self-Worth."

Having the book, along with the course, has led to speaking opportunities, and now has led to a coaching program for professional women with children. I know the challenge these women face, and I want to help guide them through the process, and beyond, so that they can get to the other side faster and easier. It can be done alone, but it is much easier with a partner. I want to be that partner for those that need it most. There is no reason to suffer through this trauma, anger, guilt, or frustration alone.

My road to becoming a lawyer, and now an author, coach, and speaker, was not a straight line. But I would not have it any other way. I've met the most amazing people, worked on important and life-changing cases, and now get the opportunity to share those experiences and expertise with others. Even though it was unlikely from the start, grit and determination made it happen!

LaDonna McAbee is founder, CEO, owner, entrepreneur, ecommerce e-tailer at Home Sweet Home Treasures, specializing in vintage, retro, new and used, and many custom-made treasures. Saving the earth one landfill at a time. Ask me about the Purposeful Shopping Ambassador Program for your next fundraiser!

Speaker, teacher, domestic goddess of the McAbee clan, wife to my high school sweetheart.

2 Beautiful Daughters + 4 Perfect Grands + Fur Friends = Love Family

Website: **homesweethometreasures.net**
LinkedIn: **linkedin.com/in/homesweethometreasures**
Facebook: **facebook.com/HomeSweetHomeTreasures1**
Twitter: **twitter.com/hshtreasures**
Instagram: **instagram.com/homesweethometreasures**
TikTok: **tiktok.com/@homesweethometreasures_1**

Chapter 3

Girl Shied Away From, But Now Found

LaDonna McAbee

Be kind to one another, be kind to our children and nurture them along the way!

~ LaDonna McAbee

Born in a small town in Arkansas, was a baby girl whose parents lived in poverty. Both were uneducated and abusive to one another, their children, and society. Sissy, the oldest of five children, became the protector of three, and the angels took care of one. Our sweet brother went with the angels after just a few hours of life. Endurance of the "childhood" journey became hardcore for Sissy and her three siblings as they were tested on every level of life.

Both parents, who came from large families as children, worked in the cotton fields to help their parents and never finished school. Sissy's dad finished fourth grade, never learning to read or write, but became very fast and accurate in basic math skills. He was a giving, helpful, rebellious, abusive, and hardworking man. Her mom finished sixth grade, loved to read, and could do basic writing. Sometimes helpful, but always thought someone was exploiting her; she was rebellious, abusive, and a stay-at-home mom.

One time, Sissy, age three, and Bubba, age two, were outside with their mom, who was hanging laundry on the line. When she finished, she said that they could stay out and play, but warned them not to go into the woods. Bubba ran straight into the woods and her mother blamed Sissy because she was the oldest, and her mother expected her to protect her brother. Sissy was spanked with her mother's shoe and then, into the house the children went.

Soon after, they moved away from the woods and into a house next door to a small neighborhood (convenience) store. Every Friday, their dad would get paid, and he came home with several friends and his brothers, to drink beer. He gave the children a quarter each so that they could both go to the store and buy a chocolate soda and a candy bar (Yahoo). Every Friday, Sissy's mother became angry when her husband showed up with his group, because they stayed too long, drank too many beers, and ruined dinner. The family didn't live next to the store for very long. Sissy was four when they moved again and this time, to their forever family home.

The two-bedroom shack in the center of the block became the family address, their playground, and where the abuse started and ended. Sissy and Bubba shared a bedroom. There was one bathroom that had no door, a living room, and a kitchen. Sissy's mother swore that there was a ghost in the house and that was where all the noises and falling objects came from.

Sissy didn't get to go to kindergarten when her neighborhood friends did because it cost money. Her parents couldn't afford to send her and said that she needed to stay home with Bubba. The shied-away girl couldn't wait to go to school, meet new friends, and show the teachers how smart she was and what a good girl they were getting.

In first grade she tried to make friends, but it was very hard as the other girls seemed to be mean. The teacher held up a picture of a cup and saucer and asked what the picture was of. Sissy raised her hand so proudly was called upon, and then everyone laughed at how she said cup and saucer. The school decided to hire a speech therapist to come in to help her with language and speaking, calling her "tongue-tied." They labeled her as "special" and started the program to correct her speaking. School did not turn out like Sissy thought it would.

Bubba started going to school as a first grader when Sissy moved into the second grade. Her mother taught Sissy and Bubba how to walk home from school. She showed them how to get home and what to watch for when crossing the railroad track. The two of them walked home from school so that she wouldn't have to come and pick them up. A stay-at-home mom, she couldn't find the time to pick up her own children in the car. She timed them to make sure they came home exactly when she wanted, with no wasting time. If they were one minute late, there would be a belt waiting for them.

In the second grade, Sissy had to start cleaning the house. The house was filthy all the time with roaches, cigarette smoke, dirty laundry, dirty dishes, etc. Sissy hated coming home from school. She would have to do the dishes that had been piled up all day from breakfast and lunch, with cigarettes put out on and in the plates, glasses, and cups. Trying to find clothes for the next day became a challenge with so many piled up. She helped cook dinner and then the dishes would be piled up again. There wasn't a dishwasher. Sissy was the dishwasher.

One day, the children walked home from school and the bedroom window was broken, the vacuum cleaner in the yard, and a bicycle in the bedroom. Their parents had been fighting and everything in the house appeared worse than ever. Of course, the house had to get back in some kind of order to even walk through it. Every time their parents fought, the retaliation would be against one or both of the children. Their mom would use anything to hit them and the dad usually used a belt. Then there was the paddle that they both would use, the one that had a ball attached to it.

As the children became older, a "switch" would be used. She ordered them to go get the switch and they'd better not bring back a brittle one, because if she had to get up and retrieve it, she would grab the strongest and the skinniest one she could find. Sissy never wanted to be home. She always went to school and caught the bus to go to church every Wednesday night, Sunday morning, and Sunday night. Anything to escape going home.

Sissy always loved it when her mom would brush her hair, even though most of the time it required her pulling and yanking to get the tangles out. Sissy's hair was always matted as a kid. Sometimes her mother would braid or roll

Sissy's hair and it would be so soft and pretty when she was done. Sissy loved dressing up and getting her hair done. Anything to get positive attention was a win.

Sissy and Bubba had a lot of scary times with the spankings. One day the children were helping their mom with the laundry and ironing and having a good, calm time. Bubba went to run his bath water and forgot about it until the tub had pooled over the top and onto the floor. He tried to be good and clean it up, but his mom wasn't happy that he used the clean towels to soak up the water instead of the dirty towels. In her anger, she took the iron cord to his back several times, until blood showed, and Sissy jerked the iron away from her. The children were so scared that they ran into the bathroom, locked the door, and climbed into the tub, crying themselves to sleep.

A new brother came into their lives, and what a joy he turned out to be. Except, now there was another brother to help take care of. Sissy, eight years old when he came into their lives, learned to make his bottle, diaper him and clothe him. Once he started walking, he did everything with the two siblings. They became a pack of three. And then, two years later, a sister arrived. Sissy became proficient at taking care of babies and toddlers.

When the fighting would get bad and scary, Sissy and Bubba would grab their siblings and run to the bathroom, lock the door, and sit in the tub with them until it was over. Then the parents would retaliate against the two oldest children, beating them and making them clean the house. People thought the babies belonged to Sissy because she was never without them.

Their dad worked at a "soda" plant loading the trucks. Their mom would take them to visit him at work and take him dinner. It was a nice time, with no yelling and fighting. Their mom and dad decided that they would build a porch and a bedroom at the back of the house. Sissy was going to get her own bedroom and wouldn't have to share a room with her brothers or sleep with the baby brother. They built the porch first and then the bedroom came later.

All of a sudden, the soda products started showing up on the back porch. Case after case of drinks were stacked up. The police came one night and found the cases, which were missing from the company. They arrested Sissy's dad and fired him from his job, all within a few hours. He had four kids and a wife to support. He had always worked, and would do anything for money to support his family and his own habits.

Both parents enjoyed drinking, Sissy's dad never knew when to stop once he started. Both started getting hooked on different types of prescription drugs and the drama just kept growing. The judge gave him 10 years of probation and that was it. The bedroom did get finished but a cousin moved into it. You would have thought that they could have shared the new large room. No, Sissy still slept in the same room with her brothers. The cousin stayed for a few months and then, all of a sudden, she moved out. Then Sissy got her own room but wasn't allowed to sleep there at night.

When Sissy was ten years old, a huge fight broke out and her mom took the two babies and left the house on foot and went to her brother's house. That night would haunt Sissy forever. While Bubba and Sissy were sleeping, her dad came in. woke her up, brought her to his bed and molested her. Sissy's mom returned to the house and the molestation continued, on and off for almost five years, until Sissy became pregnant at age fifteen. Her parents said that they would raise the baby. She knew it was wrong and didn't want to have a baby from her dad.

After a lot of fighting, and threats from him and her mom, Sissy had an abortion. Sissy's mother said that it was her fault because she would walk around the house in her bathing suit and short shorts. Sissy felt devastated because, instead of supporting her daughter, and getting Sissy the help she needed to deal with this horrific ordeal, her mother blamed her. Her mom told her to keep quiet about it and when Sissy insisted on an abortion told her she would have to arrange it herself. Nothing was put in place to stop her father from doing this again, and no protection given to the family. Sissy's mom continued to be married to him and to sleep in their bed together.

You may wonder why the parents could get away with abusing each other and the children for so many years? Because others shied away from getting involved. Family, friends, teachers, doctors, and acquaintances didn't want to get involved. Were both parents to blame? Yes! The mom never protected the children; the dad never protected the children. Sissy thought she was the only one that the dad molested, but over time, she discovered that several cousins and friends were victims as well. You may ask, what did the mom do? Nothing! The two people that should have been protecting their own children became their worst enemies. Shame on everyone who shied away from the mental illness that her parents must have endured. Shame on everyone who shied away from that little girl's plight.

As you may have guessed, that little girl, Sissy, was me. The family home still sits in the center of the block as it always did, but I choose not to go there and want nothing to do with it. I very rarely even go to the city and visit. A lot of great memories are there as well, but the overbearing and horrible events overshadow the good ones. I've worked hard to overcome the obstacles and tragedies of my childhood and have now made a success of my life.

I went right from high school to getting married and moving to Fort Hood, Texas, where I started college in the nursing program. During that time, my husband and I were relocated to Germany. So, I didn't get to finish the program. I had to choose to finish the nursing program or to go with my husband. I chose to go with my husband.

While I was there, I started taking classes on base through Maryland University, not for nursing, but just my regular English, math and required classes. Then when I came back to the States, I received my paralegal certificate in Arkansas, but it didn't count when I moved back to Texas. So, I went back to school and became a teacher for Special Needs in a private school.

Even though I didn't want children, because of my own childhood, Mark and I ended up with two beautiful daughters. We have three grandsons and one granddaughter, too. I vowed as a young girl that I would never be like my mother, so I broke the pattern of abuse when I raised my own daughters. Family is everything to me and I will protect them until the end.

Now I have a thriving e-commerce business. I sell everything from the shirt you have on your back, to vintage jewelry, to baby clothes, and everything else from A to Z. My business is all about building relationships.

Every Monday I host a live show about building your mojo, and every Thursday I do a livestream about throwback memories and events. I am building my coaching business to promote Mojo: how to become happy, organized, and successful. I want to build people up and make them feel great. I want to help people to get up in the morning, dress to impress, and set themselves up to be more positive.

Never, ever shy away from helping an abused child. Take a stand against child abuse of all kinds. The phrase, "if you're abused as a child, you will become an abuser," is fiction. Break the trend!

Be kind to one another, be kind to our children and nurture them along the way!

Dani Di Prizio is a life and business coach, facilitator, writer, avid reader, a.k.a. library nerd, and self-proclaimed java junkie. Her heart is in solution-focused collaborative coaching, inspiring projects and helping people to envision and build their own life bridges in the direction they truly wish to be. Dani is in the process of writing additional literary content.

What is your happily ever after? Let me know. I would love to hear it.

Email: dmdiprizio@gmail.com

Chapter 4

Cinderella's Sneakers

Dani Di Prizio

All our dreams can come true if
we have the courage to pursue them.

~ Walt Disney

Let us go on a journey with a teenage Cinderella who swapped out the glass slippers for a pair of sneakers and created her own happily ever after.

Cinderella met who she thought was her Prince "Charming" in the halls of the local high school. Somewhere between classes, dances, and French fries with gravy, they ended up connecting over teenage drama, future dreams, and more teenage drama that made soap operas look like a Disney movie. And Disney always has a happily ever after, right? Or so she thought.

Cinderella ignored her intuition, falsely identified the teen dream drama as love, and held out for the happily ever after with the glittering castle and the starry-eyed, together-forever ending—because that's love. Right?

Wrong.

After the so-called romance of mix tapes, roses in lockers, and after-school walks and talks, this relationship quickly became imbalanced in practically every sense of the word. In her heart, Cinderella knew this relationship was not in her best interest, but she felt love for him, felt sorry for him, felt protective of him, and was scared of him, all at the same time.

This confused the hell out of Cinderella.

She pushed away family, friends, and even school staff who were trying to help her. She, on the other hand, felt they did not understand him as she did. After all, she was Cinderella. She took care of everything and everyone. She could help him, save him, fix him.

Wrong, again.

Sometimes when you are too close to something or someone, you do not see it clearly. Hold a written piece of paper close to your face and try to read it. Chances are you are too close to it to be able to do so. Put a bit of distance between you and the distortion and you can see it more clearly. It is not that you are illiterate; at times, we are simply too close to a situation or person to see things clearly. Sometimes distance is a blessing.

This is what happened to Cinderella.

As the end of the year approached, Cinderella went off for summer vacation and came back with the hopes of going off to college/university. In her excitement, she shared this with the Prince. It was not well received. After all, this would change the direction of his happily ever after. Cinderella did not see it for what it was at the time. She internalized it as he loved and valued her so much that he did not want to see her go. Because that is what true love is, right?

Wrong.

Shortly thereafter she found out they were having a Little Prince . . . *Wait, What?!?*

Senior year is predominantly the time of the much anticipated "ball," along with the parties, school trips, and all that we envisioned our last "hoorah" to be. Cinderella watched it all go by in tearful silence.

On top of all this were the constant reminders from Prince "Something or Other" that no one would ever want Cinderella now. She was ruined. Who would want a single mother with no skills, little education, who came from a broken family home—especially in the 80s.

His abuse was continuous and hurtful.

The relationship continued to unravel quickly, becoming more and more unstable physically, mentally, and emotionally. She was not even sure which was worse: the physical, the mental, or the emotional abuse. At least physically, the pain would subside, and the marks would fade, but not the rest. Her self-esteem began to peel away like paint off a wall.

She felt as if she had cried an ocean's worth of tears, trying to hold something together with one hand tied behind her back. What about the Little Prince? He was her most precious gift.

How could she walk this tightrope with him, without falling off?

Days became a blur. Cinderella felt as if she could no longer read the paper in front of her face. There was no knight in shining armor, no castle, no glitter, and no gold; she was as shattered as a glass slipper.

Where did she go? *Within.*

Somewhere deep inside there was a very special voice that stayed with her through it all. It was the voice of her fairy **GOD**mother. You see, Cinderella had a secret she had kept to herself since she was a child.

Somehow, someway, she always knew everything would work out favorably for her, whether she could see it, or not. All she had to do was figure out what she really wanted or needed, start taking action towards it, and in time, "*Bibbidi, Bobbidi, Boo*" things would work out for her.

How? She did not know or understand. Like magic, the right people or resources would come into play, even if not right away, and Cinderella had a plan.

Sometime after the Little Prince was born, Cinderella experienced one of the most dangerous nights with Prince "Something or Other" that she had ever experienced thus far. Things were escalating and she knew she had to flee the proverbial castle . . . but, how?

Cinderella called upon her fairy **GOD**mother. "How do I get out of this safely?" Through the tears, Cinderella looked up and saw a unicorn her father had given her. Her family knew she loved unicorns and every year since she was a child, Cinderella would always add a white horse to their traditional family Christmas list. Her father would ask her "Where are you going to put it?" "In the backyard," (of course) would be her reply.

Cinderella went over to the unicorn. Something told her to turn it upside down and there was her answer.

Underneath the base of the unicorn was a hole. What she saw in front of her was her carriage. From that point on, literally every spare cent that came her way, that she could spare, went into the unicorn. Dollars and change taped together were secretly placed inside and the bottom taped shut, to keep it as silent and secure as possible, in case it happened to be moved.

You see, Prince "Something or Other" would constantly take money from Cinderella. Nothing was sacred, regardless of the Little Prince's needs. He took money from everywhere and anywhere, including jewelry and family heirlooms. Taken, pawned for next to nothing . . . leaving Cinderella heartbroken, yet again.

In shame, at times she had to ask her family and a "soul brother" for financial help with food, baby necessities, and rent. This totally crushed what little was left of her pride. At this point, she vowed to do whatever she could to never be in this position again. *This is not love, this is not "normal," and this is not safe. This is NOT me!* ***I can do better than this, and I will.*** But what did that look like? She did not know.

Cinderella asked her fairy **GOD**mother . . . what else, please? Diversify your funds. This did not mean financial investments and offshore accounts. Cinderella had an epiphany, "Do not put all your eggs in one unicorn." Enter the picture frame.

Cinderella looked around. A picture frame she had hardly noticed before came clearly into her view. She had a new spot, the footman for the carriage. She started putting money in the back of the picture frame, between the picture and the cardboard, so if the back was slid open, you could not see the money.

Phase 2, check.

Shortly thereafter, she noticed a split in the seam of the carpet. She had never noticed it before. It was raised just a wee bit as if to grab her attention; it did. Money under the carpet.

Enter Phase 3, check.

Everything was going to work out favorably. She could feel it. She would find a way to rescue herself, create her own space, and adjust her sails along the way.

Enter the A-Team. Connect with family and support systems. Cinderella's mother, father, and sister were integral in helping her to escape the castle and to getting back on track. Phase in, create a plan, and find a support team, (especially those who have your best interest at heart, even if you are too proud to admit it).

Be ready to execute the plan. Check.

One of Cinderella's gifts was her love for, and natural ability for helping people to build their bridges from where they were, to where they wanted to be. This time, the bridge was for her.

So, after the last of the "unsafe" nights. Cinderella put her plan into action. Gathering her horse, carriage, footman and sneakers, she threw a diaper bag over one hip, and her baby on the other, and then she *"Bibbidi Bobbidi Boo'd"* her ass right out of there.

So, whatever happened to Cinderella? Well . . .

She excitedly continues her journey of helping people find their direction and build their very best bridges along the way. She shares her six main keys to opening the doors to discovering your happily ever after:

- Always have faith everything is working out favorably, even if you do not see it at the time. Trust your heart and intuition.

- Take action, accountability, and responsibility for your life. Life is a gift for us to be grateful for. Let's create and live it as best we can.

- Build better stronger bridges for yourself, in the direction you want to go in, and help others to get across along the way.

- Be your own knight in shining armor and rescue yourself. Have a plan. You got this.

- Believe in and love yourself first. Validation and worth comes from within you.

- Sneakers make great *slippers.*

~ The End ~

As a refugee and immigrant from Vietnam, **Kimchi Chow** learned to be flexible and adaptable; she accepted the new life as a second chance to prove herself worthy. Today, Kimchi's vision for Asian American women is to be great role models for future generations. She uses coaching and training to help her clients create a worthy legacy to pass on to their children.

If you are an Asian Pacific Islander woman and looking for guidance in the areas of integrating western and eastern cultures, or about building a strong partnership in your marriage, or resolving multi-generational conflicts, schedule a free discovery call with her at her website or email your request.

Email: Kimchi@AsianWomenOfPower.com
Website: AsianWomenOfPower.com
LinkedIn: linkedin.com/in/kimchichow

Chapter 5

Blessings from Unfortunate Events

How an Asian American Refugee Pursues Her Freedom and Keeps Her Promise

Kimchi Chow

"What can you do to promote world peace? Go home and love your family."

~ Mother Teresa

A Nightmare That Lasts A Lifetime

Imagine waking up and seeing a rifle pointing at you while you are still in bed. You might think you were having a nightmare because what you saw was incomprehensible and impossible to believe for a 16-year-old city girl. A firm and loud voice with a northern Vietnamese accent transported you back to that chilling moment. "Get up, go downstairs, and wait for the order." At that moment, you knew that your life was about to change drastically.

I still can see that image vividly even after 47 years have passed. Because of what happened to Vietnam and to my family, I was given a second chance—to live in America, where I still live today. I have been able to experience a life of personal freedom and liberty without the fear of being put in jail, having my assets taken away, or even being killed. Nobody understands this better than a refugee. The second part of our lives is all about living up to the vows we made during the most difficult times.

My First Test - They Took Away My Freedom & Liberty

On April 30, 1975, the Vietnamese Communist Party won the war and they started to confiscate assets from wealthy families and businesses, with no legitimate reason for doing so. The Communist Party sent a troop of three to four soldiers to each family on their list, forcing everyone out of their homes at midnight. The soldiers came in with guns and rifles and these men were not local people that we knew.

After my mom turned over the keys to the safe and the cars, these soldiers told us to grab a few items of clothing, and then they shuffled us into a van and drove us to a large hotel in town. They put all members of each family in a tiny room, with a minimum of four people per room. Some of us had to sleep on the floor since there was only one twin-size bed per room.

Every day at midnight, the chief of the investigation would call the heads of each family to a private room where he conducted further interrogation. They wanted to know if we had additional assets, and where we had hidden them. These midnight interrogations lasted for a few weeks. Then the officer released the children and the elderly and moved the heads of each household to the city jail, where they were kept for another seven months. My mom was held there with my baby sister, who was only two years old at the time.

Life definitely became hard for us during that period. My mom somehow managed to survive those months in jail with my baby sister, while seven of us struggled to find work to buy food to eat. We felt like criminals because the government had "blacklisted" us. Local people and neighbors did not want to be involved with us, as they might also end up on the blacklist, so they turned away from helping us.

The only person who stepped in and acted as an angel for us was our aunt, my mom's older sister. Without her support, we would not have had shelter or food to live for another day. We would not have had an opportunity to escape from Vietnam and we would not be here today. At sixteen years old, I experienced total helplessness.

The Second Test—How Strong Was My Faith?

In 1978, the Vietnamese Communist government encouraged Chinese merchants and foreigners to leave Vietnam, with the condition that these merchants would give all of their assets to the Communist government. In exchange, the merchants would receive a permit to leave Vietnam officially.

After my mom was released from prison in 1976, she could not own or run any business because we were on the government's "blacklist." Even so, my mom was able to reconnect with some trusted friends to borrow money and gold. This enabled her to buy fake documents and identification for her family to get out of Vietnam.

I still remember the night when we escaped Vietnam. The sky was clear and cloudless, and the weather was warm on the Mekong River. After we passed the government checkpoint, the members of each family lined up quietly, one by one, to board the boat.

There were several fishing boats at the shore that night. One or two were brand new, but most were older. I don't know about the other boats and how they were structured inside, but our boat was a fishing boat, which was not designed to carry passengers. It could fit 20 people lying down comfortably, but there were at least 50 of us on board the boat that night.

The heavily-ladened boat moved slowly and quietly away from the shore. The captain did not start the motor for at least a mile. Then he announced that we were officially outside the Vietnam border, and that we would face choppy waters since we were in the sea. He told his assistant to shift the motor into second gear, so that we could move faster.

While our bodies were jerking left and right, bouncing up and down due to the choppy water, all of us were extremely happy and felt so relieved. More stars started to show up in the dark sky, as if they were welcoming us to a new world.

We sailed in the ocean for about four nights and five days with no problem. The first motor had been replaced a few days before, and then the second motor went dead. Our boat was using two motors simultaneously, but on that day, one of the motors overheated, so we had to stop to replace it with a spare one.

While our captain and his assistant were working to replace the motor, we noticed another fishing boat approaching us. As that boat came closer, we saw four men, one with a gun and the other three held knives in both hands. These men's faces did not look friendly and they began speaking to our captain in Thai.

After about fifteen minutes of exchange between our captain and the pirate leader, they agreed to tow our boat to the Thailand border. In exchange, our captain had to give them a new boat motor and all the gold we had. They threatened that if we did not comply with their demands, they would use force to hurt the people on our boat.

The pirates towed our boat for about half a mile further out, then they cut the cord that tied our boat to theirs and sailed away. Floating in the ocean after being robbed, all of us had mixed emotions: anger toward these pirates, resentment toward the captain for his decision to give up the extra motor, and relief because we were not harmed. These emotions soon subsided as we adjusted to our new reality. With no motor on the boat, how would we get to our destination?

We were floating in the ocean for another day and a half when the captain told us that we would soon run out of food and the water might only last for another day or so. This news was alarming, even though most of us hardly ate anything due to seasickness. To calm everyone our captain asked the adults to pray for miracles. For those who were aware of the situation, this was the longest night of our journey. For the rest, it was just another day at sea.

I woke up the next morning to the sound of many voices. When I asked what was going on, someone told me that the captain had spotted a large cargo ship, and he was trying to contact it by radio communication from our boat. The vibe within our boat changed completely, from hopeless to hopeful.

Three or four hours later, the cargo ship approached our boat. Once they found out that we were Vietnamese and Chinese trying to escape the Communist regime in Vietnam, they contacted the German Embassy and got approval to rescue our boat.

During the time we waited for approval from the German government, the captain of the cargo ship gave us food and water. One of the new foods I tried that day was a German cheese which was strong-smelling and unappealing. I stuffed the crackers and salami into my mouth quickly because I was starving, but I did not want to try the cheese.

We finally were approved to immigrate to Germany. Seven months later, after we got in contact with my father who had been searching for us since 1975, we relocated to America.

The Vows I Never Forget

For the first ten years, after I relocated to America, I tried to forget this journey. I tried to hide the feeling of shame every time I heard the words "refugee," "Asian," and "welfare."

Whenever I wanted to give up on school or jobs, my mom would remind me of the price we paid to get out of Vietnam, to live in a country like America, and to experience our freedom and liberty. My mom often told us there was nothing to be ashamed of when we used food stamps to buy food at the grocery store. She told us that we were using the government's aid to prepare for our independence by learning English and attending trade schools six days a week. It took us two years before we could stand up on our own feet and become taxpayers.

Two decades later, all members of our family were more established. We had received college degrees, made good incomes, were married, had children, bought homes, and lived in nice neighborhoods. We were living the American Dream. Of course, my dream and my siblings' dreams were not the same.

I have never forgotten the vows I made with God during the night our boat was stranded in the ocean; when we were out of food and water, with no promise for tomorrow. The vow began with, "When I get out of this situation, I will never complain about any difficulties or challenges in my life." Then it progressed to, "I want to be worthy of the second life I was given." And today, my intention is to make a positive impact on my family and my community. Looking back, these vows, or subconscious intentions, shaped the direction of my life.

First Crack In My Marriage

I went to college and received a two-year Associate of Arts degree in data processing. I got a job at Intel and met my future husband there. After marriage to my husband, I returned to college and earned a Bachelor of Science degree in computer science. I graduated at twenty-nine years old and then took a job as a software test engineer, while raising my daughter.

My career was good; I enjoyed working and earning good money. My parents-in-law helped us come up with the down payment to purchase our first home: three bedrooms and two baths. When I had my daughter, my in-laws moved in with us because they wanted to give us a hand, and also my daughter was their first grandbaby.

Due to the limitations in communication between my parents-in-law and me, my husband became the interpreter and referee when there were disagreements between us. Most of the time, my husband sided with his parents and told me to change and adapt to his family's perspective about family structure and customs, based on Taiwanese tradition.

My first lesson from a big misunderstanding with my mother-in-law was: I should never shout at my mother-in-law. That was unacceptable, no matter what reason or explanation I had for shouting. Shortly after that incident, my in-laws moved out. I'm not sure if they sensed the friction between my husband and me, or not. My husband didn't tell me the reason and I felt relieved at that time.

This incident caused a small crack in my marriage. I saw that I was not a priority for my husband. He would continue to execute things in our family household based on his father's wishes. I don't recall if my husband ever did anything I asked or wanted without getting approval from his parents first. Because of that, I felt unheard and unseen. I felt invisible whenever my in-laws were present.

Two years later, I had a son. We moved to another town and purchased a bigger house with four bedrooms and two-and-a-half baths. We had to sell the first house in order to get the down payment for the second one. When we bought this new house, my husband had already asked his parents to move in and live with us, which they did.

My husband and I both worked hard in our careers. We made more money, but we also spent more time at work due to the commute and long hours. We moved to different companies. For a year, things were going alright with no major disagreements. My husband still listened to his parents, and they had the final approval or disapproval for our major decisions, like what cars to buy, what jobs to take, etc. One of the decisions that his father made further damaged my relationship with my husband.

Is It My Body, My Decision?

I was pregnant with our third child, unplanned. My husband asked my father-in-law whether we should keep that child or not, since we already had two babies—one daughter and one son. At first, my father-in-law thought of giving our third child to my husband's younger brother, since he and his wife were unable to produce a child. Then, after his son refused to accept that offer, his father told my husband we could keep our third child.

It's a Chinese custom that you want to keep your wealth or power within your family's bloodline instead of being open to an outsider. It happened to my father-in-law personally, when he adopted a baby girl from his cousin, because his wife could not get pregnant. That tradition is typical and acceptable in many parts of Asia, but not in America. And what made me upset was that my father-in-law and my husband did not ask me first, to see if it was okay with me to give away my unborn child, as if I had no voice in this family.

I cried many nights in bed, and I told my unborn child that he or she was not welcome here. I didn't feel loved, appreciated, or respected by my husband and his father. I felt that I was in a battle where I was on one side, and my husband and his family were on the other. What I fought for was my own self-worth, in terms of money, power, and status.

A few weeks later, during a pregnancy exam, my ob-gyn doctor told me there was no heartbeat from the baby and I had miscarried. That miscarriage caused me so much guilt. I assumed the baby left because I told her I did not want her in my life. I felt ashamed because I thought no mother would ever not welcome her child with open arms. So I buried the guilt with many activities and business in the evening and on weekends, to avoid facing my husband, my in-laws, and my two children.

The emptiness inside me, from unfulfilled love in my marriage, lasted at least twenty years, until I forgave my mistakes and what my husband and his parents did to me. As I grow older, I have more empathy and compassion toward my mother-in-law, about how she couldn't speak up and stand up for herself. I recalled my husband telling me that his mom put up with a lot of pressure and unfair treatment from her mother-in-law and her husband's siblings. She would be the first one to wake up and the last one to go to bed. She definitely had no voice in the family, even though she was the wife of the eldest son.

The Price for Greed & Vanity

The events from when I was 30-50 years old are blurred since I kept so busy trying to fill up my time. My marriage was not getting better and I suppressed many of my emotions so it would not get worse. Both my husband and I were still working for high-tech companies. We had a Vietnamese live-in nanny to take care of our two kids and cook for us. We moved to a bigger home to accommodate privacy for everyone, including the nanny.

My husband and I accumulated more assets. We invested in multiple businesses, land, and condos in Mexico and in U.S. states. We thought this would be our legacy for our children when we are no longer here.

Then 2008 hit and the U.S. economy's bubble burst. Many fields were impacted by the financial downturn. More houses got foreclosed on because the owners could not pay the mortgage. Many businesses were closed because promised loans and lines of credit were terminated by the bank.

This affected all of our investments. We lost at least 90% of the money we had invested. Our 401K fund was left with about 10% of its value. Both the financial hit and the emotional hit left a big scar on my heart.

I blamed myself for risking our life savings and our IRA funds and making those mistakes. This was one of my biggest mistakes financially and it took me five years to forgive myself. I felt ashamed for becoming so greedy and for stupidly listening to leaders who seemed so confident, yet did not have much proof of their expertise and integrity.

Devastated, I looked for seminars to learn about forgiveness and trust, and a friend introduced me to the Landmark Forum. That path led me to pursue the coaching career I have today.

At the time I'm writing this, my husband and I are still married after 38 years. I continue working and practicing my communication and active listening skills to bring in more empathy, curiosity, kindness, and compassion. I have to let go of judgment, control, and perfectionism when I interact with my spouse and children, who are now 34 and 32 years old. I want them to know I understand what it's like to be in their shoes.

Lessons In My Life

Here are the life lessons and ideas I have learned and am still using today:

As an immigrant/refugee:

- **Be open to asking for help** when you can't do it yourself. Most people are happy to have an opportunity to help someone.
- **Be adaptable to learning new things**. You never know when this knowledge or skill will be useful in the future.
- **Be proud of your accent.** Your accent reveals where you came from. It does not indicate the level of your intelligence and wisdom.
- **The best way to pass on your heritage's culture and customs to your children** is to give them an explanation of why you honor those customs, even in this modern day.

As a businessperson:

- **Be humble** no matter how much you have achieved or accomplished. Remember you got here with a lot of help from people you know and don't know.
- **Be kind and generous to yourself and others** with your words and actions. You never know when those kind words and gestures could save someone's life or encourage them to do great things.
- **Never give your power away** by automatically thinking that just because a person has more authority or power than you do, they are smarter or know more than you. Observe their character by watching their actions and behaviors. Evaluate what they say by verifying their information independently. Always verify their motives.
- **Do due diligence** on someone you are about to invest in or with, like a business partner or a founder of a high-end program that costs more than $10K, or someone you may want to marry someday. Doing this work early and thoroughly could save many years of headaches and heartaches.

As a human being:

- Have faith and pray when things seem to be hopeless. There are a small number of things you can change and have control over; the rest leave up to God. Pray for guidance for yourself and others. Know that you have no control over many things with your children and your spouse.

- **Never give up on your values and principles**. They are like your blood type and DNA. Also, don't put down others' values and principles if they are different from yours. We are all unique people!

- **Have empathy and compassion for yourself and others**. Forgive yourself and others for past mistakes in order to gain inner peace. Remember no one is perfect, even your parents! You can forgive but you don't have to forget.

- **Find the hidden gifts from your past mistakes.** Look for a way to come back better, stronger, and more resilient than before. When you do, you will have converted those mistakes into gifts and opportunities for a better future.

I hope my story helped you see that underneath our skin tone, we all are the same with red blood, veins, tissues, and bones. As human beings, we all have the same feelings and emotions when unpleasant things happen to us. What distinguishes us from each other is the level of our resilience: to fall-down-seven-times-and-get-up-eight; to have hope that tomorrow will be better than today; and you and I are going to do our best to live our lives, today!

Whether you are a refugee, an immigrant, or native-born, I encourage you to find your top five virtues from viacharacter.org, then implement those virtues daily through your life, work, and community. When you do, you will feel happy and content.

After all, that's what life is all about!

"You should never view your challenges as a disadvantage. Instead, it's important for you to understand that your experience facing and overcoming adversity is actually one of your biggest advantages."

~ Michelle Obama

Marilyn Atteberry, a youthful 86-year-old great-grandmother, attributes her health, vitality, and success to her life's purpose to empower people to live with self-confidence, integrity, and a purpose to create what Buckminster Fuller called a "Win/Win World."

A former Sunday editor for *The San Francisco Examiner,* she taught award-winning high school journalism and media classes. In 1973, inspired by the burgeoning Human Potential movement, she co-created two businesses providing workshops to teens and adults.

She now enters her third decade as a licensed Avatar® Master, teaching the Avatar Course tools, empowering people to become CEO of their personal reality who live fulfilled, contributing lives for themselves, their families and the world.

Marilyn is presently working on three soon-to-be published books, and is excited about her latest business, "Boomers to Bloomers."

Email: marilyn@avatarsv.com
Website: TheAvatarCourse.com
Facebook: facebook.com/BoomersToBloomers

Chapter 6

Cinderella's Mind-Blowing Adventure into Purpose

Marilyn Atteberry

Inspiring someone is awakening a viewpoint that realizes that something that seemed impossible can actually be done. ~ Harry Palmer

Alas, meet Cinderella, covered in soot, ridiculed, mistreated, stuck in a prison disguised as a pretty suburban home, resigned to being more a slave than a person. She often gazed into a metaphoric crystal ball only to behold a future promising more of the same . . . or worse.

Yes, you guessed it! Cinderella, AKA Marilyn Brannan, was a woman (me) disillusioned by the broken remains of lifelong romantic dreams of home, hearth, love, motherhood, and "happily ever after."

Gradually, after years of hoping for a surprise visit from a Fairy Godmother, I began entertaining the idea that MAYBE a risky, uncertain future might have better odds than staying stuck where I was. I began to face the unquestionable fact that the marriage was going nowhere fast, and if I did decide to leave it I would need to find a job. A shade or two brighter than "dismal", I told myself that I could ALWAYS go back to working for a newspaper to handle the mortgage payments and other living expenses.

On the other hand, the thought of going to work and leaving my two young children in another's care made it difficult to even TRY to put on a happy face! Even though I felt fairly confident one of the newspapers in the area would hire me, I loved being a 24-hour, at-home mom. Newspapers don't have two-month summer breaks, holiday vacations, and hours coinciding with an elementary school day.

That year my daughter was starting kindergarten, and my son was in first grade. I casually asked my husband what he thought about the possibility of me returning to San Jose State University for a year to obtain a teaching credential and soon contribute to the family income. He heartily agreed. I doubt he had any thought about me considering divorce and I wasn't ready to take that big of a leap . . . yet, a few preliminary baby steps seemed a smart thing to do. I returned to school and, in January of 1968, received a secondary teaching credential focused on teaching high school journalism.

On New Year's Eve, fate (disguised as my husband) literally hit me in the face and at last, I decided to risk the liberation leap, mustering up the sudden courage that accompanied his New Year's after-party gift of two black eyes and a broken nose. On January 2, 1968, I stamped "No More" on 10 tumultuous years of marriage and motherhood. I secured an attorney and feelings of relief outweighed any question or hesitation.

During the next month, I received my secondary teaching credential and immediately applied to substitute teach. Days became busy as I moved from school to school, filling in whenever journalism teachers decided to take a few days off. I had fun mingling with teenagers, my two kids had fun playing with grandma, and a Fairy Godmother DID finally appear! With a flick of her magic wand, one of the teachers I'd substituted for was transferred to a new high school opening in his district. They offered me a job to replace him at Fremont Union High School in Sunnyvale. Needless to say, I leaped again and embarked on 10 years as an advisor to the school newspaper, teaching English, Film, Mass Media, Journalism I, and Journalism 2.

It was an interesting time. With the famous "sixties," winding down, I found myself smack-dab in the midst of teenagers captivated by the thrill of rock'n'roll, women's lib, sexual freedom, contraband drugs, unwanted pregnancies, illegal abortions, and the threat of being drafted into an unpopular war. Many parents were at their wits' end and I could feel their deep concern and often, hopelessness.

I somehow "knew" my Godmother had a reason for plopping me back into high school . . . one greater than teaching kids how to put together advertisements, short films, and newspapers. Something profound unfolded within me, and a desire to assist my students to make wise choices amidst the confusion, propelled me to enroll in evening and weekend university courses in psychology, adolescent development, and sociology.

A few years passed, and I eagerly adopted many of the ideas and techniques I'd learned in classes entitled:

"Super Learning", "Values Clarification", and "Adolescent Psychology", to name a few. Then, in 1972, curiosity prompted me to enroll in a San Jose State University summer session course entitled, "Techniques of Group Encounter" ala the box office hit, *Bob & Carol, Ted & Alice.* Even though I hadn't seen the movie, my interest in the current rage called "Personal Encounter Groups" was definitely boosted by the bonus of five quick Continuing Education Units that would boost my teachers' salary!

It was a week-long intensive and I found the class intriguing. Having never explored the area of human consciousness before, I found the notion that beliefs actually precede and cause our experiences both revolutionary and thought-provoking. However, I must admit that the true value of the course was NOT in the curriculum at all—it was in meeting a fellow student I initially labeled a strange creature of dreaded "hippiedom." His name was Brandon Poso.

At first, I avoided, well, TRIED to avoid him. He was scary looking to me, a suburban housewife and mother. Unkempt. Long straggly hair. He actually reminded me of a spider monkey with his skinny, hairy body exposed under, of all things, overalls! He joined a group of us "civilized" appearing people when we decided to have lunch at the coffee shop across the street from the college. Of course, we had to be polite. All morning, noticing and attempting to avoid his intense eye contact, I took great care to sit down at the far end of the lunch table. Within moments I heard the scraping sound of a chair being pulled up near me and, lo and behold, Brandon plopped down beside me. Within minutes he managed to engage me in a most interesting conversation.

Despite my snap judgments, he was entertaining, intelligent, and even charming. Before the week's end, we became great friends and even met each other's families. My daughter, then age 12, started her babysitting career watching over his two young boys on summer days, as he and I held regular brain-storming sessions around my kitchen table. Brandon was 10 years my junior and had just started substitute teaching. He devoured stories about my classroom experiences, and we enjoyed discussing and comparing what we had learned in the unique class we had shared. Again, I integrated some of the ideas I had learned into my fall high school classes. Students responded well.

Our friendship grew deeper. During one of our more personal kitchen table chats, we compared past experiences and what had occurred to motivate us to decide to go into teaching. He remained quiet when I spoke of my 10 years of marriage and how disappointed I was that I couldn't "make" it work. Then, meeting my eyes with his most penetrating gaze, he recommended I attend an introductory EST Guest Event being held soon at the Masonic Auditorium in downtown San Francisco. Already having experienced the full two-weekend seminar himself and finding it fascinating, he invited me to join him and three of his friends to attend the event.

"I know you will find the course fascinating and life-changing Marilyn," he said with certainty. "Attending this two-hour Introductory Guest Event will give you a chance to decide that for yourself." I sat quietly.

"Exploring your beliefs is beyond valuable for anyone wanting a happy life, and I know attending the event and feeling the seminar's value will be good for both yourself and your children." After waiting a moment for that to sink in, he added, "And why don't you consider the added value you could bring to the students in your classrooms."

I was hooked! The day arrived. Brandon, his three buddies, and I hopped into his ancient VW Bus on the hot, muggy summer afternoon and charged down Highway 280, excited to try something new.

I must admit that proper Marilyn, in her pink and white herring-bone suit and three-inch heels, was initially a bit stand-offish in the company of four hippies in worn jeans and "questionable" T-shirts. Regardless, I decided to be a good sport and try to look beyond my evaluations. After all, I trusted Brandon and it was for a good cause. And, well, some of my favorite students also wore worn jeans and "questionable" T-shirts.

So, seated in the van, I went back and forth in my head between imagining what my mother would do if she ever found out about my reckless decision and the conversation the guys were having about the upcoming Giant's game. Both dialogues were rudely interrupted by deafening banging sounds that shook our vehicle. Clang. Knock. Rattle. Kerplunk. Thud! Shake. Silence. Shock! There we were, dumbstruck and stranded on the side of a rapidly moving racetrack of a freeway. We looked at each other.

After what seemed an eternity, my rational mind began working, and almost instantly, relief flooded my body as I realized we were still pretty close to civilization. Perhaps this unexpected automobile failure was actually the answer to all my back-and-forth considerations! Whew. I smiled with confidence and was the first to speak, removing a small plastic card from my girlie wallet, pink to match my proper pink and white summer suit.

"No worries," I said, gallantly waving my American Automobile Association card in true heroine style. "We can use my handy AAA lifesaver to get your van towed, Brandon! We can always attend another event another day."

"What in the world are you saying, Marilyn?" Brandon responded with an accusing tone and fierce eyes. "Didn't you say you wanted to go to this shindig tonight?"

"Well, yes," I answered, defensively matching his tone, but it's obvious we don't have any transportation. Your vehicle is decidedly dead!"

"You made an agreement," he returned incredulously, "and now you want to break it just because my car isn't working?" I stared at him in amazement and looked around at the three other guys for a little backup support. They stared back.

"You created this whole situation, you know," Brandon said, matter-of-smugly. Sweating profusely in my little pink suit, I sat speechlessly.

"You have doubts that beliefs precede our experiences in life," he continued. "Those doubts were strong enough to cause my bus to break down. Just think about it! You now have a golden opportunity to follow your innate wisdom, drop your doubts, test your power and create getting us to San Francisco on time. Don't you want to prove to yourself that you're on the verge of discovering you are much more powerful than you've ever dreamed?" I sweated in amazement, wishing I wore loose pants and a t-shirt like the rest of my travel mates.

"What are you saying?" I replied.

Brandon surveyed the guys and asked, "Are you game? Do you want to continue on to San Francisco, stepping it up so we can still make it on time? Thank God we left early. We still have a good 45 minutes!" They shrugged and slowly began to smile.

"Sure," grinned a friendly, curly-headed guy named Jim. "The bus is safely off the road and there's a steady flow of traffic. We've got plenty of time to hitch a ride and make it on time."

"Hitchhike," I sputtered in matronly horror. "What are you talking about? I don't hitchhike. Never have. Never will! That is a solemn vow I made to my mother."

"Well," Brandon said, this time kindly, "Do you want to keep playing by old indoctrinations or do you want to trust your ability to make your own rules, and even create miracles? I guess it truly comes down to that. Can you trust yourself? You're not alone you know. We're all learning together to grow."

I felt a familiar feeling rising in me: part disbelief and part stubborn inclination to prove I wasn't some frilly, sissy female. The latter won.

After about 10 minutes, firmly asserting my unconditional "rules," I was standing on the side of the road in my suit and high heels, thumb extended, and surrounded by four questionably attired young men. They had all agreed to my conditions: 1) we would not separate under any condition; 2) we required an air-conditioned vehicle with bucket seats; and 3) if a ride didn't show up within 10 minutes, we were using my AAA card!

Within minutes, with me as part of this motley crew, a vehicle pulled up! It was so roomy we all could fit comfortably. Oh yeah, it was a pick-up truck with paint buckets in the roomy bed, one for each of us! While not exactly what I expected, it certainly did meet my stated requirements, and I am a woman of my word! It took two of the guys to help me board the truck in my tight skirt and spike heels. As modestly as possible I perched upon a seat made of four paint cans and tried to figure out what to do with my legs! After we were all as comfortably arranged as possible, the truck slowly accelerated and joined the flow of traffic on the busy Friday afternoon.

Fifteen minutes later our chariot slowed to a stop. Seconds later our driver appeared, leaning on the side of the truck bed, announcing he was taking the next off-ramp and we needed to find another ride. Both relieved and puzzling over our next move, I mustered up a smile and awaited my turn to leave the back of the pickup truck. Disembarking became a challenge, despite the polite efforts of my comrades to help a woman with a tight skirt and heels retain her dignity. Maintaining a calm demeanor was almost as challenging, but I managed to make it over and down with a degree of aplomb.

All ten feet securely on the ground again, we thanked our chauffeur and, straightening my skirt and windblown hair, I used my classroom voice to announce, "I have a few additional conditions, you guys! Our next vehicle has a roof!" No one seemed to mind the new rule.

I really had little time to build up any concern because again, within minutes, a car drove up. Granted, it was tight with five of us crammed into the back . . . but it was air-conditioned and the lap I perched upon was friendly enough. After all, I'd known the owner for about an hour now.

The new driver was a cordial and amusing fellow who dropped us off at our next layover: the freeway exit to Half Moon Bay. We now had about 30 minutes to make it on time to our destination in downtown San Francisco.

Rather intrigued by the strange events of the last hour, I was courageously encouraged to really go for it, continue to test this fascinating "belief creates reality theory", and dream big. I made my final amendment to the travel requirements.

"Okay guys," I declared with authority, "our next ride will drop us off on time in front of the entrance to the Masonic Auditorium. We will each enjoy a comfortable seat, in a cool, air-conditioned vehicle with soothing music. It will be large enough for all of us to relax and catch our breath." Then I added wistfully under my breath, "A glass of wine would be nice."

Minutes later up zoomed a brand-new motorhome driven by a lovely young woman with a big smile. She gestured for us all to get in and make ourselves comfortable. Classical music filled the air and I settled back with a sigh on a lusciously upholstered bench along the side of the van. After asking us where we wanted to go, she laughed at our answer and assured us the auditorium was "right on her way." We quite animatedly shared our exciting and magical travel story. I even managed to admit the "belief-precedes-experience theory" might have some merit.

"Oh, by the way," she added a few minutes into our tale, "in the cupboard in front of the sleeping area, you'll discover a pretty good bottle of Pinot Noir. I regrettably won't be able to drink, but we must memorialize this extraordinary achievement! Glasses are in the cupboard above the sink."

We looked at each other in stunned amazement. My mumbled request for a glass of wine had not been a demand! It was merely an off-handed remark by a woman who was pretty much out of her mind, blown away by the startling events of the day. For the first time all day, I couldn't think of anything to say.

I sipped the wine, clinging to my glass, marveling at the gigantic turn I had put into motion, whether planned or not. I knew I embarked on a direction I couldn't predict yet knew was inevitable and right. She dropped us off at the front steps of the Masonic Auditorium with ten minutes to spare.

I don't remember much of what Werner Erhard, founder of EST, had to say, but I do remember the emphasis was on learning how to take the driver's seat of our lives and use deliberately created beliefs to move us toward our goals and dreams, instead of living at the whim of others and circumstances. Of course, I signed up for the seminar.

I don't want to over-stretch any reader's ability to believe this story, but there is actually "frosting" on the proverbial "cake!" Although the enlightening events of our trip were definitely enough to motivate me to register for the course, I also had to put some attention on getting back home to San Jose. I mean, really, how long can any sane person expect such magic to last? I received a clear answer.

Prior to this day's enlightening trip, I would have labeled this last bit of magic "chance" or "good luck", but from the perspective of "beliefs create experience," VOILA! Hold on to your seat! Each one of us traveling adventurers, mingling amongst a crowd of thousands, just "happened" to bump into a friend who was willing to take us home. Mine was an almost next-door neighbor who loved hearing my story on the ride home and dropped me off at my doorstep. And there is still more!

The next day, I picked up Brandon in my classy Nash Rambler and we drove to the abandoned Volkswagen Bus on the side of the freeway. Before deciding which direction would be the closest walk to a phone booth to summon AAA to come to our aid, Brandon decided to try, one more time, to start the vehicle. It started up immediately, purring like a baby! Go figure.

In retrospect, as my entire life flashes before my eyes, I know this lightbulb hitch-hiking adventure was not just an event that transformed my life path into a superhighway. It was a re-directional U-Turn that simply tossed me, AKA "Cinderella," into the lap of a trusted inner GPS that had actually been guiding my journey ever since it was launched in 1936 when I landed in my mother's arms.

I have never hitchhiked again. Didn't need to. I learned the intended lesson that beliefs indeed precede and create our life experiences. I also learned what I really came here to teach. Fellow teacher Maureen Ortiz and I created a business called Excel'ent Ventures to empower high school students with tools to build self-esteem and find their reason for living.

Together, Brandon and I founded and trained "The Sage Experience," a seminar company designed to empower people to uncover their inner wisdom by exploring the beliefs and emotional blocks preventing them from experiencing unconditional love for themselves and others. He passed away at the age of 38 in 1985 and, after 18 years of continuing with Sage, I chose to close that company to become a teacher for The Avatar Course®.

It's been 28 years now and my present husband and I are creating a business called, "From Boomer to Bloomer," a company inspiring people over 50 to experience The Avatar Course® and make their remaining decades the happiest and most fulfilling yet.

Grateful for the guidance of my faithful and wise inner "Fairy Godmother," I invite you, dear reader, to take your own Fairy Godmother by the hand and let's all wave our "magic wands" to create a peaceful, win-win world.

Nadine K. Thompson, is an ESL teacher, poet, writing doula, international speaker and writer. Her first book, *Encounters*, a book of poems which looks at a variety of life encounters, was published in 2021. She appeared as an international speaker on the Voices of Women Summit hosted by Kimberly Crowe on March 6th. The title of her talk was called "Woman Transitioning to Self-Love." Her talk is now part of the first *Voices of Women* book, which became a best seller on Amazon. She has also spoken at the Sing Your Heart Song Summit. Her talk title was "Love Un-choreographed" focusing on the SAVERS acronym to help writers to journal and get into the flow. She has shared on the podcast "Book Talk" and has hosted her own writing and journaling workshop.

Nadine is presently writing her first nonfiction book which will be out by the end of 2022. She continues to collaborate with other writers and is a contributor to the Gratitude Book Challenge with Donna Kozik. She presently lives and works in Hangzhou, China.

Email: nadthom@hotmail.com
LinkedIn: linkedin.com/in/nadine-thompson-1852283a
Instagram: instagram.com/afrosensei10
Facebook: facebook.com/Iamawomanrising

Chapter 7

Go Kick Out the Horizons

Nadine K. Thompson

Wherever you go,
go with all your heart.
~ Confucius

In August 2008, I arrived late in the evening at the Charles de Gaulle airport in Paris, and it took us some time to find our hotel. My first impression of France, as I waited to collect my bags, was that it didn't seem as impressive as I had seen on TV. A friend and I were traveling together; we got our luggage and then got on the metro. As we moved along the tracks, I was surprised by the graffiti I saw on the walls of the metro. The train sputtered on in a long and winding way. We were tired after our long flight and wanted to get to our hotel.

Finally, we got off the metro, then sauntered around looking for the exit. We kept seeing the word "sortie," but we had no clue that it meant "exit." We decided to ask other passengers; most were in a hurry and others didn't want to answer when they heard English. We exited the metro station, our patience had been tried and tested, and our emotions were tearing at the edges.

We were now on the streets of Paris. Then came another challenge. We couldn't figure out the numbering on the buildings. After walking for more than twenty minutes, a wonderful lady helped us to find our hotel. The hotel wasn't posh by any degree. It was a mid-ranged hotel, run by an Algerian man. When we checked in, he offered us mint tea, which I gladly accepted, and afterward I had a shower and crashed into bed. This was my first night in the city of Paris.

How did I get to Paris? Why were we here? Let's backtrack to October 2006. I had applied to the Japan Exchange Teaching Program (JET) in December 2005 to work as an Assistant Language Teacher in Japan. Those who were selected got notified in May 2006. I received no response from the Japanese Embassy in Jamaica, and in my mind, all participants had already been selected. I, therefore, went back to work as a high school teacher in Jamaica. I chose to forget all about the JET program. Then I got a call near the end of September. It was late to be heading to Japan, as the school year had already started, but I knew this would be a great opportunity for my life. I grabbed it with both hands and ran towards the mesmerizing thrill of the unknown.

Japan was filled with countless surprises for me. The first one was that I was placed on an island. In one sense that seemed amazing, moving from my island of Jamaica to an island in Japan. There were tons of similarities between Jamaica and Amami Ōshima, Japan. One Jamaican guy repeatedly told me that he felt bad for me because I would not garner the real Japanese culture because I had been placed on a small remote island.

Living on Amami Ōshima proved challenging, especially due to the language barrier. I made learning Japanese a priority because I needed to communicate, and this communication was necessary for daily survival. I tried to do my best to study, based on the textbooks that were sent to us from CLAIR, the office responsible for the JET program in Japan. Despite my willingness to practice and learn, it became very difficult to learn Japanese on my own. Living on an island meant that there were no language schools or people who were teaching Japanese to foreigners.

In July 2007, I saw an advertisement online that the YMCA in Kobe City would host a free summer camp to teach foreigners Japanese. This, I felt, would be a remarkable opportunity to learn and grow while soaking up some culture on mainland Japan. I told one friend who also desired to improve her Japanese and both of us decided to spend three weeks in Kobe City learning Japanese. This is quite a preamble to explain how I got to Paris, but hold on, the pieces of the story will come together as if fitted together by a seamstress who sews a ball gown for a royal event.

There were different levels for the Japanese classes at the YMCA. I started at the beginner's level. Our gathering was also quite multi-cultural. In the group of students were Koreans, Thai, French, Chileans, Jamaicans, Indians, New Zealanders, Chinese, Indonesian, and many other nationalities. People came with varying reasons for wanting to study Japanese. My friend and I struck up a friendship with two international students, one from France and the other from Chile.

During the afternoons, with classes out of the way, we rummaged through the city taking in museums, shopping malls, street food, and festivals. We even hung out at daytime karaoke places. We took the special Japanese pictures called "purikura," where we went into a booth and snapped crazy group photos of ourselves. These girls were high school kids, and we were teachers, but we felt as if we were all the same age, rushing along with excitement, everything capturing a new feeling for us. I enjoyed their company and the thrill of finally being able to explore mainland Japan tickled our hearts. One magical treat we gave ourselves was when we went to Kobe Harbor at night. It infused us with joy as we rode on the Ferris wheel and had a meal together, as we took pictures and settled ourselves into teenage frolic.

The friendships we built those three weeks felt lasting. We celebrated my French friend's birthday with her and we all discussed the future and where we would meet again. On a whim, she mentioned that we should come to Paris to visit her. Neither my friend from New Zealand nor I had ever been to Paris, so this invitation rested in our hearts. It continued to be nurtured even after we went back to Amami Ōshima. My French friend returned to France after completing her year of international study in Japan. My friend from New Zealand and I made plans to visit Europe. The story threads are now intertwined taking this idea that was planted in our heads and making it a reality.

The journey to France proved to be hard. The fact that I was not from a country with a strong passport meant that I needed to apply for a Schengen Visa. We wanted to start our journey from France, visit the friend we met in Kobe, then travel to Italy, Spain, and Germany. I set to work trying to get a visa. The information I got from the French Embassy in Tokyo outlined that to get the visa I had to meet several criteria, one of which required me to have proof of where I would stay in France.

I could not just go online and book a hotel. First I would have to pay for the hotel in full. Then I needed to have a letter from the hotel in France saying that I had booked the reservation. The hotel had to approve it by affixing their stamp and the signature of the manager to it. This became quite challenging for me. Many hotels were not willing to sign this letter for me. Living on Amami Island limited the fact that there were not any travel agents who could help me to get my flights and hotels organized in the way the French embassy required for the documentation.

My friend had her heart set on traveling to France together, but she could not fully comprehend why I needed a visa to travel. She felt it was because Jamaica wasn't a good country, without understanding that countries are ranked in different tiers based on their economic standing. This affected whether one could travel and move freely to other countries. I pressed on, holding on to hope. I called several hotels and hostels in France, Italy, and Germany trying to find accommodation that would be willing to send a letter of proof that I could stay in their hotels. Finally, I got everything organized and I had to go to the embassy in Tokyo. I bottled up a collective nervousness in my heart, and worry pulled my head down.

I got to the French embassy in Tokyo and waited in a long line. I handed in my documents and there was one glitch—one hotel's address could not be verified. My heart sank. I had run a marathon trying to get all the documents they wanted. I had also spent a lot of money to pay in full for my flight and hotel. There was no way I could walk away and call it a day. I made my case to the guy who collected my documents. They would give me a few days to get the hotel's correct address and submit it to the embassy. I went back to Amami Ōshima broken. What was next? What could I do? My friend felt disappointed for me and I told her it was probably time for her to go on this trip without me.

After resting for the night, the following day I got back on my phone and made more calls. We could not get through to the hotel with the missing information. I had to cancel the payment I'd made to the hotel. My friend finally had a breakthrough with another hotel that was willing to provide the proof of stay and a valid address, as long as I paid for the hotel. I grabbed hold of this latest straw thrown to me and quickly paid the money, and they got the document ready. After that, I had to get it faxed to the embassy in Tokyo. I got everything completed in the last few hours before the cut-off time.

I slept well that night and didn't worry about the outcome; I had done all I could to fight, pray, and plan. This dream of visiting a country I felt to be glamorous and representative of high class had rocked my confidence and shown me a side of the world that held disparities based on race and other types of discrimination. I later received news that I got the visa; my passport would be sent to me by courier.

You might surmise about why I put up such a resistance; why take on this battle to get to Europe? The trip to Europe was massive in what it stood for to a girl who grew up in a rural village in Jamaica. As a child my family did not have disposable income for us to travel anywhere as a family. I remember staying at home during the summer holidays; books became my friends. I would go to the public library in my small town and borrow books to read because I didn't have many books at home. In books I read about far-off lands and that was how I traveled and explored the world. I had even written a poem about a couple caught up in a romantic walk along the streets of France. These were only ideas that I had in my head. Going to Europe was, in a sense, expanding my horizons.

One thing that seemed unattainable for my family was traveling. Luxury was not something that we could afford in any area of our lives. I went to a high school with one area for boarding students and another for day students. It meant I did not live on the school's campus; I went home every evening because I lived close to the school. Many of the students at my high school had parents who worked in the bauxite industry as engineers and managers. They were known to be well-paid. These kids had the luxury of traveling around Jamaica and staying in nice resorts, as well as being able to go to Florida and the Caribbean islands. Other parents were doctors, nurses, teachers, and government workers. Like me, some had parents who were farmers, and in my case, my parents had not received any higher education. We all ended up at the same high school. For me, it was based on the fact that I received high scores in the National Primary School exams that placed us in different high schools. High school in Jamaica starts when students are ages 10-11, which is equivalent to middle school in the US and other countries.

Growing up in my small village, the church was the pivotal place that brought us together. We didn't have a cinema close by, so we would organize movie evenings at church. We also had a games evening, and we even put on our own music and drama productions. I spent a great deal of time at home with my family and helped my parents on their farm. Being quite agile as a child, I used to climb trees and help my mother pick tangerines and oranges that she would bring to the market and sell, or use at home to make juice. I fed the chickens and helped with the goats. These things we did because there were four of us girls at home and we did not have a brother growing up with us. While feeding the pigs, I would daydream about many things: a life in which we had disposable income to enjoy good food, good places, and true elegance.

As a child growing up on a farm, in a village where life was slow, we seemed to be at the bottom of the food chain. Most of my clothes were quite unflattering and not in the fashion of the day. As a teenager, I felt out of place. I became a bookworm with very limited social skills. My routine was home to school and weekends at church. Most of the trips I took around Jamaica were with groups. Dreaming of living or visiting exotic places was a way in which I felt we could enjoy some of the blessings of the universe.

The first night I arrived in Amami Ōshima, the other foreign teachers on the island organized a party for me. It coincided with their Halloween celebrations. This was a party where alcohol was being imbibed. The talk turned to me and one question they asked me was, "Where else have you been before coming to Japan?" I answered that I had been to Cuba, transited through the airport in the US, and now to Japan. Some of them were surprised, "So you have never visited the US and didn't travel to other Caribbean islands as a child?" My answer was "no." One person responded, "Wow, that's crazy you haven't been anywhere." She then went on to tell us that her parents were in the military, and as a child, she had lived in many countries on the continents of Africa, Asia, Europe, and North America.

In that moment I felt small and uncultured. I hadn't been anywhere, and I hadn't done many interesting things. By their standards, "loser" would probably be the best word to describe me. In my interactions with the group after that, I became very quiet. They had a wealth of personal, firsthand experiences about the world that I had only read about in books or seen in movies. I felt like I was really out of my depth, grappling to understand Japan and the Japanese culture, and also measuring myself against the other foreigners and second-guessing myself.

Being on the Jet Program proved to be different from teaching back in Jamaica. Here they expected me to bring real-life experiences to share with my students. I felt deficient in this area, like somehow I had missed the boat somewhere. These were just thoughts I had in my head—my limiting beliefs hanging around and causing me to doubt myself. Despite battling with my inner critics, I decided to dig deep within to learn and engineer a positive atmosphere. I was determined to be the best Assistant Foreign Teacher for the students I had the privilege of teaching.

After a long digression, let's get back to France. On our first day in Paris, we procured a map, got on the metro, and decided to explore the city. We exited the metro at the Main Street intersection. We looked around and I was swept off my feet: in awe of the buildings, their architecture, and the feeling we got stepping out onto the historic Parisian boulevard. There stood the Palais Garnier Opera House. As we breathed in the city, we bought pastry from beautifully decorated shops and sat outside drinking delectable coffee at elegant cafes. Our explorations led us to the River Seine. We took a boat cruise on the Seine and there it loomed above us: the Eiffel Tower. Imposing and strong, the Iron Lady could be seen everywhere as a soldier guarding the city. I could not wait to see it up close.

The streets on the banks of the River Seine buzzed with life. Many people were peddling their wares. In an area where they were selling photos of artistic prints, I found an A-3 size photo of Bob Marley. This represented something wonderful: to be able to connect with another Jamaican on the streets of Paris, if only in spirit. There were tons of Eiffel Tower models in all different sizes and materials. This eclectic street of merging world cultures resonated well within my heart. It provided a good dose of what I needed on my first full day in France.

Our first day culminated with us visiting the Eiffel Tower. There were throngs of tourists and we came face-to-face with the reality that France was a popular tourist destination. It held us tightly, as if in a sardine can. We got discouraged at different points but decided to stay in line until we got our tickets and were able to get to the top. Part way up the elevator broke down. We walked up for much of the way. The very top eluded us, but we were happy that we got to stand on the Eiffel Tower and see the city of Paris below. One of my bucket list activities was crossed off my list and the drive to see more of France was ignited.

Eventually, we met up with our French friend. We had been missing each other's phone calls since landing in Paris. She arranged to show us around the city for a day. She also was not originally from Paris, and had come to stay with her brother while she worked through the summer. It seemed like we had not been separated from each other since we last met in Kobe City, Japan. The continuous banter and our languages interspersed with Japanese created an international potpourri.

It amazed us to see her in her French surroundings. We heard her speaking to other natives and we joked that she was so different when she spoke Japanese, English, and French. She had picked up Japanese quickly and also spoke English well. I, too, wanted to become proficient in Japanese and switch comfortably from one language to the next.

Our day out took us to see Mont Marche, the beautiful and amazing French church. The journey there proved to be an interesting one. While on the metro we met a Black Muslim woman wearing a burka, with her baby strapped to her back. Somehow in France, this image seemed out of place, but this was due to my limited understanding of the diversity of races and religions in France. At Montmartre we were entertained by a very cheeky guy with a painted body who stood like a statue, then started chasing us when we went up close to him. It was all in good fun. We stood at the highest point surrounding the church, our awareness glued to the camera lens; a lens that captured our heartfelt memories.

Street-side cafes piqued my interest, and I appreciated the ambiance of the street leading up to Montmartre. Lunch, however, was not at a café. Instead, we went to a goat cheese restaurant that had a talented Greek chef. I had never had goat cheese before and they offered a wide variety of delicacies. The chef made several recommendations. In the end, we had the chef's special. During this delicious meal, we had a lot of laughs, and as I write this I can't help but stop and smile at how great that day felt, having good food and good friends.

That afternoon we saw our French friend off at the train station. Tears welled up in our hearts, but we promised to meet again. We explored Paris for one more day, getting in some shopping and culture as we visited The Louvre, another popular tourist destination. Locked behind a glass case, the *Mona Lisa* failed to impress us, as museum visitors were not allowed to go up close to see it, and snapping photos of it was not allowed. I enjoyed the Egyptian exhibit, which seized my attention with its display of history and useful information. We got to see the Arc du Triomphe, but we didn't make it to Versailles.

Before leaving Paris, my traveling partner had a great idea. Why not send postcards home to our friends and family? She thought it would be cool to send postcards of

Paris, while we were in Paris. I bought a set of postcards and wrote some messages to my parents, my sisters, and some other friends. In getting myself ready to send the postcards off, I felt mixed emotions. I did not want to be someone boasting and reveling in my newly acquired status as a global traveler. I spoke to one friend from Jamaica who knew that I was traveling in France and she expressed that she felt a tinge of jealousy. She had studied French in high school and always wanted to visit France. I wanted it to be a stirring celebration with my family. I hoped they would see how far I had traveled in my life journey. From a little girl who walked to school because we didn't always have the bus fare; or a girl who wore unfashionable clothes to being in the fashion capital of the world; and a girl who had barely traveled around her own country to experiencing life in Japan; and now was able to get a taste of life in Europe.

On a train bound for Nice, we left Paris. Our first night was rough, but we managed to capture some treasured memories. In Nice, we met another friend who was also living in Japan and traveling around Europe. Nice held its charms and we saw how the rich and famous lived. There was a famous beach packed with so many people we could barely find space to land our feet. Our hostel seemed to be the hip strip for young people who were traveling across Europe for the summer. Dinner and a drink went for 5 Euros, and was quite tasty and filling. The camaraderie and youthfulness was enjoyable. We took a day trip to Monaco. Wow! The Ferraris were impressive. I did not know much about Grace Kelly; I learned a bit about her when I heard about the palace there.

The next leg of our journey took us to Rome. We planned to stay for three days but, little did we know, that was nearly impossible. We got on a hop-on/hop-off bus and got to see a bit of the vast city. The Colosseum stood large and looming. We were told we would have to "jump the line"—meaning we had to pay some guy at the side a few Euros if we were going to get ahead in the line. We decided that we would wait our turn instead. It took some time, but eventually we got in. At the exit, a group of men acted out a gladiator scene and persuaded us to get dressed up and join in. It was good fun and resulted in the sort of photos you look back on and laugh at when the memories flood your mind.

When we visited Vatican City, I felt carried by a deep sense of awe. I did not know until then that the Vatican was regarded as a country and had its own governing rules. The Sistine Chapel blew me away. The work of art on the ceiling can only be described as extraordinary. There was so much history and knowledge in one place that I could have stayed there for hours and hours. We didn't realize that Rome shut down on Sunday and most tourist places were closed. We found some walking paths, explored the city and enjoyed the pizza and pasta. I can safely say that I had the best-ever pizzas in Rome.

Rome, with its sprawling history and quick-tongued and expressive people, took us on the dance floor for a bit, then twirled us and pushed us back. We gathered our bags and headed to Frankfurt, Germany. I had always wanted to visit Spain since studying Spanish at high school and university. But, a tiff brewed and I canceled my trip there, losing most of the money I had paid in full to stay at the hotel. I should have spoken my true feelings to the person I was traveling with. I lost a lot in deciding not to go to Spain.

We got a flight to Frankfurt from Rome. Many people asked us later, why Frankfurt? We were departing from Frankfurt so we thought it might be easier to get there and then we could travel to other parts of Germany. The truth of the matter is that because I needed a visa to travel, I didn't get a lot of legroom to plan spontaneously. If I could do it again, I would chose to read more about the places I would visit and then plan a better itinerary.

Frankfurt slowed us down and allowed us to reflect on the whole journey up to that point. We took time to get a good rest, visit interesting museums, and enjoy apple wine. It is a city full of banks, and we got a chance to go to the top floor of the highest bank and look down at the whole city. Frankfurt is known as a premier transport hub of the world. Surprisingly it had a very complicated metro system. Well, that is what we thought when we compared it to Rome, which had just one major line. The city grew on us and I loved the greenery. I did some shopping and we enjoyed an array of good chocolate and cheese.

My friend wanted to go to another city to see the home of Mozart, which was quite a journey away. I decided not to go. In the end, she did not want to go on her own. Deep down it might have been me putting up resistance because I had to cancel going to Spain. After that, the thin air between us cut like a sharp knife. We gave each other space. I went off to get some fresh air and after that things were fine again.

The trip to Europe opened my eyes to many things in the world: the hardships of people with third-world country passports, and how hard it is to travel as global citizens due to visa restrictions. I saw glimpses of racism with people assuming that my friends would pay for me; thinking I was not financially competent to pay for myself. I saw the disparity in life with a woman who did not want to sit next to me on the Eurostar.

On the other hand, it was a victory for me. I come from the rural village of White Shop, Clarendon Jamaica. If you look it up on Google Earth, you probably will see the topography, but not see my house clearly. Despite all my struggles, I took the gumption that my parents instilled within me, bolstered up my courage, and faced the nay-sayers. Many people did not believe that I would ever amount to anything in life because my teachers described me as unassuming. Many also thought I did not have big dreams. I did not voice a lot about the life that I had imagined for myself, but something inside wanted more and pushed me to claim more from the universe.

I lived most of my life hooked on one side by limiting beliefs, and on the other side by imposter syndrome. I felt that in some ways I did not deserve it. I was rising too much above my status. In writing this story, I am reflecting on my journey. I pushed towards the horizons with all my might and I shattered the glass ceiling holding me back in the cocoon of being a woman, being black, and being from the third world. No dream is too big; go conquer your horizons. The journey will present overwhelming obstacles and pressures that will cause you stress. Be strong!

"You may not control all the events that happen to you, but you can decide not to be reduced by them."

~ Maya Angelou

Katy Maag is a BSN, RN, CCRP, Certified Stress Management Coach, Uppiness Facilitator, Presenter and a Laughter Yoga/Therapist and Teacher. She offers tools for stress management and laughter in order to provide more joy in current times.

Katy works with professionals who want to master their state of wellness. She has been a presenter for over two decades on health and wellness, with a side of laughter, adding an element of edutainment as a stress-relief tool.

Email: Ikatymaag@gmail.com
Website: KMwellnessconsulting.com
Facebook: KMWellness Consulting
Linkedin: KatyMaag

Chapter 8

Seasoned with Wisecracks

Katy Maag

If you laugh a lot, when you get older
your wrinkles will be in the right places.

~ Andrew Mason

The first memory I have is at the age of three years old and my brothers were four and one. Our grandmother dressed us up and drove us to a big, old building. Everyone was sad, crying and saying, "He was so young." My mother remained in another room. The three of us walked silently into the big room where Dad lay on a tall, raised bed. We had no idea what was going on. As we walked away, hand-in-hand, my grandmother knelt and whispered, "You have to be a good girl if you want to see him someday."

I only remember a few things from when I was three years old. I remember when my Grandma taught my mom how to drive a stick shift in her blue Opal, a car we kept for more than 15 years. We did not go out much except to church or to visit a few relatives. That car held many memories of laughter and one big life lesson: don't hold on to the door handle when someone is driving around a curve. My brother fell out of the car that way—and his only concern was his orange popsicle that got dirty.

As I grew older and went to school, I knew I was different, because in those days a single parent household was not very common. I always felt grateful that Father's Day came in the summer. My mom had a hard life and was not well mentally. Looking back, I became my mom's caretaker. My mom's mother and dad passed away when she was young.

As time went on, my mother became more troubled and unwell. She would often wake me up in the middle of the night saying she was dying because she ate a sock or a button which she could not find. Of course, this made it difficult to get up and go to school the next morning. I wasn't very good in school and they enrolled me in the special needs room.

In the second grade my aunt, Mom, and I were in a car accident. My mom sat unresponsive in the front seat. I was terrified, thinking that she had died.

In third grade, I started handling the checkbook, and even ordering pizza for the family dinner. We didn't have much money, so pizza became a special treat. I first started gaining weight in the third grade. The neighbor boy and I were found "playing house"—it was innocent, nothing happened. But my grandma said I was pregnant, and being so young, I thought it might be true—I thought I had to eat for two. By fourth grade, I weighed 200 pounds. Being overweight also added to my problems of fitting in at school. I felt tired, isolated, and confused.

At age twelve, I was in a serious car accident with my uncle, his three sons, and my brother. The car flipped, which ejected me from the car. I had a head injury and a crushed right elbow. They did surgery on my elbow that night. Two days later when I was allowed to walk, they discovered I had also broken my left foot. I had a cast on my right arm and left leg, not something you see every day. Looking back, I had begged my uncle not to go down that road. I had a dream the night before that the accident was going to happen. At times, I see things before they occur.

My great grandmother was Madge Laird, a bareback horseback rider in the circus, and part Cherokee. When my grandmother passed away, (my Dad's adopted mother) his half-sister attended the funeral and told me that, in fact, we have some Cherokee ancestry.

Throughout most of my school years, I was picked on and bullied. Now that I am older, I realize most people have had this experience in some capacity. One year I ran to be a county officer in Future Homemakers of America—the Historian. I managed to be elected as the Historian and I even arranged to present a plaque to President Ronald Reagan when he came through our county by train. Well, as often happens when using public transportation, the train ran very late, so we didn't get to present him with his plaque as an "honorary homemaker." But, his office did send me an interesting letter and the first embossed paper I had ever seen. I still have that as a keepsake.

Back in school, I felt very unsure of myself and my abilities, as I thought I was not good enough. School did not count high on my list of things to do. I was tired from being up all night with my mom or studying, or working at a carryout, and suffering from being overweight. At home, I would sometimes worry that I might get injured when a family member would get violent if he didn't get money for drinking, or other illegal substances.

My junior year was probably the worst, as I missed a cumulative forty-five days of school which is over a quarter of the school year. I did not want to do anything but keep working after high school. I felt I wasn't smart. Was I wrong! I was a caretaker and a survivor. It is amazing, looking back, at how seasoned I became at an early age, doing many things most people never have to deal with. I did them and I kept on going.

I even went on and earned the highest degree in Future Homemakers of America, but couldn't go to the state capital and walk across the stage to be awarded the plaque. I had no money to go and I had to work. The guidance counselor tried to find a way for me to attend with the other students, but I refused due to work. When I graduated from high school, I didn't even look to see if the diploma was signed. Well, to my surprise, it was.

After high school, I worked one full-time and three part-time jobs as a carryout worker, bartender, and nurse's aid. After working for a year, I decided I loved being a nurse. My aunt was going back to school to be one also and I decided to attend as well. Going to nursing school full-time and working so many hours became overwhelming. I failed two classes by only a few points. One was pediatrics, and the other pharmacology. Now, looking back, the knowledge from those classes came in handy.

I moved out of my family house in a hurry. Something inappropriate happened to me and I told my Mom—she didn't believe me. I left in fear of more abuse and couldn't live with it anymore. So I moved in with my grandparents who owned an apartment building. I lived with them until a nearby apartment became available.

One of the first months I lived with my grandparents, their eldest son, who was in his 40s, died of a massive heart attack while they were at bingo. They had adopted him when he was three months old, and my dad and my uncle were nine and ten. The night he died is a memory that sticks. I had to sit them down and tell them—one of the hardest things I have had to do in my life. Life is precious, and they were elderly.

My name changed while living next to them, as Grandpa would answer the phone and call me "Katydid," and it stuck. We did have some laughs, a bond that strengthens many relationships.

After a few years, my grandfather's health worsened, and we asked hospice to come to care for him. I was still working and going to school. The night before he passed, I stayed up late watching him and finally decided to get some sleep, as I had a test the next day. Oddly the test was on the respiratory system. I fell asleep and had the oddest dream that my barefoot Dad and my uncle who had died, suddenly came back to me and said they were "taking Grandpa home at around 5:00."

I woke up at 4:00a.m. and Grandpa woke up and wanted to know why I was awake. I said because I was studying. I went to school that day and just wanted to be quiet—not my norm, as I was always lively and encouraging everyone. My classmate asked me what was going on, and I told her about my dream. I got home from school half an hour before I had to go to work. My grandma said he had a great day.

While working at the nursing home I had witnessed the signs of the process of leaving this world and knew I should have stayed home. At work, a close friend told me to go home, that it would not be long before he would pass. The next day, when Grandma and I talked about the dream, I asked if my dad was barefoot when he was buried. She looked shocked and told me: in those days they didn't bury people with shoes.

Two months later, my grandma needed back surgery and I became her caretaker as she recovered. Then my mom started to have problems with her blood pressure. They admitted her to the hospital, and sometime in the middle of the night, she had three strokes.

After six weeks of caring for her, we moved her to a rehabilitation unit in Dayton, although she came home on weekends. I took care of her, and even had to insert a catheter to drain her bladder. I did not have help to take care of her and after everything that had happened I'm not sure why I did it. I used to put everyone's needs before my own. I learned later that you cannot pour into anyone else's cup, if you have nothing left in yours. I kept working full-time hours between three jobs, going to school full-time, and caring for my mother.

I graduated—the first person in my family to graduate from college. I went to work on the night shift at the local hospital. First, I floated to different units in the hospital, which became a great experience. Then I learned that I enjoyed critical nursing and started to work in the Intensive Care Unit. Soon, I was approached to be the Nurse of Hope for the Cancer Society. That is when my speaking engagements started.

I loved working in ICU until one night when I switched shifts with another nurse. We were all busy. In the next room the patient was a baby with Shaken Baby Syndrome. I had another adult patient who was having difficulties. He rolled over and fully fisted me right between the eyes. I had an instant headache and water running from my nose. I could not think clearly but figured it was due to the headache. I stayed with the baby in the next room while that nurse went to lunch. The baby's oxygen went low, and I couldn't even think clearly enough to know what to do.

After my night shift I drove home, still not thinking clearly. Later, Grandma found me with my car still running, the car door open, my apartment door open, and me lying on my bed. Good thing I lived in a small community! Later that night, I went out with my friends. They insisted I go to the Emergency Department because I was not acting right. I could not even carry or follow a conversation. So I went to the ED and the doctor said, "Oh, it's just a head injury."

It did not get better. I had injections in my head for the headache. The doctor also tested my memory skills, and I could only remember two numbers in any order. The average person can recall seven numbers, which is why the telephone number has that many. It turned out to be a long healing process. I felt grateful that I kept my humor as it was hard to think straight. I even went to a head injury support group.

After eight months, I didn't feel ready to return to nursing. Mentally exhausted, I could not register red lights and stop signs. It took maybe another year to recover. In the meantime, I weighed 350 pounds and felt men wouldn't be attracted to me at that large size. I had stomach weight loss surgery. I know some people think that is the easy way out, but they are wrong. It is still hard work every day.

After a year-and-a-half, I met my current husband. We were older when we got married and I had medical conditions that made it difficult to get pregnant. We started trying. After being married for only two months, we found out I was pregnant with my first child. Most of the pregnancy was difficult, with many related medical issues.

When first pregnant, I worked in a hospital in Cardiac Rehabilitation, the Healthy Lifestyle Information Center, and the Occupational Health Unit. I went in to apply for a full-time job in the occupational unit. I had a doctor's appointment when I was 24 weeks along. Not feeling well when I got to the doctor's office, he checked me and told me I was already 2 cm dialated and my cervix was 30% effaced.

I got a very quick ride over to the hospital to be admitted for surgery in the morning. They put a stitch in my cervix called a cerclage, which is used to keep the cervix closed. In the morning, I didn't progress, so surgery was in the cards. After surgery, they wanted to move me to a bigger hospital used for high-risk pregnancies. They said I was 3 cm dilated, and had a 50% chance of having the baby because labor was progressing. I got to Ohio State University Hospital, which was on strike and people were put wherever they could find space.

So after I was put in this big room, the residents checked me. They told me they were removing the stitch because I was going to deliver that day. After they removed the stitch, they moved me to the maternity ward to wait. They put me in bed with my head down and feet up because my bag of water had ruptured. So I had slow-leaking water from that point on. I remained in that position for eight days. I always wanted to be a mother, and at 32 years of age, I became one. I delivered at 4:30 a.m., five minutes after the doctor checked my cervix and had reassured me I was not in labor.

I rolled over and felt like a gunshot had gone off in my belly. I didn't even have time to put my glasses on. I put the call light on and when the nurse came in, she screamed down the hall that I was delivering. I had no glasses on, so I couldn't see anything. I just heard a weak cry that sounded like a cat. They rushed him off very quickly. I lay there and was in shock at what had just happened. Did it happen? After a while, I put on the call light as I did not feel well. Having a baby, you bleed a lot, but something seemed off. Yes, I was correct. I had a uterine tear and had bled more than average. I couldn't get up, as I had been on bed rest for over eight days.

Every morning the minister came in to talk with me and to ask how I was doing. Then she asked about my son's details. I looked at her and said I had no idea. She said she would fix that. She went down, took pictures, and baptized him as 1lb. 12 oz. and 13.5″ long. At 26 weeks, he was a preterm baby, 14 weeks early, and had only a 50% or less chance of survival. They didn't allow me to see him because I had developed a fever and was ill.

I didn't see him for two days, and ironically, the first time happened on Mother's Day. So, trying to be a good mother, as he needed extra nutrition, I decided to breastfeed. A nurse came into my room with a breast pump. I learned how to use it, and she reassured me that at first I wouldn't produce much milk, but that it would come. I was released from the hospital and able to go home for one night and pack. I planned to go back down and stay in a nearby hotel. My aunt, uncle, and my grandma were so anxious to see him that they drove me down on 315, a major highway. I sat in the back seat using the breast pump so I could keep on schedule. The machine malfunctioned, and the batteries leaked all over my clothes.

The first thing I did when I got back to the hospital was to go talk to the nurse. When I told her what occurred with the pump, she looked at me and said she didn't think this had ever happened in all her years on the job. I asked the nurse to get another machine. We laughed together for a moment. Honestly, I needed a bit of stress relief. It is an understatement to say that having a baby who is a micro-preemie is a roller coaster ride, with many ups and downs.

The first major unfavorable hurtle came when the doctor said my son, Mason, needed to learn to breathe without a tube. That turned out to be the worst decision. The doctor let his oxygen go too low, to 80%. When checked the next day, Mason had developed areas in his brain that lacked oxygen, which would result in a stroke in adults. In these kids, it is an indicator of cerebral palsy. The doctor let us know it might be just his legs, or both his arms and legs, that were affected. Mason had all four extremities affected, so they decided to transport him to a children's hospital to be treated. I went home, and the next morning I got a call that, in two hours, they were planning to move him. That is approximately how long it took to drive to the children's hospital. Fortunately, the transport went well.

Mason had to have many surgeries; the first one was to open up his airway. After surgery, the area became infected, and the doctors at Columbus Children's called to inform me that a tracheostomy tube for breathing was his only option. I felt devastated, getting that news over the phone. As a nurse, I knew what all it could entail. I hung up the phone, lay in a fetal position in the corner of my new house, and cried for over an hour, as my mind swirled with fear and worry.

I found myself in a new home and in a new community. I knew I could somehow take this on. I always wanted to be a mom, but not like this. It took a long time to realize that we all have something that we choose to do; "picking your hard" is an understatement. After many surgeries and much education, Mason was able to come home after 14 weeks in the hospital. The family room in our home became like a mini-hospital room. We had an oxygen tank, a baby heart and breathing monitor, suction equipment, and the regular baby basics.

We had only been home for about a week when my niece came to visit. Mason was not even four pounds. She was holding him close to her body. As she pulled him away from her shoulder his tracheostomy tube, which was not snug, came out. He turned blue instantly. I laid him down and reinserted the tube and started CPR. At that time, the EMS was on their way to take him to the hospital. Well, thank goodness they did not keep him. He just needed the tube to breathe no matter what, which meant we had to pay attention to all the clues of an ongoing breathing problem.

For the first nine months Mason was at home, his nighttime care had to be concise. Mason had to eat two ounces of formula every three hours, in addition to having breathing treatments every three hours, and postural drainage. With severe acid reflux events after he ate, I had to keep him upright for 20 minutes, except for changing his diaper. This would take over two hours. By the time he fell asleep, and everything was completed, we would get another 20 minutes of rest until the next round.

Mason had many surgeries for multiple medical issues during the first three years of his life. However, the tracheostomy tube was not going anywhere. Finally, they sent us to a specialist who was considered the best in the world. On our first visit, he flat out told me, "When this tracheostomy is gone, you will think I am like God." He was noted to be number one in the world for his success in getting children to have the tracheostomy tube removed and to be able to breathe naturally. There were multiple surgeries to get the tube out, including reconstruction.

Even with all this, we had hoped to have another child. I found out, just before corn harvest season, that I was pregnant again. We had planned to keep it quiet; however, I was sideswiped and had to tell them in the ambulance that

I was expecting. The first few visits, we saw a heartbeat, then at the 13-week visit—no heartbeat. Therefore, I had a D&C to remedy the non-viable pregnancy. A few months later, I became pregnant again. This one was similar to the first, where I felt nauseated most of the day—the first clue that I was expecting.

For multiple reasons, I had to have a cerclage (the stitch to keep the cervix closed) at 14 weeks and was put on bed rest, so was not allowed to take Mason to his medical appointments. That pregnancy became difficult as I stressed about both Mason and my unborn child. The night I went into labor with my youngest I had my favorite meal—crab legs. I got up and felt something happen, like I wet my pants. In the bathroom, I thought my water broke but it hadn't. Since it was a very high-risk pregnancy, we drove quickly to the hospital. I knew I was in labor. They checked me and said they weren't sure. So the doctor came in and took the stitch out of my cervix, as my water broke, only three weeks early this time.

The doctor stayed and in the morning, reassured me that if I were in labor for twenty-four hours, I would have a cesarean section to deliver the baby. Lucky me . . . they administered an epidural for pain control way too early. It had worn off by the time the doctor arrived, 30 minutes before I was scheduled for the c-section. I attempted to keep pushing, but then they instructed me to stop. The baby's cord was wrapped around his neck two times. Mitchel finally emerged and was fine.

Life continued to be a struggle. Mason often would pull his tracheostomy tube out as a way to get attention, which was difficult to deal with. Meanwhile, my boys grew older and went to school, while I still cared for my mother, along with the help of my younger brother, who proved to be an amazing caretaker.

Then, it was highly suggested that all nurses get their bachelor's degree in nursing before 2019, the year I turned 57 years old. The first thing they told me was that I just wasn't on my game anymore. Therefore, I decided to prove to myself that I could do it. I went on to become a certified Cardiac Rehabilitation Specialist. When I took the exam, I was one of the first to do it, a demanding test that had a 60% passing rate on the first take.

I continued going to school and became active in the American Cardiac Pulmonary Rehabilitation Organization. I have been a representative for our part of Ohio, and even president. They also asked me to be on the Mac Committee, a liaison for Medicare and companies, so they know the documentation and criteria for rehabilitation. I have been to Capitol Hill, talking to Senators and Representatives, to help get legislation changed for heart health. I have been going to D.C. approximately twice a year for the past six years with American Associated Cardiovascular Pulmonary Rehabilitation and American College of Cardiology.

I enjoy working with cardiac patients, as heart disease is the number one killer in the United States. I have been working in cardiac rehabilitation for over 23 years now. About four years ago, we started to do intensive cardiac rehabilitation, in which the patients get exercise and education every day. I work off-site by myself most days.

One day while watching information videos, I learned about Laughter Yoga as a stress reduction technique. I researched and discovered the nearest training was three hours away. I decided to sign up, as I have naturally used laughter as a stress reducer for most of my life. I try to find the humor in most situations and that can be hard at times. I found myself pleasantly surprised how easy it is—Laughter Yoga has helped keep me grounded in many situations.

I am now a seasoned professional trainer for Laughter Yoga. Along the way, I learned that people's behaviors are about them, not about me. I realize that there are adult bullies who want to retain their power and position. I wish someone had told me earlier in life that "laughter is the best medicine" and that it feels like an instant vacation. I have always used laughter, but was not sure why until recently. I have learned to implement it into my work life and into my presentations. I have also started to work on becoming an Associated Applied Therapeutic Humorist. I am learning and growing where I feel necessary. I've also learned it's best to always light your own fire and energy first because if you don't, it goes away.

I am a caretaker to my sons, patients, family, and Bob who is my adopted dad, and anyone else I meet. I try to be seasoned and let things go, like Teflon. Laughter is a great vacation and a buffer. I enjoy presentations and spreading humor and joy.

Lori Blum Sugarman is an imagination coach, a youth motivator, a writer, illustrator, teacher, conference presenter, and a believer that written expression for children and teens is as essential as oxygen.

Her writings include: *Plumdiggity! Developing Student Writers*, two volumes of poems, 26 songs of alphabet characters, five children's stories, three plays, three short stories including "General Ruckus and the Peepcircles," "The Gingerbread Village," "Adventures of Penelope Sugarplum," and a book of lullabies.

Lori has devoted the past 15 years to developing student writers through the Plumdiggity Writing Method of Creativity and Imagination.

Email: infullblume@gmail.com
Website: Plumdiggity.com
Instagram: lorisugarwriter

Chapter 9

Writing Will

Lori Blum Sugarman

I can shake off everything as I write;
my sorrows disappear, my courage is reborn.

~ Anne Franke

Your heart and my heart have emotions, protests, observations, and moments of exhilaration to voice. Imagine being a big blob of emotion inside a silent vessel, without windows.

"Let me out of here!" screams Miss Furious, who had to suppress herself when her "friend" acted selfishly.

"No, no!" said Mr. Conscious Restraint. "You can't make a scene. Be quiet!"

"That's not fair!" Miss Disappointment protested in silence, losing a promotion to someone less skilled.

"Shhhhhh," cajoled Mr. Conscious Restraint, "don't be a poor loser!"

Ugh! All that heart and emotion with nowhere to go. I hope my story convinces you to explore more written expression for yourself, and/or for the children in your world. It is your best friend in hiding.

For me, writing has been that non-judgmental best friend, a boredom rescuer, a frustration receiver, a sadness dumping ground, a creative observer, and a vehicle for expressing the impossible, imagining the unreachable, and speaking the unspeakable. Writing has been my home for rhyme and rhythm, both in absurdity and actuality. It lets me philosophize over anything—even ants—and gives me nods of approval when the words express their intention. Writing allows me to express myself in ways that orally would never happen.

My parents were role models for written and expressive language, not intentionally, but randomly. It is just the random personalities they were. Life is so random, isn't it? You and I are here based on the union of one egg and one of 200-500 million sperm. What if I was the result of a different sperm? Would I still have green eyes, brown hair, and a penchant for practical jokes? Would I have a mind that quickly hops from subject to subject? Would I have grown to love writing, with different parents?

Both of my parents were unusual and not like other parents I knew in childhood. Most parents want you to memorize your math facts or know the state capitals or memorize some religious or secular wise teachings. My dad, Jack Blum, insisted we memorize this verse:

I was gleaned in protoplasm by the prehistoric chasm
that separates the monkey from the man
By means of valued data
and geologic strata
I can tell you which day the earth began.

He even made us learn to say and spell a-n-t-i-d-i-s-e-s-t-a-b-l-i-s-h-m-e-n-t-a-r-i-a-n-i-s-m.

Additionally, we were constantly peppered with his one-liners in lieu of back and forth conversation. They were a mix of life commentary and humor. I think his one-liners served to elevate him beyond the mundane details of life. Instead of discussing the nuance of a sibling squabble, he would say, "When two people agree, one is unnecessary." Jack was not attuned to nitty gritty details.

Other "Jackisms" we heard a million times:

- "Say three words, Poochie (our dog) and I'll never have to work again."
- "The wounds of life—don't nurse them, don't rehearse them."
- "You have to see the world through rose-colored glasses."
- "Buh-buh-buh-but officer . . . (said as he ran a red light).
- "1-2-3-CHANGE (waiting for a red light to change) 1-2-2¼ -2½-2¾, Ch ch ch ch ch CHANGE!"
- "I have a ten-state territory: North Carolina, South Carolina, Georgia, Tennessee, Florida, Alabama, Mississippi, plus the states of Frustration, Fatigue, and Anxiety."
- "Minkschool Dinkschool Olivier Flickerschool" (what he said when trying to break us out of a pout).
- "The guy at Eckerds said . . ." (Giving us his advice but tricking us to believe the drugstore clerk said it.)

My mother, Barbara Blum, engaged us in car word games like GHOST and ABC (being the first to find a road sign word or license plate starting with A through Z) whenever on an errand or family trip. We loved playing the word game "Perquacky" which can now only be found on eBay. Her routine after fixing, clearing and cleaning breakfast dishes for seven eaters began with the daily crossword puzzle, while her cigarette lay upon a glass notched ashtray, burning slow twirly smoke—a habit she couldn't kick until nine days before her death, declaring 65 years too late, "I'm never smoking again."

She broke the doldrums of mothering, policing, refereeing, nursing, cooking, and laundering with a book in hand. We even had a dictionary about a foot wide with its own chest-high stand. Because it was there, and accessible, we often walked over to it, closed our eyes, fanned the pages, landed on a random word, and read the definition. Some words had pictures. I always loved words with pictures.

Those darned thank you letters we were forced to write to relatives for holiday and birthday gifts! But I found it to be a pleasant experience. If you have young children, use the thank you letters as a forced opportunity for your child to put thoughts to paper. I think my enjoyment came because I could write what I wanted without interruption or opinion from a sibling or a parent.

My father was a language humorist, and it was fortunate that his industry at the time was ripe for humor. As a bra and girdle salesman, before the era of "Me Too," you can imagine the jokes we heard around female anatomy, living off the fat of the land, supporting half the population, and the new bra sizes that included ping pong, ding dong, king kong, and holy cow. In today's no humor climate, his cups would have runneth over straight to the firing squad.

Random Encounters

I am the firstborn, to Jack and Barbara Blum, of five siblings. The moment my parents met could not have been more random. My mother, a Los Angeles-born and raised 25-year-old, was two years engaged and taking a final "girl" summer trip, with her best friend Marion, across the country before her wedding in the late fall. My dad, Jack, a 35-year-old New York native, had recently accepted a position as a bra and girdle salesman and was traveling his seven-state territory.

He came out of the same movie theater in Miami, Florida as my mother and Marion, but through a different exit. He headed to the nearby newspaper stand, where the girls arrived 10 seconds earlier and had purchased the last newspaper. Jack asked to buy the newspaper from them and then suggested they all have dinner the next night. The trio had dinner two nights in a row and on the third day, the girls began the trip back to California.

Long story short, my parents married one year later and lived together for 55 years until death. What if they sat somewhere different in the theater and never crossed paths at the newspaper stand? Mr. Random strikes again.

The Pearce and Crawford Families

It seems to be developmentally "normal" to want to be like everyone else, until you are way past your teenage years.

My family was different from our southern neighbors on many counts. First of all, we were Jewish and that made us different in terms of all holiday celebrations, feeling uncomfortable singing Christmas songs in school, and not going to church on Sunday mornings, like everyone else. Second, my mother was from California and my father from New York, which brought different values and humor from Southern culture. Third, my mother was a screamer and a yeller; our house was noisy and rambunctious.

Everyone else in the neighborhood had calm parents who did not yell. The exception was the Crawford family, who happened to have six children all about the ages of the Blum kids. I felt perfectly normal and comfortable at the Crawford's. It was no different than ours— a lot of activity, board games, and Mrs. Crawford yelling at one of the boys in her New England accent . . ."CHRISTOPHA! GET IN HERE RIGHT NOW!"

In second grade, my new friend two houses up, Susan Pearce, and I sat upon big round concrete pipes that lay on the dirt lot of a house being built next to mine. We talked about our mothers crying because John F. Kennedy had been assassinated that day. The first time I went to play at Susan's house, her mom let us take Coca-Cola (which I was not allowed to have) and Saltine crackers outside to snack on. Susan and I ended up having a "cracker-in-Coke toss fest" on each other, and her mother was not pleased. I remember being curious that Mrs. Pearce didn't yell, but you could still tell she was mad.

We played tetherball all the time, raked leaves into piles, covered them with sheets and jumped into the piles.

In the winter the Pearce's had a roaring fire in their fireplace and hot chocolate ready for any neighborhood kids needing to get warm and dry from the hours of sledding in a hearty snow. The Pearce house stood at the top of the hill which we had to walk up, in order slide down the fantastic slope Hobbs Road gave us, for perfect sledding. The fireplace was always filled with random gloves and mittens needing to dry before returning to the frigid, but thrilling, outside elements.

I loved Susan's house. As the youngest of four, and the last child living at home, Susan's house seemed calm and peaceful. Our house was loud and chaotic. My mother was a big yeller and screamer. You've heard me repeat that already, but—just like the rabbis say, "when the Torah repeats, pay attention." Her yelling was defining! Her irritation happened often, as the only adult, alone in a house with five kids, due to my dad's weekly out-of-town travel.

She ran a tight ship and expected us to hop to it when she barked an order. If she called us to the kitchen table for a meal, or to come inside and we weren't there almost immediately, the Barbara Blum natural bullhorn erupted! I think that is why she never had cancer. She yelled out all her anger and kept nothing suppressed. Her emotions left her through her vocal box, instead of stewing inside and saturating her cells with stress chemicals.

Humans get mad. Children can be maddening. If you are a yeller, I am here to say we were not harmed for a moment by our mother, who mastered the art of yelling. Her yelling communicated to us that our delay tactics or ignoring her commandments were no longer an option. You may not have to go to the extreme of yelling; it could be a just stern tone of voice, but children are geniuses at hearing the wiggle room in our tone of voice. So say what you mean with firm conviction, and do not add the word, "okay?" at the end. "Okay" implies you are seeking permission. It gives your child too much authority and undermines yours. Plus, it invites an argument. Isn't life easier when children are trained to agree without protest, at least until "rebellion-hood," aka adolescence, arrives?

Susan Pearce's parents were gentle, kind, committed to the less fortunate, and gracious. Mrs. Pearce took us roller-skating many Friday nights at the First Baptist Church skating rink. In fourth grade, she took us to read to underprivileged kindergarten children every week. On the night, once a year, when *The Wizard of Oz* aired on one of three stations: ABC, NBC, or CBS, I was at Susan's house. Together on the blue leather den sofa, we watched, spellbound and excited when the second part of the movie (I think when they made it through the poppy fields) turned from black and white to color.

Mr. Pearce was superintendent of Guilford County Schools, but I just knew him as Susan's daddy who sat in his armchair when I came over, reading the newspaper or watching TV, always engaging with us, always soft toned. I never heard him raise his voice except one time when my sister and I decided to disguise our voices and call him at 5:30 a.m. to see if school would be canceled due to the night's snow.

"LISTEN HERE YOUNG LADY!" he growled, highly

irritated. "I DON'T KNOW HOW YOU GOT MY NUMBER BUT DON'T EVER CALL ME AGAIN. YOU'LL HAVE TO GET YOUR NEWS LIKE EVERYONE ELSE—FROM THE TELEVISION!" and he hung up. That voice was a shocker! I've never confessed to Susan (until now) what we did.

Mr. Pearce took it upon himself to put an end to my dangling teeth that were stubbornly hanging on by a thread. On more than one occasion he tied one end of a string to my tooth and the other end to an open doorknob. One-Two-Three-SLAM the door—and out came the tooth!

Susan's older sister, Sarah, had a closet full of prom dresses. They were satiny elegance, in all colors, flowing in length to the floor. We both went into a trance stepping into Sarah's closet, imagining in our young minds being at a prom, in one of these dresses, with Prince Charming.

Susan's house was a split-level. The entrance door, under the carport, opened into her den with the kitchen off the den, separated by half-sized wooden, saloon-type swinging doors. Down seven or so steps was the basement, where Susan and I made up and performed plays. From the main floor den, up another five steps or so, was another room set up as a den with a sofa, a couple of chairs, and an in-cabinet record player. The room closed off completely with folded doors.

Susan and I played 45s every afternoon from second grade on. We danced and danced. Sometimes one of us would get stuck on a song and insist we play it over and over and over again. I remember getting stuck on "Crimson and Clover" by Tommy James and the Shondells and "I Want to Make it With You," by Bread. I was in love with

George Harrison. That was THE question we always asked everyone, "Who is your favorite Beatle?"

I wish my children had discovered the joy of dancing as I did, beginning in early childhood. Dance with your children! Dancing is joyous, freeing, confidence building, and a great shredder of self-consciousness.

I was occasionally invited to stay for dinner by Mrs. Pearce, and the family had a beautiful tradition. Before eating, everyone would hold hands and Mr. Pearce would thank God for the food. I remember being moved by this as a child. It felt intimate, even though I didn't have the word in my vocabulary.

The only time I ever heard Mrs. Pearce yell was when Susan and I doubled up in her mother's rocking chair and rocked so hard the chair crashed back and broke. Mrs. Pearce became so upset and started crying. I never felt so bad in my life.

Living in the south and being Jewish was not like living in a community where people understood your religion or practice. I remember Mrs. Pearce teaching Susan a little bit about Judaism in front of me and that felt wonderful. I always got to string popcorn for their Christmas tree decorations, which was fun because we never had a Christmas tree. In seventh grade I had to make a dress for Home Economics and my mother was not a sewer. I had picked out this orange and green material and the pattern for a puffy sleeved high bodice dress. It felt like Mrs. Pearce saved my life by helping me learn to sew that dress and pin in those curvy sleeves.

Teenage Years

You may wonder why I share some of these stories. Perhaps I will share something that informs you of how your own child is thinking.

My teenage girlfriends who came over did not know what to make of my Pop. He would ask my 13 and 14-year-old girlfriends their bra sizes, so he could give them some samples, and he asked it as naturally as if it was a shoe size. Speaking of bras, it is quite strange that here my dad was in the business, but I felt too embarrassed to bring up the fact to my mom that I wanted one. I didn't need a bra, but all my friends were wearing them and I wanted one too.

Girls used to wear half-slips and full slips under dresses, and I remember having this stretchy elastic full slip that I cut and made into the length of a bra. Guess what I wore the next morning? A white blouse so EVERYONE could see Lori Blum was wearing a bra too! In the sixth grade, Mrs. Pearce was taking Susan and me to a square dance and my mother took me shopping for an outfit. When I tried on a knitted top, two little mini points were sticking out and I mustered over my embarrassment to say, "Do you think we can pick out a bra?" We did. That was the first and last bra I ever purchased, until my dad retired when I was 42 years old.

Teachers Matter

As I write this, the past two days were spent with my dear friend since third grade, Lu-Anne Winfree Deaton. We pulled out the high school yearbook. Do you realize everything is stored in your memory, no matter if you never retrieve it? She began mentioning names from high school that I had not thought about since then, and could have died without ever thinking of these people. When she said the name, it formed a mental picture and when I looked at the photograph in the yearbook, the two matched up! Our brains are SERIOUS computers!

Lu-Anne and I began talking about our fourth-grade teacher, Mrs. Andrews, who sat in a child's desk facing our class, with speckled age spots on her small, elegant hands and fingernails. One day a new student walked into the room with her dad and there was an awkward silence. Debbie Simon was only ten, but about 5′9″ or 5′10″ tall and her father had to be at least 6′5″. There were no extra desks for Debbie and Mrs. Andrews asked a boy to go to the office to request a desk. Debbie just stood there awkwardly. I raised my hand and offered Debbie to share my seat until the boy came back with her desk. Our families became good friends, but I will never forget the shock of seeing a fourth grader who was almost twice the size of our teacher.

I adored Mrs. Andrews, even if she did write on my fourth-grade report card "Lori talks too much." She let the class free-write once a week and I discovered how stories could just come out of your brain and onto paper. My hand would start moving and stories came out. The magic was the ending, because I started off with no ending in mind and by the end, there it was. It's like walking in the woods, and not keeping track of how you came in, but somehow your exit appears. Our minds are jars awaiting the chance to remove the lid. Mrs. Andrews freed us once a week from the more mundane tasks of formula writing and allowed us to take the lid off for discovery.

Fast forward 30 years . . . In my short time on earth, I've figured out a way to put creative writing programs into dozens of schools and help hundreds of students discover the joy of writing. An unbelievable episode initially slammed the door in my face, but time healed my paralysis and kicked in my determination. More about that later.

Love

Love is happy, joyous, peaceful, painful, heartbreaking, and disappointing. Writing saved my broken heart and helped me heal. If for no other reason than love, it pays to journal. Children grow into adolescents who will likely experience love as both exhilaration and heartbreak. The ability to express and process emotions on paper is a lifetime productive tool, in my opinion. Writing helps release emotion. Plus, you can change endings and put the morons who broke your heart, or bad bosses who broke your spirit, into a popped hot air balloon. Turn the other cheek, but on paper you don't have to!

Creating What Does Not Exist

My dad took a transfer from Greensboro, North Carolina to Atlanta, Georgia during my first year of high school, ninth grade, and then moved us back to Greensboro at the start of twelfth grade. My three brothers had become soccer fiends, and so had my mom, becoming the second female referee in the state of Georgia. Our return to North Carolina brought the reality of an entire state void of youth soccer.

The void was huge for my brothers and mother. Returning to Greensboro, Barbara went to the Parks and Recreation Department and requested a soccer program be offered to the youth of the city.

"No thank you, Mrs. Blum. We have baseball and football. That's all the kids want or need."

The next day she enlisted about 50 neighbors to call Parks and Rec requesting soccer. Parks and Rec called my mother the following day. "Mrs. Blum, if you find the coaches, we'll give you fields to practice."

There was a lot of resistance to soccer in the 70s. There seems to be a natural instinct to resist new ideas. My mother became a tiger-driven force for youth soccer. She went to the Guilford College men's soccer team and found coaches. The demand, and interest in playing, were instant. She opened a soccer shop to provide cleats and uniforms. She organized a statewide soccer association and supported local communities eager to bring soccer to youth. She organized an international tournament bringing Brazilian youth soccer players to Greensboro, N.C.

In fact, at her eulogy, the sports reporter for the *Greensboro News and Record* recounted a story we grew up with. Mom had gone to Grimsley High School and asked Principal Glenn for permission to use the fields for practice over the next several weekends, as city fields were in shortage due to other sports. Glenn said, "No."

That first weekend, the team—including my mom—climbed over the fence. The following week her letter to the editor appeared, regarding a certain school's refusal to permit weekend soccer practice on their empty fields, to prepare for Greensboro's FIRST-EVER INTERNATIONAL YOUTH SOCCER TOURNAMENT. The day after her letter was printed, Principal Lodie Glenn saw the light and welcomed all practice teams. I am proud that my mother's contribution to youth soccer resulted in her induction into the North Carolina Soccer Hall of Fame. She showed you don't have to accept "no" for an answer if you want something that does not already exist.

More Writing Please

When my son was in fifth grade, I approached his teacher and asked her to request that Matthew read one book a week, of any level, and write a summary of the story, because I didn't see him writing enough to build skill. I said she did not even have to read it or grade it but coming from her, he would do it. She refused. In sixth grade, I asked his social studies teacher to request Matthew interview the bakery staff at Publix and write up what he learned about their native countries. Again, for no grade, but just for the exercise. She refused.

Teaching is a huge task and sometimes "one more parent request" comes at the wrong time. I should have found a way to structure more writing for my children at home. I could have bribed them, or sat down with them so we all could participate. Three children, a combined 15 years of elementary school, and only my daughter, when in 2nd grade, had a teacher that pushed the students to write every day.

When our youngest child, Gabe, was in second grade, his teacher agreed to let me come in once a week and do a 45-minute creative writing class. Until he finished 5th grade, I ran an after school creative writing club, plus an after-school drama club that performed three plays, which I wrote for 25 child casts.

Because of the feedback from students, parents, and my own experiences, I initiated contact with five elementary schools and secured principal agreements to give the after-school writing program a go. My beloved cousin, with whom I had been pen pals from age 14-22, had only a few weeks left to live, due to her battle with pancreatic cancer.

I decided to spend two weeks with her in California and schedule the writing clubs to begin upon my return, so I would have something joyous to redirect my energy into. The day before I left for California, about 5,000 parent informational flyers, grouped by grade and classroom size, were delivered to the five schools.

On the way to the airport the following day, I received a call from the media specialist at my son's school, where I had conducted the writing clubs. "Lori, I did not give you permission to use my testimony on this flyer and I forbid you to distribute them."

To this day I do not know why the, "This program is valuable to the writing development of our students and I can recommend Lori Sugarman," sentence created such a visceral response from the media specialist. It's not like I was selling cars. I was flabbergasted and speechless. Too overwhelmed with my cousin's impending death to think clearly and vehemently protest, that phone call stopped the after school creative writing clubs for a couple years. I made a call to a friend who retrieved the 5,000 flyers.

Fast forward beyond this bump in the road. Two years later, I sent 52 letters to 52 principals in the adjoining county and one said yes to having an after school creative writing club. The following year, one more school said yes, and then another and another . . . the program continued to grow and turn hundreds and hundreds of reluctant writers into enthusiastic ones over the past 15 years.

Several years into it, I compiled and published a 350-page book of exercises called *Plumdiggity! Developing Student Writers*. A year after that, in collaboration with musician composer Chris Foster, we published 26 songs and videos with lyrics to sing along to while growing beginning reading foundations. All 26 songs are stick-in-your-head fun and playful; some are zany, and many include character lessons of friendship, kindness and sharing.

I became fixated on the alphabet in my sixth decade: 26 songs; 26 beginning read-write-color-trace-draw booklets; a volume of poems and poem stories around 26 letters; a 26-page booklet of coloring pages; and 9 out of 26 short stories written to play off the 26 song themes. Why couldn't our alphabet have 5 letters?

The reward for me is turning attitudes of "I can't" into attitudes of "I did it." For the past 15 years I have also worked with hundreds of school-aged children and teens in private practice, as a hypnotherapist. Hypnotherapy empowers young people to experience changes in attitudes through their own brains' capability. It is a critical life-skill to not quit, to not give up, to persevere, and to believe that you have capability. This is what I teach.

I will share a discovery made working with children as young as four years old. It came while reading Eric Carle's *Slowly Slowly Slowly Said the Sloth,* which contains lots of adjectives for the word slow such as lethargic and lackadaisical. Young children LOVE repeating big, long words after you! They giggle and repeat with frequency. Teach big vocabulary playfully!

Thank you for taking the time to read *The Cinderella Monologues* and my chapter. Do yourself a big favor, even if it's just dedicating a spiral notebook to recording one thing about your day or an emotion you feel, do that! Our dog Poochie never said the three words my dad begged for, but we, as people, have the great capacity for spoken and written language.

Writing is the physical evidence of the very short time we get to be on this earth with our adventures, trials and turbulence. You may just be surprised at what comes out. There is NO judging your writing! If you stare at the blank paper without a flow, simply write about the last meal you ate and those observations. Soon you will find yourself replacing one word for a more expressive one or seeking out a thesaurus for more options.

One final tip: If you have children and they fight, insist they write about the fight. Either they will figure out the solution themselves, knowing a writing task is at hand, or they will become excellent writers with all the practice!

There is no recipe, there is no one way to do things—there is only your way. And if you can recognize that in yourself and accept and appreciate that in others, you can make magic.

~ Ara Katz

Corinne Lalanne has a background in accounting and a passion for helping others. She is a Certified Holistic Health Practioner, an accomplished group facilitator, and a public speaker focused on topics of healing from separation, loss, grief, divorce, hospice, and trauma awareness. She is a life transition advocate and soon to be published author. She has been featured in the Sacramento Diocese monthly publication.

Email: corinne@balancedhealthandlife.com
Website: balancedhealthandlife.com

Chapter 10

A Cycle Broken

The Journey from Victim to Warrioress

Corinne Lalanne

Fight for the things you care about but do it in a way that will lead others to join you.

~ Ruth Bader Ginsberg

A friend recently said to me, "Corinne, you have had such a tough life," and until that very moment I never thought of myself, or my life, in those terms. My life wasn't tough, it was just my life. Since that moment I have found myself compelled to write these words.

My life lessons have always been held close to my heart and, for the most part, undercover. I've spent the last 25-plus years doing all I can to hide my true self, and trying to discover who that true self is, and how I can be of any use to the world around me.

I was the only child of a controlling, domineering, yet loving, mother whose life mantra was, "What they don't know won't hurt them." My father was an abusive, mean-tempered alcoholic, Marine Corps Drill Instructor. As I write these words I can now vividly feel the "tough life" and the pain I kept undercover for so many years. I became nothing more than one of my father's recruits having learned to say, "Yes sir" and "No sir" or "Gunnery Sergeant Grand's residence, Corinne speaking." Who answers a phone like that at age seven? This lost and lonely little girl spent many hours being quietly obedient, as any child of a violent alcoholic learns to be. Her best friends were imaginary except for a Barbie doll and a Terrier dog named Cindy. I was always told I could go out to play when all my chores were done. The problem was, they were never done. So much in common with Cinderella, as I see it now.

The sense of "humor," which was so much a part of my father's personality, seemed so confusing. Was it the result of being an alcoholic or of being in the Marine Corps? In either case, to a seven-year-old child, it became cruel. I am reminded of the time my little terrier, Cindy, spent the weekend at the local vet getting spayed. Meanwhile, my dad bought a rabbit from the local grocery store, put it on the bar-b-que spit, and jokingly decided to tell me that we were having Cindy for dinner that night. I couldn't eat for the entire weekend until my father redeemed himself by collecting the dog from the vet, returning her home to that little girl (me) on the following Monday.

At age eight, I had to give away my dog Cindy, as we were transferred to a military base in Hawaii; where my parents would eventually get a divorce, and my mother and I would be allowed one last move. We chose to return to California.

As I look back on those years of my parents' divorce and the toll that alcohol and the military took on my life, it's hard to hold back the tears. My father remarried a very strong and dominant woman who only allowed my dad an occasional visit during my high school and adult years. She was never able to have children. I would later find her medical records that noted a botched abortion in Mexico leading me to believe the reason she was unable to conceive. Her job as a Social Worker for San Diego County put her in charge of picking up kids who were removed from their homes for various reasons.

A year after my high school graduation, my father was in a terrible car accident. We were told he'd never walk again and would most likely be a vegetable if he even survived. He'd been out drinking and managed to remember where he parked the car but had no identification with him.

While driving home on a San Diego freeway, he hit an off-ramp guardrail in a VW bug, totaling the car, with equal and major damage to his six-foot seven-inch body. He lost four pints of blood before ever reaching the nearest hospital, not more than two miles from the accident.

As miracles would have it, my dad survived, just as he had in Okinawa when a hand grenade blew up under him. He'd spent months on a hospital ship as a guinea pig for a new salve that would hopefully heal and reduce the evidence of burns on a large part of his body. He had to be tied down, so he'd not touch and reopen or infect the wounds.

Several years later, he'd practice yet another miracle by surviving a Southern California flood that washed the truck he drove several miles downstream leaving him clinging to a branch, stripped of all clothing, and filling his lungs with mud and water. The Marine Corps certainly taught him survival skills.

I remember a time in the third grade when I felt I needed to be the "perfect child." I had not been able to complete a homework assignment on time. The evening I was supposed to have worked on it, my parents got into a huge argument at the dinner table and my dad threw a plate of spaghetti at my mother, missed her, and hit the dining room wall.

Obediently, my mom and I spent the rest of the evening cleaning up and hiding any evidence on the wall, discarding broken dishes, and hiding the tears we shared. We were lucky that night, it was only plates and not us.

The fact that my homework had not been completed got me into trouble. I couldn't give a truthful reason for not completing my assignment, so I wrapped my hand in an ace bandage and told my teacher I had sprained it, in order to give myself additional time to complete my assignment.

I thought I had done a good thing keeping the "family secret" in the family, but when my father learned that I had "told a lie" to get out of my homework, he wanted to be sure I never told a lie again. The usual "spanking" now had a weapon. He hit me with his military belt. Unfortunately, those belts have big, brass Marine Corps emblems on the buckle and when used in this fashion, it caused the blood vessels on the back of my leg to be broken and left a lifelong scar.

That man, my father, stood 6'7" inches tall and was in top physical health and strength, aside from being a drinker and smoking for a number of years. At eight years old, I barely came to the man's waist in height and would have been lucky to have weighed 70 lbs. I learned my lesson. I NEVER told another lie . . . out of fear for my life.

When we moved to Hawaii, my father was sent out of our life by the military, to God-knows-where, for two and a half years. Letters and cassette tapes were our only form of communication in those days. NO computers, cell phones, or news media on the war we were fighting or where. Our only connection became an FPO box in San Francisco.

As I have written these words, I have come to the revelation as to why I write in the third person so often. As I have written this entire piece, I am still trying to protect that little girl who, in reality, is me. Over the years, I have come to a greater understanding and compassion for the way God took this man out of my life. This allowed me to recover from those childhood wounds mentally, and understand that I was not to blame for my dad's alcoholism and abuse, or my parents' divorce.

It took several years to sort through many pages of self-help books on Adult Children of Alcoholics and *Toxic Parents*, as well as visits to an occasional counselor and Al-Anon meeting. I have managed to put a much better end to the story than many who have walked in similar shoes.

My mother remarried a wonderful man who became a model father figure for me, but was also an alcoholic and ended up in a 12-step recovery program. He and I celebrated my birthday and his AA anniversary on the same day. We used to laugh and say it was the only time I could be older than him. When I celebrated my 25th birthday, he celebrated three years of sobriety.

After my father's accident and recovery, his physical condition was nothing short of miraculous. The bigger mystery was that after spending several months in the hospital, going through what seemed to be "withdrawal," rehabilitation on how to walk again, and losing close to 100 pounds, he became a changed man. The good news: he no longer drank alcohol. His mind and brain injury had blocked out everything having to do with drinking and being an alcoholic. He had, in essence, lost a large part of his life. He simply became a man with a short temper and a controlling wife, who beat him down constantly with her brand of control. My few interactions with her proved her to be nothing less than the wicked stepmother.

I didn't get a full grasp of what he'd lost until my grandmother, his mother, lay dying of cancer while living with my mom (her ex-daughter-in-law) and husband (my stepfather)—a tricky situation at best. My dad traveled from San Diego to Walnut Creek, to visit his mother. Surprisingly, she and my mother always remained close over the years.

As my father and I drove to my mom and stepdad's home in Moraga several times one week, I saw my dad and my mom talk: reminiscing and remembering times when they were kids together, laughing, and just enjoying the visit. It wasn't until the ride back to my home in Walnut Creek that my father posed the question, "Why did your mother and I get a divorce?" Well, that was the million-dollar question.

If you have ever been with an alcoholic, there is THAT moment when you fear you might say the word or words that cause the violent alcoholic to "snap." This became that moment of truth. If I lied, I would fear for my life and if I told him the truth he might remember everything that his mind had forgotten. I couldn't lie—I wore the scar that reminded me of the lesson so many years ago.

I asked my dad if he remembered being an alcoholic. He muttered that his wife, Marianne, had told him he wasn't a good person and had a drinking problem. He shared with me, "She told me she used to have to come and pick me up at bars because I couldn't remember where I had parked my car and stuff like that." I asked him if he ever remembered hurting my mom or me and he said, "Absolutely NOT! How could I have done anything like that?"

I knew, in that moment, that he really had no capacity to understand the great pain he had inflicted on my mother and me over those early years. I also felt that if we were to "unearth that monster" he could do as much harm to himself with the realization of the man he had been. He stayed quiet and in contemplation during the rest of the ride home.

Later that afternoon, which was a very warm summer day, while we were in my backyard, he noticed what looked like a birthmark on the back of my leg. He said he didn't remember me having a birthmark on my leg. Again, I felt terrified that I might say the one thing or word that would bring his memory back, and he would snap, right there in my backyard.

I took a deep breath and asked him if he remembered putting that scar there or what I had done to acquire it?

"Don't you remember, Dad?" This man, my father, died a thousand deaths that day. He turned white as a sheet and tears welled up in his eyes. He could barely get the words out, "I did that to you? What kind of a monster was I?" I had no words for him except to say that I was okay!

We said nothing more, but I know the pain he felt must have been a thousand times greater than any of the tragic events he'd lived through: the hand grenade, the car accident, being washed away in the flood.

My father remained with my stepmother until she died in 2003, of complications from Alzheimer's Disease. My stepmother hated me and never really allowed my father and me to have a relationship. Maybe that was a blessing, too. Since we only saw each other a couple of days a year during those last ten years, I had no idea of her illness. By the time my father called me to say he didn't know who else to call, he seemed to be a broken man, worn down by his wife's disease over the last few years and unable to handle the task of finding proper care for her.

My oldest daughter, Stephanie, was attending her second year of junior college at that time, studying for a nursing degree. She and I headed down to San Diego and spent a couple of weeks getting his life in order and finding a safe place, with proper care, for my stepmother. This woman spent so many years breaking my father down, much like the military had done, that he had no clue how to handle this kind of crisis.

He shared his frustration with me, in a rare conversation, by admitting that he had taken his military-issue revolver and asked a friend and breakfast buddy to hold it for him for safekeeping. He made it sound like a protective action or measure for my stepmother, but by all indications, it was also to keep him from using it, as well.

It wasn't easy and it's taken a number of years, but I have learned the art and healing powers of forgiveness. I continue to thank God for taking him out of my life when I felt most threatened and vulnerable. I thank God for Alzheimer's Disease and for giving me back my father without causing conflict between my stepmother and me. She wasn't able to remember who I was in her last months, so he didn't have to hear her opinion or criticism. She despised me for simply being my mother's daughter. I think she always felt the remaining love and admiration my father had for my mom, his childhood sweetheart.

And finally, I have been able to piece this whole story together and realize that I have accomplished an incredible feat. I have been able to "break the cycle" of abuse and alcoholism. Statistics show that 75% of children of alcoholics and abusers end up being alcoholics or addicts themselves. I did not attract an alcoholic when I met and married the father of my two beautiful daughters. They stand firm in who they are and have been loved and cared for by two good parents who were active in their upbringing. Abuse or alcohol never got in the way of their health, identity or dreams.

The story to this point became an original presentation I gave to my daughter's psychology class. I felt honored, yet taken by surprise, when my youngest daughter, Danielle, asked if I would speak to her group psychology project in junior college. She explained that they needed a victim of child abuse but didn't quite know how to ask for one. She knew about my relationship with my father, her grandfather, but not much in the way of details, other than the scar on the back of my leg, or the rare occasion when we visited with my father and stepmother in previous years. She just said she admired my strength and that I always wanted to help others.

I told her I had to think about her request, and after some contemplation, I said I would speak. But under one condition: that the story did not portray a victim's story, but rather one with a positive ending, in the hopes that it would help or give hope to someone listening.

The room had been darkened for a slide show that was a backdrop for my presentation; the lights went on and I was gratefully acknowledged. As I said to them, I felt honored that Danielle asked me and had allowed me to share this story with them.

When the teacher came to thank me, she asked how long I had been speaking? I had no idea she was referring to anything outside of this current event. She further noted that she recognized that almost all of her 32 students had wiped away tears, and she believed that everyone there had been touched by some element of the content. It became an experience I will never forget, and I will be forever grateful for Danielle asking me to share my story.

It must be noted that despite all my experiences, I managed to recover enough to marry a man who knew the importance of creating a loving family and making it a priority to be parents our girls could be proud of. We were determined to create the foundation for a family life that would build healthy values and a nurturing environment where children and a family could thrive.

I am delighted to say that we did just that and have two daughters who are making their own impact in the world. One is a registered nurse in the Sacramento area, with three thriving children. The other is a graphic artist with a San Francisco firm and is raising two daughters of her own. Both are happily married and insist on a style of co-parenting that I believe was modeled to them. Their father and I were married for thirty years, and although we divorced, we have always made it our goal to co-parent and be there for them.

My father remained on his own for several years. I began looking after him long-distance, hiring a woman from within his mobile home park to clean, help him pay his bills, go to doctor visits, RX pick-ups, shop, and accompany him to occasional meals. She appeared to care very much for my father and lived in the park with her own mother. Meals on Wheels wasn't well received, and he seemed much better off just going out for breakfast and dinner. This seemed a reasonable solution to getting him out to socialize.

After a few visits, once or twice a year, I soon realized that this arrangement was not working out. On a surprise visit, I discovered that the woman was "looking after" a lot more than my father's needs. She began helping herself to my father's stash of cash after his monthly visit to the bank, had never opened the brand-new vacuum cleaner I purchased, or even cleaned the house, as she had assured me was being done.

When I finally had an extensive and private conversation with him, I learned that his doctor had been led to believe my father was still drinking, as he thought was evidenced when my dad came to his appointments with the caregiver. He was bouncing off the walls and had trouble walking with a steady gait. The doctor had prescribed one-quarter of a Seroquel pill, to give my father less anxiety about going to the doctor, and she was giving him an entire pill. This caused him to be unable to drive and gave her full access to his car. I explained to the doctor that my father had not been drinking since his accident some 30 years previous.

The pieces of the puzzle began to fill in, and I realized that long-distance care was no longer an option. I needed to figure out a way to move him closer to my Auburn, California home, from his location in the San Diego area, some 600 miles away.

Seven years after my stepmother passed away, I found myself in a position to decide how best to help my dad as he entered *Life's Third Act,* as described by Patricia W. Bernham in her book. He would need more care and supervision in the coming years. I barely knew this man, so how did I expect him to listen to anything I could offer? I had to do an immense amount of healing on myself to get past all the pain and trauma I had buried, and the reality that I was taking on this role as a medical advocate.

The effects of his own brain trauma from the accident were becoming clearer to me with each day of my involvement in his life. While my stepmother remained ill and deteriorating, I caught glimpses of my father's inadequacies. He spent twenty years in the Marine Corps, but they never realized that he couldn't read, and now I understood why he'd turned down becoming an officer four times.

He had such strong women in his life: my mother, my stepmother, and even the Marine Corps took care of him. I felt saddened when my stepmother no longer recognized him shortly before her death. I explained that he should continue to visit her, and he simply said, "She doesn't know I'm there. I'm done," and he refused to visit her anymore. Where do you draw the line between brain trauma and the realities of life? I told him, "She took care of you, Dad. She deserves to have you there." "Nope, I am done."

He never paid bills on his own, or read any books, that I recall, and survived on what Walter Cronkite and Johnny Carson dished out to him on a daily basis. He did subscribe to *Life* magazine. This was his best attempt to keep up with current affairs. Or, he listened to my stepmother interpret what he needed to know since she always reminded him that she was the one with a college degree.

Now it all started to make sense to me. They both blamed it on his brain trauma from the accident and maybe that was so, but later I had to jump in as his only child, his advocate, and his family member.

I learned how to forgive the unforgivable and started down the path of compassion for my father. Not an easy task, but one that I felt committed to. After all, he was still my father; I became all he had left. I believed I'd find some military retirement facility in northern California and eventually get him settled in.

I gave the orders for cleaning out the house and downsizing. I explained that I wanted to move him up to be closer to me and, as long as his car was coming with us, he seemed good with it. I found myself in shock and in gratitude, all at the same time, for his acceptance. I was coming out of a 30-year marriage, recently divorced, and now bringing my father to my home to live with me. I managed to reduce his meds by simple nutritious cooking; getting him out of a pre-diabetic diagnosis and off his anti-anxiety pills.

I now understood my passion for getting my Holistic Health Certification, becoming a Life Coach, and facilitating Divorce Recovery for some 13 years at Saints Peter and Paul Catholic Church in my hometown. My entire life has been devoted to some sort of caregiving or healing. Passionate about those abilities, I had no idea how much they would be needed in this part of my life.

It became evident that moving my dad to any kind of facility was going to be very expensive, and an impossible task, given his financial position. Plan B would be for him to live with me overseeing his care and well-being, while keeping him as healthy as possible. I believe I succeeded, as he lived in my home for the next eight years.

It wasn't easy, and certainly not what I had planned. But over those eight years, I had a life partner who had spent four years in the Army, so he and my dad spoke a similar language when it came to the military. My dad was never really able to talk to me, but managed to relay to Mark stories about his past that I overheard. I think he just didn't know what to do with me.

My mother had a close resemblance to Elizabeth Taylor. One evening there was a special on television, an anniversary tribute to Elizabeth Taylor's death. My father blurted out stories to my partner that I had never heard before. He couldn't tell me the stories, but he shared them with my partner. He was clearly still in love with my mother.

My father and I were able to purchase a home together three years before he died. He thought he was the wealthiest man on earth. He and my stepmother had owned a mobile home, but not a "real" home, as he would say. He finally believed he would be able to leave me with something and he felt it helped him redeem himself as a father in some way. He shared with his caregiver, Anita, how proud he felt of me and how I had taken care of him these last years. He could never say those things to me directly, but I am blessed to have heard them from her.

My dad's health deteriorated in his last couple of years due to several urinary infections and prostate issues. At the end of his life, Hospice knew that, even in his frailty, he was a big man and could be a handful. They were expecting a rough time for us, as he was so grumpy and unpleasant at the obvious loss of his dignity.

Anita, visiting in Seattle one weekend, had scheduled to be back on Saturday, but her flight was delayed until Sunday. I hoped that Hospice would come on Saturday to help me with getting him cleaned up, his bedding changed, and making him reasonably comfortable. By this time, he was pretty much bedridden and comforted by his pain meds. I told Anita not to worry about coming, as he was sedated. But she insisted on coming straight from the airport Sunday, arriving at around 2:00p.m. I had tuned to a calming, meditative music station 24/7 the last few days, instead of his normal *Gomer Pile* or *Gunsmoke*. It seemed to be working to keep him calm, in his waking time, between doses of morphine and haloperidol.

When Anita arrived, she agreed to help me clean him up and change his bedding. She was so sweet and, though he slept, she offered him comfortable dialog, reminiscing about the good visits they'd had, the drives to various errands and labs, as well as the many breakfasts and lunches she took him to. As she reminded him of the good times they had shared, I found my opportunity to say what I wanted to and "give him his orders," as I was told I needed to do. "Dad, we've had a crazy run with you living here these past eight years. It's okay for you to go now, we're going to be just fine."

Anita and I stepped out of his room and at the door I paused, stopped, and watched for him to breathe. I stood for several moments—his chest wasn't moving. I called for Anita and we both independently checked his pulse—nothing.

I stood there stunned. My dad got his last wish: to die in his own home. His passing seemed so perfectly peaceful after he got his orders, knowing it was okay to go, and I was able to make that happen. Like a good Marine, he followed his orders and took on his task immediately. Once a Marine, always a Marine. When I called the Hospice nurse, she seemed shocked that he went so peacefully. They all anticipated a tough and aggressive transition.

What a crazy journey, one of healing for both my father and me, and one that I will always treasure. Maybe, in my succeeding to help him transition I am a "healer" after all.

The most beautiful people I've known
are those who have known trials,
have known struggles, have known loss,
and have found their way out of the depths."

~ Elizabeth Kübler-Ross

Renée Michaud (she/her) is a self-taught multidisciplinary artist (Rapper, DJ, Poet & Expressive Visual Artist), student at the Kutenai Art Therapy Institute, and Associate Certified Coach who uses creative arts to improve the quality of life and work of individuals and teams. Renée is passionate about social justice work and helping people of all ages communicate in ways that are more authentic, creative, and productive. She is skilled at facilitating memorable community events and creating safe spaces for sacred work to occur. Everyone is creative. Art saves lives.

Renée is of mixed ancestry: French and European, Algonquin-Métis on her mother's side, and Mi'kmaq on her father's side. She is grateful to live and play on the unceded territory of the Algonquin and Nipissing First Nations, also known as North Bay, Ontario, Canada.

Website: uneety.ca
LinkedIn: linkedin.com/in/reneemichellemichaud/
Facebook: facebook.com/uneetycoachingcreative
Instagram: instagram.com/uneety.ca

Chapter 11

Introducing A Reclaimed Creative Voice

Renée Michaud

Being oppressed means
the absence of choices . . .

~ bell hooks

I've been talking my entire life. For those who know me, or have seen me speak to a crowd, you wouldn't think I had lost my voice, but I had. It's surprising that such a "chatty Cathy" of a child turned social butterfly, turned public speaker, could feel voiceless. In school, I played Snow White in a theatre production and later gave the valedictorian address. I even studied communications in university for God's sake! And still, so many words never left the confines of my skull for fear of the pain they could bring me and those I loved. It's as if there was a piano in my throat, with a range of notes that were not allowed out.

I learned growing up that my voice did not hold equal weight in our house. Patriarchy raised me just as it raised my parents and their parents and their parents. Somewhere in my family tree, a matriarch tipped the scales of gender justice—among my Indigenous ancestors, no doubt. For all the women of the past, present, and future, this mini midlife memoir is an echo of collective female words, both spoken and unspoken. This is a short story, still in the making, of how I reclaimed my voice and myself through the power of creative expressive arts.

There is a pervasive belief that male voices and values are normal, right, and central. Thus, we tend to compare "circumscribed second-class female citizens" to the "male ideal." I say *we* because many women have internalized the oppression they experience and end up believing their voices are less important than men's. I was a case in point. Hear ye, hear ye, this is false! We have made progress in the area of women's rights, but there are still too many workplaces, social spaces, and homes around the world where HER thoughts and feelings are ignored, interrupted and silenced.

This will not do, and so our work is not done. In fact, according to the 16th Global Gender Gap Report by the World Economic Forum in 2022, gender equality across politics, work, health, and education will now take 132 years to reach full parity compared to 100 years before the pandemic. We have lost ground and must speak up for ourselves, for the great sisterhood, and for Mother Earth on whom all humans depend for survival. Men, this may be uncomfortable for you as you may not be used to hearing wolves howl so often. However, discomfort and change travel together. So, let's safely get uncomfortable together as I zoom back into the personal side of this story . . .

Finding purpose in the pain

I know in my bones that I'm not the only one who has ever lost their creative voice. It is in this shared experience that I find purpose in writing to you here. Storytelling itself is a form of creative expression, which I trust will only contribute to strengthening my creative voice. That's art! It just keeps on giving! Many times, someone else's story has touched me deeply and left me feeling less broken, less alone, and more connected, hopeful, and inspired to take a small, brazen step in the direction of a more loving world.

The mistreatment I experienced as a girl has made me compassionate to the oppression that many people feel—thwarting them due to their trans, non-binary, or gender-fluid identities. My emergent allyship for the queer community is one of the silver-linings I've gleaned from my unfortunate subjection to gender-based oppression and violence. I feel purposeful in creating more compassionate spaces for the full rainbow of gender expression and sexual diversity to burst out of the outdated and rigid collective tolerance to only pink and blue boxes. Fly away with me as we travel through space and time to inner dimensions of my life/world previously untold . . . a creative voice in the remaking.

Sharing one's story: a gate to deeper, wiser lands

On most workdays, for nearly 10 years, I told stories to classrooms and gymnasiums full of students trying to figure out what they wanted to study after high school. As a college recruiter, I was mostly talking about things around me, not about myself. I was telling an institutional story with pieces of my superficial story in it, anecdotes for emotional effect. It was a fun job with amazing people that allowed me to travel and learn crucial life skills like public speaking, adaptability, and keeping my meal receipts organized if I wanted to get reimbursed. However, after thousands of presentations about how great postsecondary life was at a bilingual institution, the enthusiasm in my voice began fading. A sign that a change in me or around me was to come—or both. I needed to discover and share a deeper story.

I love clarifying and expanding the meaning of words, so I'll share my enthusiasm for the definition of *enthusiasm* here with you. You're invited to think about what enthuses you in life.

Enthusiasm:

1 - *absorbing or controlling possession of the mind by any interest or pursuit;*

2 - *an occupation, activity, or pursuit in which lively interest is shown;*

3 - *any of various forms of extreme religious devotion, usually associated with intense emotionalism and a break with orthodoxy.*

What are you passionate to learn, talk about, and do? Pause to name at least one thing to yourself!

Thank you, Mr. Merriam, and Mr. Webster for that, who, by the way, I learned were the founders of the oldest dictionary publishers in the U.S. This gets me thinking, I wonder how the all-male leadership of a dictionary company impacted the meaning and underlying values of the very words we use to tell our stories as women, if at all? Power-over patriarchy is not always overt. It hides in the spaces between words and in the shadows of punctuation, so keep your question marks handy as you read, write, and move in life.

Now that I think more about it, my story actually starts well before working in public relations. It was the summer of my second year of university in beautiful Ottawa, Ontario, Canada. I had an elective to choose, and selected *Women in Media,* not knowing exactly what to expect. *I* liked media. *I* was a woman. Done! I took a break from biology classes and stepped into the world of gender politics. At the time, at the whopping age of 20, I had not even heard of the term *feminist*. This means that in my complete high school education, the mandatory curriculum failed to integrate gender equality as an essential topic. Boo. Shame! We must do better.

Sitting in the air-conditioned auditorium with 100 other strangers, I looked at the projection screen, with squinted and curious eyes, as the professor showed us images and videos, proof of how women were infantilized, objectified, and portrayed in the media to sell goods and worse—to withhold power from them. I was quietly astonished. I felt like a fish becoming aware of the water in which it had always been swimming. Or a bird being told there was pollution in the air it had always depended on to breathe and fly. This would be the beginning of looking at my place in the world more consciously and critically, and with more discerning eyes.

Crossroad Moments

Contemplating my life for this project has been a fruitful experience, and I don't mean pineapple stress-eating between pages. The task demanded that I reflect on which of life's unexpected moments most significantly shaped my story thus far. There were times of change that cued me to question and redefine who I was and who I wanted to be. At every milestone, I was the Hermit Crab becoming aware of the tightness of my shell. Under new external and internal pressures, I scavenged for a roomier home that would allow me to be and do differently, as I became a new version of *moi*.

Anyone I've ever met has impacted me, some more profoundly than others. Come to think of it, countless beings I've never met have impacted my life: the people who paved the sidewalk out front, the trees that give me oxygen, the startling bug with too many legs. A great reminder of the web of life and our universal interconnection.

Here are the top 20 life moments that sent me inward to figure out who to become next:

1. Studying at what felt like an exclusive university rather than an inclusive one. Switching two weeks later to a new city with a more inviting student body and meeting some of my best friends to date.

2. Beginning my first job after university and feeling like something weird was going on there, but not being able to put my finger on it, or knowing how to act. Turns out, the new territory was politics.

3. Being offered a managerial position and feeling anxiety and depression for the first time at the idea of getting up and going to work. In hindsight, I didn't know how to be anything but positive, nor ask for help when debuting in a leadership role. Why did some men keep cutting me off?
4. Leaving my job and city to follow my fiancé for his work. Then leaving said fiancé who became increasingly manipulative and violent. I broke his heart; he changed the locks. I lost most of my stuff but became less attached to material things moving forward. Gratitude to the people in my life who helped me get through this. If you're reading this, I love you!
5. Being introduced to electronic music and festivals (some see these as spiritual pilgrimages). Rekindling my love for dance!
6. Questioning my sexuality and exploring sex with a woman. We both went back to dating men in the morning. Was I that bad? Ha!
7. Meeting a man who facilitated a major spiritual awakening and introduced me to rapping. I glimpsed a larger Self. The inspiration was palpable and the breakup inevitable.
8. Every time a romantic relationship ended, reflecting on what I learned about myself, others, and life. Get up and try again, but respect and enjoy singlehood.

9. Encountering an advocate for ending homelessness whose empathy filled any room she entered—my interest in social work exploded.

10. Meeting a coach who asked me to think deeply about who I was and what I wanted to give and receive in life.

11. Taking too many drugs and drinks on Canada Day and experiencing a short psychosis, layered with more spiritual awakenings, including trauma resurgence. Starting my sobriety the next day.

12. Quitting my Masters in Communication due to burnout, but also with the newfound aspiration of becoming a musician. I had a vision that I would meet Beyoncé some day! I am still hopeful . . . My thesis supervisor supported gracefully with the difficult decision to make the change. Asking for a one-year work sabbatical to explore my budding enthusiasm for creativity and spirituality. It being declined, then quitting my job to dedicate more time to the callings of the wild!

13. Being asked to volunteer and work as a facilitator and coach with youth seeking direction after high school. Eventually, becoming trained and certified in a more empowering coaching approach to thinking, conversing, and helping people.

14. Taking a DJ course because I just didn't see enough female DJs out there and being offered an out-of-

the-blue artist mentorship opportunity on a rad community mural.

15. Covid, duh. Never have I spent so much time with myself, with so little access to my usual distractions for emotional coping and numbing. Feeling the depths of what was unfelt in the dusty corners of my inner cupboards.

16. Starting to write poetry and rap to process experiences and emotions. Finally meeting another local female rapper! (Noticing where I'm putting punctuation to express *enthusiasm*.)

17. Communicating with many of the men whom I felt had disrespected my too-porous boundaries in the past, be it sexually, emotionally, physically, or materially. The unresolved content was screaming from inside me for due attention, discussion, forgiveness, and resolution.

18. Moving back to my hometown to be closer to family and nature where I could feel more supported, as Covid continued to change society in waves.

19. Going back to school to become an art therapist to heal thyself and help others in their healing. Synthesizing my story herein!

What would be your top ten or twenty life moments that changed your sense of self and life direction? You're invited to pause, write your list and even share it with another trusted soul. This memoir thang is proving to be a great way to accept the past and solidify my sense of self in the present. Ego integration baby!

Going deeper: childhood healing

Like many others, I'm now more aware of how childhood adversity has shaped me in life-affirming ways. Do you remember the perspective-shattering moment when you realized your parents or guardians weren't as perfect and heroic as you once believed? They're human and imperfect like us. This moment comes at different times for everyone. I love my mom and dad and appreciate how much they gave to support my becoming. And our family, like all others, had their struggles. Everyone has difficult moments when suffering is really alive, which prompts us to ask questions—of ourselves and others—to make sense of the discomfort.

As I became more self-aware and literate in psychoeducation and feminist studies, I started to recognize that, like many other households in patriarchal societies, I was raised in a home where my dad held most of the power, had the loudest voice, and carried the heaviest hand. That made speaking up scary, because the response was unpredictable and at times violent. It's amazing how long the stress of walking on shattered glass can live in the mind and body if not fully felt and transformed to build up a new, stronger self. I suspect Mom and my brothers felt some of this too, but those are their stories to tell. My dad was also fun, loving, funny, and generous which made for a disorganized attachment style with him, one I would later work at making secure.

I learned through reading, training, and therapy to be more assertive and empathetic when communicating with Dad and in life, in general. Here is my voice coming back! This makes me want to sing like Ariel in *The Little Mermaid*: "Aww-Aww-Aww!" Some moments required me to be as strong and loud as him, while others needed a gentle and soft approach. Looking back now, I don't think that always being fierce, or always being compassionate, would have improved our relationship over the long-haul. There were times for rigid boundaries and fiery interjections, and other moments for open, calm discussions.

I've seen changes in us both: more democratic decision-making, less button-pushing, more empathy, and greater open-mindedness, less fear and stress, more calm and togetherness. I know our quality time with family in this lifetime is limited. I've therefore chosen forgiveness (of my-self too) and personal growth, in order to have a loving relationship with my father.

Rhythm & Blues

Canadian R&B artist Alessia Cara sings about the maturing process in her song, "Growing Pains." God, I love that album! Sometimes, life experiences call for rhyme, melody and harmony to hold and transform the depths of our feelings and falls. While on the Red Road, we must not lose sight of its delights, for it will appear darker and longer than if viewed from a higher, wiser perspective, with eagle eyes.

The "Red Road" is a term used to refer to the healing path in some Indigenous cultures. This inspired the title of my first collaborative hip-hop release written with Solaire, another talented female rapper. The hook goes like this (imagine a boppin' beat in the background and women belting in unison):

We wanna hear your story
We wanna share your glory
We wanna talk with you as you do what you feel
    is right for you
Let's walk that Red Road
I'm listening to you

I'm imagining all the wounded healers around the world singing this together, echoing Carl Jung. He coined the term to refer to people who chose a career in healing because they themselves had experienced a significant wounding experience. Pain is great for bringing change. It's hard to ignore.

Luckily, we have modern science and medicine to support us. And sometimes meds are needed. I myself have been on and off medication for anxiety and depression for a decade. If you have been on this up-and-down roller coaster, you're not alone. I've always been determined to heal deeply, learn coping skills, and live without them. It's a personal choice I made again recently with the confidence that art-making would support a deep and long-lasting mental health recovery. Stay tuned!

My biggest breakdown (and eventually breakthrough) was uncovering that I had been sexually abused at the age of seven, by someone I knew and loved. This difficult realization came to me in puzzle pieces scattered over time, handed to me from the protective chambers of my unconscious. I slowly unfroze and began to explore the trauma in my body with trained professionals. Visual art-making has helped me slowly accept my past and safely feel the emotions of confusion, sadness, fear, and rage. Rap played a big part in owning my story, recovering my voice, and taking back the control and power that was stolen so long ago. Here's part of my verse, again from "Red Road":

I'm a warrior
*Making f*cking order here*
Telling stories dear
Better open up your ears
Make my point crystal clear
Dropping all my fear
Dropping all my walls
So I can say what's really here

Really here barely there
Under where Sacred gear
Her no is gold
Stop drop and roll
Cause she's on fire and can't be told
Won't lay cold
Best grab ahold cause
Mother Earth's outta control

The time is now stand up
Louder prouder
Make room cross time and space

Feel the crowds gather
Resurge Reclaim Reborn Rename
His height - turning tables
Her weight - Inescapable!

What a meaningful performance memory! A gathering of femme and non-binary folks offering the soul medicine that comes from reclaimed stories of resilience. Rapping for me naturally followed DJing which taught me about rhythm and emotionality. It also calls attention to smoothing out transitions between songs. A good DJ brings in ease and grace to spaces so that crowds flow seamlessly in and out of changing songs and the feelings they evoke. An aspirational way of moving through life, really.

Because I'm not a technically trained singer, rap is more accessible to me right now. It's fun, feels powerful, and allows me to tap into some deep emotions while channelling Spirit to bring through some higher messages. I'll keep developing my DJ and rapping skills knowing full well that soulful singing is the land way over yonder where I'm heading. Music is a such a magnificent way to give voice to people who have had it thwarted over the years and even across generations.

Changing the systems that created us

Gratefully, I discovered Feminist Therapy on my journey. It holds at its core that mental health issues experienced by women and other marginalized populations can be caused by the psychological oppression they face in the world. I distinctly remember the moment when my feminist therapist said, "It sounds like you are starting to set boundaries." I responded naively with "What's a boundary?" Can you believe it?! I was in my late 20s before coming across such a pivotal concept for human well-being! I had never fully understood the choice, voice, and power I had to say who, and which behaviours, were physically and emotionally welcome in my space.

It turns out that speaking and singing are not the only ways to help us reclaim our voices, whole selves, and health. We can get creative with it! Writing, making art, and dancing connect us more deeply with our authentic selves, with each other, and bring about social change in beautiful, curious, and compelling ways. We must all work to end people being spoken over, ignored, erased, looked down upon, and cast to the sidelines.

Men are great—toxic masculinity is not—and it hurts men, too. Toxic masculinity refers to cultural norms related to male stereotypes such as to be a man, you must be dominant over others. This belief can lead to misogyny, homophobia, sexual assault, and domestic violence if left undiscussed and in control of our collective beliefs. It also does not give men the social permission to be humble, ask for help, and be emotionally vulnerable, which all humans need throughout life to feel healthy and grow. As we know and have all felt at some point in our lives, isolation and emotional problems can lead to psychological distress. Using our voice and making art are both political ways of saying "no more." We want inclusion, not oppression!

Expressions of inward transformation

It was Christmas Eve when I had what I call my "Brittney Spears moment." (Deep respect for the anti-conservatorship advocate.) In my parents' hers & his washroom (see what I did there?) I looked at my dyed blonde bob hairdo, complete with Cleopatra bangs, and said with a quiet dramatic sigh, "It's time." With the clippers on zero, I bic'ed it. Took the whole thing off. It felt ah-mazing! Absolutely liberating. I could feel myself letting go of a previous romantic relationship. It was an outward expression of the inward transformation that was happening.

It's funny how tied our hair is to our identity, values, and beliefs. I truly think all women everywhere should shave their head at least once and see what life's like with so much extra time to spend on something other than hair. It's also an interesting experience to see how people around you interact with you . . . possibly differently. If you have, or decide to shave your head, I want to see before and after pics! Write me about your inner/outer life on the balder side.

I continued to drop traditional expressions of femininity that I felt were imposed on me to appear more desirable to men, or to fuel the shallow parts of materialism. I stopped shaving my legs, pits, and bush. Quit wearing makeup, jewelry and bras. Got rid of nearly all my high-heels. Why should I present as taller and wobblier to be seen as respectable or desirable? I kept my wedges in case of a special event, and leather mules from Spain because they were so unique and comfortable. And yes, I am a confused and tormented vegan/vegetarian. I might always have parts in me that keep such debates alive. I dressed more masculine during this phase until I realized a new trap—I was subjugating femininity to masculinity again!

I express myself more androgynously now, sometimes more "femme" and other times more "masc." I want respect for myself, and any person who beautifies or not, and presents as any gender. It's about having the choice and confidence to express ourselves authentically without the pressure from society to look one "right" way. How open are we really as a society to the fluidity of gender expression and sexual orientation? Or do we still live in an old-school rigid protocol for these categories of expression? Our brains can struggle with spectrums and ambiguity, but we can open our thinking and be more flexible, less fixed. Life is not about things staying the same and remaining comfortable. We'll keep being asked to change . . . in this case, it's about individual empowerment and collective inclusion.

Leaps into creativity, spirituality & emotionality

While working in public relations, I found myself looking for ways to be more and more artistic in my job. I would step up when there was a PowerPoint to design, a video to produce, a cultural event to coordinate. I even found a way to produce a dance flash mob, back when they were all the trendy rage. I would feel so alive and in the flow when working on these creative projects. There was a calling inside me bubbling.

Eventually, I mustered up the courage to put together a letter to my employer requesting a one-year leave without pay. What were the reasons for my request? Intuitively the words to put on the page came to me: "to take the time to explore creativity and spirituality." These two areas were fascinating to me and I felt like my 9-5 job left little time to dedicate to these growing areas of interest.

In my cubicle I had an intuitive painting I had made that read "Express that." Looking back, I see how these themes are connected to one of my purposes. I think we have many purposes in life and to try desperately to find a single act that feels purposeful, and is valuable to our community, creates undue stress. Plus, my mission statement keeps shifting as I grow.

Currently, one of my purposes is to improve individual and collective quality of living through art-making and creative self-expression. Beyond having savings to cover my living expenses for a year, I didn't have much of a plan when quitting my job. I went with the flow, immersed myself in more spiritual and creative spaces, and freelanced in communications and event planning, where I had strong skills and experience.

I also cried a lot while learning to be an entrepreneur. I still do. But my relationship with crying has changed. I now understand tears as a healthy expression of temporary emotion. What another unfortunate social script that "real men don't cry"! Toxic masculinity in the works handed down by generations. Imagine not being allowed to cry, or never having your tears touched by the compassionate gaze of a trusted witness? Yikes, sounds like a cold, isolating world.

Art makes you feel the full range of human emotions. I'm told there are 2,000 of them. Every human experiences fear, sadness, loss, grief, and overwhelm—some of the hard things to tolerate in our minds and bodies. As a society, we suppress our full emotional expression. For example, there is shame around crying and, worse yet, being witnessed in our tears! God forbid you're seen someone bawling outside the privacy of your home. Crying is actually a good sign of emotions resolving one drop at a time.

I'm so passionate about shedding the collective shame we carry about tears that my forthcoming book is dedicated to this very mission. It's called *Fine Places to Cry* and is a compilation of people's surprising and heartfelt moments of crying in (not so) unusual places for good reason. Think poetry and short story have a baby—but by surrogate or adoption. So let yourself be moved to cry! Tears fell many times while writing this chapter, including in a public café, and I'm ok with that. I survived.

A case for self-awareness

As I furthered my self-exploration through art, journaling, meditation, and yoga, my identity evolved. I believe it's helpful and moral to regularly contemplate our thoughts, feelings and inner workings. It helps us figure out what we love, what emotional baggage we carry into spaces with others, and which feelings tighten our throats. Creative expression is one way to do just this.

Sometimes our life experiences can be so heavy, we cannot express and transform them fully and completely without the help of more powerful tools, like art and community. Color, shape, rhyme, stories, and movement invite people in to witness a story that is both unique in its iteration and also in some way connected to others. No matter the tragedies in a story, it holds some degree of a happy ending because it was told and heard with compassion and appreciation.

Art saves lives. Read the bumper sticker. And when it can't, it improves the quality of living while we are still here. Experiencing it is one thing, creating it is next level. It is a carrier of beauty, hope, awe, universality and much more. Without these experiences, our Spirit fades and the light in our eyes loses its glimmer. Think back to the worldwide pandemic when these expressions of soul were significantly stifled. What a gray world we lived in . . . but this greyness actually compelled people to tap more into expressing their forgotten, but necessary, creativity.

Artmaking is an act of reconnecting with ourselves—our values, beliefs, and the unknown parts that wish to be recovered. Our creative expressions magically mirror our souls and reveal broader parts of our identities: the good, the bad and the sublime. Now, a single doodle, collage, or song won't be a quick ticket to everlasting happiness. Nothing really is. Artmaking is a practice, and we must trust the process enough to keep coming back to it. It takes faith in ourselves and in the creative Spirit to remain steadfast. It ain't a sprint, it's a marathon—a spiritual pilgrimage that lasts a lifetime and definitely keeps living interesting! So "art it up," as my therapy professor would say, and let your creative expression flow! The community needs your gifts.

Art has always been the raft
onto which we climb to save our sanity.
I don't see a different purpose for it now.

~ Dorothea Tanning

Sandra E. Jackson is a Shiftologist who globally empowers men and women to become Shift Ambassadors by supporting them on their journey into purpose to find their true identities. She is an enthusiastic and self-motivated author, life insurance agent, facilitator, panelist, and ordained evangelist. Sandra has turned her adversities into becoming an entrepreneur, author, and radio show host.

Sandra was married for 20/12 years and birthed nine children. She pursued her education and received her bachelor's degree in 2020, during the pandemic.

Sandra is ecstatic to be a #1 Amazon Best Selling Author several times and a few of her books are: *The Greatest Mother in The World, My Hidden Strength, Trauma, Grief, Pain-Bodies, & Healing; Joy Comes in the Morning, I Am Woman, and Life After . . .*

Email: journeyintopurpose22@gmail.com
Website: sandrarumph.com
Linktr.ee: linktr.ee/60423sandra

Chapter 12

From Wealth, to Poverty, to Abundance

Sandra E. Jackson

I'm still here for such a time as this, and I am ecstatic to be alive.

~ Sandra E. Jackson

Childhood Bliss

I celebrate my parents today for their contributions to making my childhood simply delightful. Although they have served their time on earth, gratitude remains in my heart because I know it could not have been as easy as they made it seem. I am the twelfth child of fifteen children born to the Rumph union.

A few years after I was conceived, my dad owned a block of residential properties on Pennsylvania Avenue in Rochester, New York. He and my mom also pastored a fiery Pentecostal church on Pennsylvania Avenue. The congregation grew exponentially and reasonably quickly. People traveled for miles around to be in attendance and the lines outside wrapped around from the side door to the back door. We were activating our heavenly gifts by serving the community. Souls were filled with salvation, and the city of Rochester shifted and transformed remarkably.

I was born on Columbia Avenue. At the age of five, the family moved to the suburbs of Penfield, New York. They lived in abundance, never lacking anything. The children were given an allowance but always knew that if and when we ran out, daddy's pockets awaited us to ask. I enjoyed being the twelfth child. I rode my bicycle daily, going up hills and around the cul-de-sac.

Being the only African American in my class made school challenging. Shyness gripped me, and I refused to let go. It became overly noticeable, which impaired my ability to speak up when called upon. On the other hand, everyone showed a sense of caring. Nonetheless, I always had friends and associates during school. I adapted a habit of bringing Twizzlers to school and made my locker the meeting place where everyone gathered before class to get at least two Twizzlers. This was my way of feeling connected. Everybody loved me and could hardly wait for me to open my locker, so I thought!

Bullying Is Wrong

During homeroom, I sat next to a small male. He liked to whisper racial slurs. One particular morning, something rose in me. I couldn't believe it. He was to my left, and when I went to my seat, he said THE N-WORD! I ignored him and gathered my belongings, as he continued his bullying. He said the word over and over again until I snapped. I grabbed his shirt collar, twisted it and threw his body across the room. I must have been in shock, and the entire classroom became instantly silent. Never had I become violent, but looking back on that moment, people can cause you to come outside of your personality and do things you would never dream of doing. Have you ever experienced that at a young age? Bullying is wrong! After that, I learned to take the higher road and not allow anyone's lack of knowledge or hatred to affect me, or my personality.

Mealtime

Meals at our house were like being at a buffet restaurant. Breakfast, lunch, and dinner times were enjoyable, filled with laughter and updates on the news. We enjoyed an array in a buffet-style setting, as the many items on the table conveniently pleased each palette. Every Saturday, we met around the extended kitchen table filled with the most delectable entrees, both hot and cold dishes. While waiting on each item to be placed on the table in front of him, my dad sat quietly reading his daily newspaper, which was faithfully delivered every morning. My mother worked succinctly, ensuring every dish that was supposed to be hot arrived piping hot, with the steam rising for proof. My dad wanted it no other way. She aimed to please Daddy with grace, humility, and love. The children always wanted the grace to be said quickly so we could dig into the scrumptious cuisine.

Momma always cooked multiple items from the same categories: Smucker's strawberry and grape jelly awaited the homemade biscuits, wheat toast, homemade oatmeal, grits, rice, bacon, ham, Bob Evans sausage, fried chicken, scrambled eggs, sunny side up eggs, biscuits, raisin bran muffins, coffee, tea, orange juice, and Welch's grape juice. Our dinner meal during the week was often: roast beef with carrots and potatoes, collard greens, candied yams, potato salad, cornbread, fresh lemonade, and watermelon drink. Each dish was prepared with love from Momma's special home recipes.

During our mealtime, I can recall my mother telling hilarious stories. My dad would burst into laughter before she could complete the story; she would laugh while sharing. Consequently, it was nothing to hear laughter around the breakfast and dinner table. Thinking back on my childhood makes a smile come across my face.

Our home was active, with people coming and going. We often awakened early in the morning to a loud lawn mower making sure the grass was properly manicured, the maid ringing the doorbell, and the dog barking when let out in the fenced area surrounding the in-ground swimming pool. Every morning after breakfast, Daddy and Momma would meet at the front door to kiss and say their goodbyes, and then she watched him pull out of the garage, drive down the driveway, and up the street.

Family Time

Thursday nights were our time with my mom. She took us on long drives up into the hills and down into the valley, to look at the vibrant colors of the autumn trees. We always went and got a bite to eat, and her favorite fast-food spot seemed to be Wendy's. She ordered the turnover, a double with cheese, medium fries, and lemonade. She then said, "You all can order what you want." Before returning home, we stopped at Abbott's Frozen Custard Ice Cream to get the soft vanilla swirl ice-cream cones. We drove home in the cool of the evening with our windows down, the wind lightly blowing, trying to eat as quickly as possible so it wouldn't melt all over the immaculate Lincoln Continental. Sometimes napkins couldn't save us. Family time was the best time.

Home Training

Our parents raised us with morals, values, and qualities I can appreciate today. A few in-home lessons were: if they had company when we walked into the home, we were to speak. When you woke up, you said good morning to everyone. When you walked into the house, you took your shoes off. Never leave your curling iron plugged in if it wasn't in use. The same for the boom box, where I loved listening to my music all day and night. At times, to my surprise, when I returned home both would be missing. When I asked Mom, she said, "Yes, I know where they are, but you must promise never to leave them plugged in when you aren't using them. I was slowly learning, and she confiscated them multiple times.

We were taught to bring our tithe and free-will offerings to God's house, because it is the first 10% of all of our income. As children, we obeyed and followed in our parent's footsteps, and we remained blessed. I have realized that there is truth in scripture that says it is more blessed to give than to receive. There is an art to giving; the more you gift, the more you get.

Gifting

Giving is a part of my life and always has been. In 2021, I started a business which is close to my heart, Journey Into Purpose, LLC. Our mission is to shift, empower, and uplift those who have struggled in life, by moving them from the place they are in right now, to the place God wants them to be. One evening, while speaking with a lady, she said her van was impounded. We acted as a liaison and reached out to people who could assist her with paying the fees so she could have her van back. We are searching for willing investors who can donate, as the list of clients grows daily.

Rewards

I felt so rewarded as the woman expressed her enthusiasm and gratitude for having her vehicle back. She took a picture as she drove out of the lot. I now put singles on my dashboard so when I see homeless people, or people holding a sign requesting help, I can assist them before the red light changes to green. Stay ready to bless people without asking questions. I live by the adage, do unto others as you would have them do unto you. I am so pleased that my children have adopted the same principles. My college student came home a few days ago and said, "Mommy, I just gave a lady a few dollars. She was in the Walmart parking lot." I said I did as well. We looked at each other and smiled. I remembered a time in my life when I needed someone to gift me.

Near-Death Experience

I lived with my parents and graduated from Penfield High School. After graduation, I worked diligently at the

Champion Factory Outlet in the nearby town of Henrietta, as a cashier and the 2nd assistant manager, while I attended college at Rochester Business Institute. Then one cold and snowy evening, asleep in my lavender-flowered bedroom, my sister awakened me, saying I needed to take her home.

I willingly arose, not realizing the inclement weather. While trying to avoid an older lady driving slowly at the top of a hill, the car began to slide. I quickly thought *I must avoid her and go to the left*, which would allow me to go around her. I swerved and we crashed into a super-duty tow truck on the right shoulder of the two-lane road.

We burst into nervous laughter; why? I still can't explain why we laughed, because we already knew we would be in trouble. Our parents were out of town with pastor friends of our family. How will I tell my dad that the car his attorney friend gifted him was totaled? My niece, in a car seat in the back, was now in the front with us, and to make it worse, my sister looked at me and said, "My neck is hurting."

The tow truck driver came to my window, asked if we were all right, and tried opening my door. At that moment, we all realized the extent of what had happened. The door was mangled, and we were stuck inside. We told him her neck was hurting, so he called an ambulance, and she went to the hospital. I called my sister Jackie, the third oldest in the family; she called Daddy and Momma on the phone. But what happened to the lady driver that we tried to avoid? She never knew what happened behind her. In life, we move at a pace that may hinder others. Make sure to move at the correct pace because we can either contribute to harm or death, never knowing.

The Beginning of Love and Suffering

A few days later, I received a card from the son of the friends my parents had been visiting, which led to us becoming an item. The card was adorable to the eye, but what struck my heart was that he took his time and hand-wrote the enclosed letter. As I began to read it, it went a little like this. *I heard we might have a lot in common, and I would like to get to know you better . . . Sorry for your car accident. I hope you are doing well.*

We traveled to Gary, Indiana for their church convention and had a great time. He asked to take me to dinner after church. When I asked my parents, they gave me a list of "do's and don'ts." First, I had to drive them to their hotel in our family limousine and get them situated; then my sister Jackie would take me over to Denny's Restaurant. We arrived along with a few of Jackie's friends. We all sat at one table and had a great dialogue. He and I then left everyone and sat outside the restaurant, laughing, talking, and building rapport.

When I traveled back home, I delved into work and he began calling me, sending me roses, Avon products, and a Gucci purse. Soon after, I found myself having thoughts about him more often than not. I was standing at the counter at work when a florist entered holding a bouquet of the most beautiful roses. This will cause the heart to palpitate for sure. Finally, he came to visit me. We went out to dinner, and he drove with precision and love. The ride was smooth as one can imagine; I fell asleep, and he didn't mind.

After a long dating period, he finally popped the question, and I said "yes." He came back to visit and the time for him to leave came too quickly. When we went to take him to the airport to return home, separation became more complex. My mom once asked me why the wedding date was set so far away. She said, "I see the way you all look at each other. You should move the date up."

He treated me like a princess, opening and closing my door, pulling my seat out, and showing generosity whenever he could. The roses were the primary purchase that caused my heart to flutter; his voice was also enticing. I fell in love, but could not verbally speak these most important three words. He said, "I love you, Sandra," many times before he hung up the phone. We talked morning, noon, and night for a long time. Listening to him express his love made me feel good inside. However, I remained calm and responded, "I care for you."

His aunt died and he was grieving when he called one particular day. I felt I needed to render compassion, and suddenly, the words I have always held so dear came flying out of my mouth. He said, "Repeat that, please. What did you say?" Unfortunately, it was too late to make those three words seep into the specific place where they were reserved for a different time. So, I repeated the words aloud, "I Love You." And then the ship left the dock, and we married.

Married Life

Our honeymoon was delightful. We drove to Niagara Falls and slept overnight, rose in the morning and had a fantastic flight to Georgia. We then took a cruise to the Bahamas. We gelled, finished each other's sentences, and everyone began to say we looked like each other. I enjoyed being with him and cooking, cleaning, and laundry were not chores. They were a pleasure. I later enjoyed going on walks in the neighborhood and on outings with my children. Married life was blissful for a while.

We lived a daily life of trying to make ends meet. In our union were born nine talented, brilliant, genius children. But unfortunately, many years of suffering had taken a toll on them and me. My long hair was short and my healthy body was now a tiny frame. If one were to look into my eyes, they would see the pain in my heart. I was distraught, devastated, and worked into the ground. My everyday thoughts turned to how could I better care for each of them, while feeling the effects of our daily turmoil. Each day I made plans for how our day would unfold. It wore me out because I realized I was doing everything and he was gone all day long trying to make ends meet.

Great Losses

After birthing our first son, when we first got married, we lost our two-bedroom apartment with the swimming pool in the back. We moved in with his parents. I received a message from someone who said, "Sandra, I just read in the newspaper that they are tearing down your home and everything inside will be placed outside." I tried to hold my breath but couldn't continue, or I would have died holding the phone. Why? Because I had saved everything new and placed it under my round bed, preparing for my dream home. I lost everything I had worked hard for. But I didn't let it get me down, and we never discussed it. When we lost our home in Fairport, we moved to the house in Penfield,

New York. We lost the home where my baby son was born in Webster, N.Y. We lost everything many times, and I still tried to remain present and continue my many duties.

Temporarily Rescued by Employment

While at the playground one early morning at Plank Road Middle School, I watched my children swinging and playing. A car pulled up, and a young man got out and spoke to me. He said he had watched me with the children and asked if I wanted a job. I said, "I would love a job. What would I be doing?" He responded, "Watching children after school until their parents arrive to pick them up after they leave work." Oh, that was precisely what I needed, because I would have many perks and be able to watch my own children while getting paid. Boy, oh boy! That was the best of both worlds for me.

We were lodging in a motel not too far away. We then lost that spot and moved again. We moved so much that I can't recall every place we lived. Finally, after work one day, my husband picked me up and said, "Let's move back to Illinois." It was payday, and we packed up in our green F-150 van and traveled to Illinois to reside in another hotel. We stayed in hotel after hotel until, finally, we moved into a condo in Crete, Illinois. At that time, we had seven small children, and I had developed a love and passion for cooking.

When the children got off the bus, they ran home so they could eat. I took pleasure in this. They said, "I smelled your cooking from the bus stop, Mommy." Another fun thing about this location was that the neighborhood had many children, so they would ring my doorbell and say, "Mrs. Jackson, can all of your children come outside to play with us?" I couldn't send everyone, but the older group had the liberty to go and play for a few hours before coming back inside. This gave me a little break to clean up the kitchen from dinner and attend to the three little ones left behind. I enjoyed living in Crete, Illinois at the time.

Loss and Eviction

Then, we lost the condo and again moved into a series of hotels and motels. The last motel was in Frankfort, Illinois. We lived there for an extended time and it was not fit for living. We had a room with the three girls and when I wanted to see the boys, feed them, and spend time together, I had to walk out of my room and go next door to their room. I didn't complain. I endured it, but inside of me, I couldn't believe I had accepted this lifestyle like this and wondered how long it would take for us to get our act together.

One day my husband said we would close on a magnificent home in Frankfort, Illinois. I awakened that morning and asked what the plan was. He said he would call to borrow money so we could close on the house by noon. Well, the person he was going to borrow the money from was unreachable. I asked if I could try to borrow the money and he said, "No." So I went outside for a walk, looked to heaven, and said, "Father, God, I can't stay another day in this Abe Lincoln Motel. I walked and walked until 10 a.m. I reluctantly went back, and when I entered he said, "You can try to borrow the money." I went right back out and walked to my friend's store.

Miracles Still Happen

When I walked inside, she said, "You look horrible. Are you alright?" I was beaten, hot, drained, perplexed, and despondent. When she finished helping her customers, I said, "I need your help. I need to borrow X amount of dollars." She said she had to ask her husband. I told her, "My husband says he will be able to repay it within two weeks, but I have to move *today*. I can't stay there any more." She called her husband and I spoke with him while he was at his insurance company. I repeated what I said to his wife, and he said, "Yes, but I have to talk to your husband first."

God Showed Up

It all panned out, and we moved into a $499k four-bedroom, brand new, brick home with an acre of land. The yard was manicured, the rooms were lavish, the basement unfinished. The house was carpeted, the kitchen stove was a stainless steel double-top, the front room had a brick fireplace, and the whirlpool in my bathroom was like heaven. It was my happy place where I could relax and zone out for a brief time.

We lived there and I thought things would get better, however, they managed to get worse and worse. We had a three-car garage with three cars. We lived in a safe neighborhood and had beautiful front, back, and side yards. I had a friend with whom I rode my bike on a nearby trail, walked for miles, conversed, and went to lunch. She became my support system. When I needed someone to watch my children, she was there and likewise. She was someone I could confide in. She didn't repeat what I shared, but took it to God in prayer. I appreciate her to this day, and when I travel back to Illinois she welcomes me with open arms.

The Dismantling of A Union

One of our pastor friends died in Savannah, Georgia, and my husband ended up taking over the church. It was not something I approved of. However, I knew I couldn't stop it from happening. Soon, I received calls about him being seen out on the town with another young lady and at a home location. He returned to our home once a month. Then three, six consecutive months went by, and he still did not come home. I began to pray and ask God for help, saying, "Father, how long will I have to suffer like this?" Raising nine children was not easy. I carried a massive responsibility on my shoulders.

One day, I arrived home, after dropping everyone off at school, to see a sign on our front door. I knew it was a shut-off notice—the water was turned off. Nervously putting my key in the door, I walked inside and flipped the light switch on; nothing happened. This could not be happening—the electricity off, oh no! *Quick,* I thought, *I'd better hurry and cook dinner so when the children arrive they will have a nice meal.* I went to the gas stove to turn it on, and nothing but a click-click. In one day, we had no water, electricity or gas. As a mother, I was devastated and as a wife, I felt frustrated.

What am I to do when the water, gas, and electricity are off? I sat in the van and prayed, and a song came on the radio. *Jesus, Jesus, Jesus!* I listened to the lyrics and tears began to run down my cheeks. I quickly dried them and said, "Sandra, you got this!" I called the water company and spoke with a woman named Renee. She said, "Sandra, I provided you with an agreement, but it's been two months since you made your last payment. Something on the inside would not let me get off the phone with her. I continued saying, "Renee, there has to be something you can do." Finally, after 35 minutes on the phone with her, she said, "Sandra, a gentleman named Roy came in the office the other day and said, 'If you meet someone nice that needs my help, you can forward my number.' Give me a moment and I will get it for you." She returned and said, "Call him and tell him I referred you."

God Sent Help

I had called on God to send Roy, but I was too embarrassed to tell him about all three utilities being turned off in one day. So I told him about the water and the gas. He said, "Give me ten minutes, and I will call you back." Fifteen minutes went by, and the phone rang. He said, "I apologize for being late, but they should be there to turn on your water any minute." He added, "They will be there to turn on your gas Monday. Because today is Friday, there is nothing they can do until Monday morning." When Monday at 9:00 a.m. came, the gas came on. But what could I do about the electricity? It remained off for a long time. I called my husband in Savannah, and he said there was nothing he could do. I was speechless.

I said, "You have to turn the electricity on, and your children need you." I wrote emails asking him to come home and help with the children. I told him that I could not raise them alone, to no avail. Finally, he wrote a check and turned on the electricity. But, within two mornings, the switch no longer worked. I called ComEd Electric Company, and they said he wrote a bad check, and they would not turn it back on unless I sent a certified check or paid with a debit card. I had neither at the time. I didn't even have a checking account. I had to get a paper check from my job, walk over to my neighbor's home, sign the back over to her and bring the cash back home after work. Or, I could drive to the currency exchange and pay money to cash my check.

Because my paycheck was never enough to meet the needs of the home, I cringed when it came time to cash my paper check. But I held it up high in the sky and said, "Lord, I thank you for each penny. Please help me to stretch it and make it accomplish what I need it for." And He always tried; I am eternally grateful. My neighbor, Jane, would ask if my sons could help her, and she paid them for moving furniture and doing little odds and ends. I always felt grateful because they needed money in their pockets as well.

Trouble Doesn't Last Forever

Although our lives were tried, God has proven faithful. I am now an author, an ordained evangelist, a licensed insurance agent, and much more. The irony is that I am in the place to empower, shift, and enlighten others on their journeys, which is fulfilling in many ways. My children are all out of high school and living their lives. The last few are still in college, pursuing their degrees in the fields of their passions, which I am eternally grateful for.

I am free to be me. I travel, host events, and shift men and women from where they are right now to where God wants them to be. I have been blessed beyond measure to be the visionary of the book *Life After...* and to have 21 courageous co-authors boldly share their stories in a raw, passionate way. I have two children left at home and my life has reached a calm plateau, and for that, I am grateful.

There is life after divorce, cancer, raising your children, and suffering. No matter your life experience, you have a giant inside you that will protect, cushion, and evolve into what God has deemed you to be. God weaved every experience for my good, for the benefit of those who are suffering, and for His glory. My story is a Cinderella story, and it only gets better from here . . . *Blessings.*

"I will ascribe to love myself, morning, noon, and night and that's a fact; it is better to love yourself than to hate yourself."

~ Sandra E. Jackson

Debora J. Hollick, The SmashThrough Mentor, is an international speaker, intuitive consultant trainer, coach, and international #1 best-selling author. Debora motivates pleasant human interactions that optimize powerful work performance. Her clients say, *"It feels like receiving a warm, energy hug while also receiving a gentle kick in the pants!"*

She is the founder of *Live Life In W.O.W!, Nuggets of Wonder~Openness~Wisdom* compilation book, a companion Playbook, and various events. Contact Debora if you would like to find out more about how you can be part of ***Live Life In W.O.W!***

Email: Debora@smashthroughmentor.com
Website: smashthroughmentor.com
LinkedIn: linkedin.com/in/deborajhollick
Facebook: facebook.com/SmashThroughMentor

Chapter 13

Cinderella, Cinderella Why Don't You Listen?

Debora J. Hollick

True forgiveness is when you can say, "Thank you for that experience."

~ Oprah Winfrey

Oh, the things we think, do, and say when we are young. We think we know it all. At least I'm pretty sure I did.

My parents adopted a bit of a different philosophy of raising teenage kids—or at least me, which, in my opinion, was quite modern for the times. To be honest, I really don't know how they dealt with my siblings when it came to dating, curfews, and such things, but I do know that I didn't have many restrictions. Maybe I should have had some.

I remember my very first date. I was fourteen. Very early in my teens to be dating at the time. Maybe even for now? I never had a curfew. That doesn't mean to say I could be out until all hours of the night. Quite the opposite, in fact. I was expected to use my judgment and it had better match what my mother thought it should be! I was very mature for my age. My maturity developed out of necessity.

I grew up on a farm. There is a lot of work on a farm. Everyone works. At least they did in my family. We all had chores to do, some outside in the barns, others of us in the house and garden. I'm not talking about a tiny little backyard garden, either. Oh no, indeed!

There was fieldwork in the spring, summer, and fall. Animals had to be tended to, twenty-four seven, three-hundred, sixty-five days per year, at least once per day, usually twice.

My first experience of having to step out of my comfort zone and become very "adult-like" and responsible in short order, was at age thirteen. It was two days before school was let out for the summer. My mother was admitted to the hospital. My older siblings had all left home and my father had to be in the fields, as well as do the outside chores in the early mornings.

I was the one who became responsible for my younger brother and sister. Add on to that, barn chores in the evening, while watching them both, along with taking care of that huge garden I mentioned earlier. It is amazing how creative one can get when having to occupy a three-year-old while you and your six-year-old brother, are slopping hogs!

While doing those tasks, there was also the house to keep clean, meals to cook, and laundry to do using a wringer washer and the clothesline. No easy task for someone not even five feet tall! Are you familiar with a wringer washer? Perhaps you haven't even heard of one? Remember, we didn't have all the modern conveniences of today.

Then there was the garden to weed and harvest, as the weeks of my mother's hospitalization continued until two days before I started school, right after the long weekend in September. My grandmother, bless her heart, did come to help me which I appreciated. I know her efforts came from an intention of much love. She taught me many things in the four days she stayed. Her way of doing things in the house was, however, very different from my mother's.

I remember she would start something in one room, take an item to another, start doing something in that room, and so on. It continued throughout the day. What this accomplished was disarray in most rooms, especially in the kitchen. I loved my grandmother. I always enjoyed spending time with her, but the disorganization became confusing and challenging for me. It became more than I could cope with. Who knew what OCD was back then?

At the end of four days, I asked my dad to discretely get my grandfather to ask her to come home. That didn't turn out to be all that difficult because my Grandpa, whom I also loved dearly, was an old-school, needy sort who expected his wife to wait on him hand and foot. And she did.

I felt on edge pretty much that entire summer. We didn't know when mom was going to be discharged. She, as a perfectionist, had her expectations. Of course, I wanted everything to be exactly the way she would like it because she had been so sick, and I didn't want her to be upset with anything when she came home. It wasn't fun when mom became upset. Believe me.

My second major experience of growing up and having "adult-like" responsibilities was just two years shy, following the first one. I was almost 16 years old. Again, a summer of growth.

I want to respect the privacy of my family members involved in this situation. Consequently, I'm not going to go into specific detail here. Suffice it to say, my parents had to leave the farm on less than an hour's notice to drive nine hours to be with one of my siblings and her newborn, both of whom were in life-threatening, medical emergency conditions.

This time, they left me totally in charge of the farm and my two younger siblings! Not only did I fear for my family members, but being thrust into the role of "farmer" and "fill-in parent" for an indeterminate amount of time was, at the very least, daunting! Maybe terrifying would be a more accurate feeling.

Not only did I have those roles to play, but I also had just started my very first "real" job. I had no clue as to how I was going to get there. I think that was when I first realized I am a pretty good organizer and had sales and leadership qualities. It didn't take long before I arranged for rides to and from work, as well as someone to look after the kids while I was there.

I'm ever so grateful for the kind, caring neighbors, friends, and extended family members nearby, who stepped up to help when needed. I'm happy to say it all worked out well.

It's Hard to Write About Personal Stuff

It just is. It opens us up to all sorts of vulnerabilities and emotions. Judgment. Fear. Anxiety. Rejection. Anger.

Regret. Frustration. Not to mention, feeling downright stupid for some of the choices made.

Relationships

From the time I started dating, I found myself attracted to older men. I also got along well with older women and had several as friends. I often wonder why I was that way. Was it because of my maturity level? Perhaps their immaturity level? Who knows?

One thing I'm pretty certain of is that I caused my parents' hair to gray prematurely! Now that I am much older and, I'd like to say wiser, I can understand why my dad didn't want me to date men several years older than me.

The good news is, I was a well-behaved teenager, for the most part. Not perfect by any means, but nothing that could land me with any lifelong regrets. At least so far.

Leaving Home

At age sixteen and a half, I left home. Looking back, I wouldn't recommend it.

As I have mentioned, we lived on a farm. We only had one vehicle at the time. In May of that year, I got a job—a really good job, working in one of the hospitals in the city close to where we lived. I had shift work while I still attended grade eleven in high school.

It made perfect sense to me that if I lived in the city, I could get to school and work, without my parents having to drive me. It would have been nearly impossible for them to be able to get me where I needed to be in the short time frame between school, work, and home.

My mom often served as a buffer for me when I wanted to talk to Dad about something I knew he wouldn't be in favour of. Not that I was afraid of him or anything. It just seemed easier that way.

Not this time! She wasn't having anything to do with my idea. If I wanted to have any chance at all, I would have to broach the subject myself.

Here goes ... My dad had a tendency toward raising his voice on occasion. I knew this, quite possibly, was going to be one of those times. Bracing myself, I told him I wanted to talk to him about something I wanted to do, and he had to promise not to yell at me until I finished explaining. He agreed.

Again, I'm realizing I just might be pretty good at sales, even though I didn't correlate the two actions at the time.

We had our conversation. He only started to interrupt me once and caught himself. He cautioned me and told me it would be difficult. In the end, he granted his permission on the condition that if my school grades fell below 75%, I would be moving back home, no arguing.

Our deal was struck. Now I knew I could sell! Still, I didn't recognize what I was doing. I didn't even know what sales were. Of course, I thought I knew it all.

Cinderella, Cinderella, why didn't you listen to your dad?

Memory Revisited

Toward the end of our talk, I recall my dad saying to me, "I can support you until you are eighteen." Of course, I knew this to be true, but memories have a way of rising up, sometimes causing havoc.

We didn't have a lot of cash flow. Not that we were poor. . . we were the first in our area to have a colour TV, as well as many other material items that might be considered luxuries at the time. We had plenty of food, clothes, and pretty much everything we needed and more. Still, at times, it felt that we were one of the less affluent families in our area.

I remember one time, I think I was eleven or twelve, and I needed money for something at school. I asked my dad for it that morning. He said he didn't have any money and opened his wallet to show me. Completely bare. The feeling I experienced, which I remember as if it was yesterday, was one of sadness, embarrassment, and mostly, fear.

I felt sad for my dad because he was a proud man, and I know that wasn't easy for him. In fact, my guess is he felt ashamed and embarrassed. I was embarrassed because I had to go to school and say I couldn't buy, or participate in, whatever it was that I needed the money for. I felt fearful because there wasn't any money, and I knew we needed money to live.

My dad saw the look on my face and said, "Don't worry, the bank will make more." Even though I believed pretty much whatever my dad said, from that moment on, I developed, unconsciously, a feeling of scarcity.

It doesn't take much for kids to develop a negative imprint that is long-lasting.

I'm A Big Girl Now

Off I went to the big city. Well, truth be told, not so big—just big to this young country girl!

I continued with my schooling and working at my wonderful new job. I excelled at my job. So much so, that when it came time for me to go into my final year of high school that September, they created a shift for me that would accommodate my studies as well as my being able to catch the last bus home.

During that time, I always dated guys older than me. The results of that weren't always favourable. I will leave it at that in this story.

When I turned seventeen, I met someone much older than I was. Much, much, older. We became friends. Let me assure you, he remained every bit the gentleman. I didn't have a vehicle so he would lend me his candy apple red, Pontiac convertible, so I could go out to my parents' farm when they needed my help, or I wanted to visit.

I felt very special and quite fancy, driving that beautiful car. I remember my long, blonde hair, blowing in the wind as I drove along the highway, feeling free, rich, and full of life. I felt an immense amount of appreciation. Still do. It was his pride and joy. He trusted me to take care of it and I did. It was a privilege and an honour to be trusted to this degree and I knew it.

Time Moves On

Almost two years passed. We began dating. I'm not quite sure how that even happened? He was twenty-three and a half years my senior. You would think we wouldn't have anything in common—quite the opposite.

We had a lot of fun together. We went out for dinner and dancing at least two to three times a week. He proved to be quite the ladies' man, and he was with me! Wasn't I special! Or at least I thought so.

Oh, Cinderella, this was a bright red flag. You should have paid attention.

I'm sure you've guessed by now my parents weren't too happy with me. They made certain to point out the pitfalls this relationship would most likely have. Did I listen? I wouldn't have a story to tell if I did. I'm not going to bore you with the details of our life. Let me just say that, as in all relationships, there are good times, and some maybe not so much.

Trust Issues Begin

As time went on, I finally began to see the signs that he was cheating on me. I even confronted him about it and let him know I knew. Of course, he denied it. Being a very independent woman, even then, I let him know that while I didn't have proof, I knew, and when or if I had such proof, that would be it. One chance and one chance only.

Are you asking yourself, "Why, if she is so independent, would she put up with his behaviour? I must have been getting something out of the relationship that, at the time, fulfilled a need. I loved him and other than this, he treated me very well. I thought he loved me.

He was good to me and my family in many ways. At the time, I guess I thought that was enough. Was it really?

Tragedy Strikes

People change when something happens that is monumentally sad. At least I did, I was twenty-one. I miscarried a set of twins. A boy and a girl. Even now, so many years later, as I write this, my eyes well up with tears. Who would they have become, had they survived?

Most people don't even know I was ever pregnant. It may come as a surprise if they are reading my story. At the time, only five people were aware. One of them was my Dad. I didn't tell him. He came to visit me one day and, even though I didn't realize it, I guess my body was changing. He noticed and flat-out asked me if I was pregnant. Gulp!

I remember closing my eyes as I mustered up the courage to admit I was. It wasn't something a nice, Catholic girl like me would want to have to face. And face it I did. Right then and there. I wasn't going to lie to my father. To his credit, he didn't get upset or berate me in any way. He just gave me a big, loving hug.

I asked him not to say anything to anyone, not even Mom. Thinking about it now, perhaps he told her, although she never mentioned it to me at the time. We did, however, talk about it many years later. Why didn't I want anyone to know? Was it the feeling of shame I had, being unwed and expecting? Or did I have a sense that something wasn't quite right? Maybe it was both.

Regardless, the experience changed me, as a woman, and as a person. There is a sorrow that you never wholly recover from. It feels like something is missing. Yes, you learn how to cope and move forward but, at least for me, I now looked at life differently.

Brief as it was, I had been a mother. While it saddens me that it was for a small window of time, physically, I still am. I feel their Spirit with me. Often. My sweet, baby Cherubs. I love you.

Time To Move

We decided we needed a change. "Let's move," we said! Well-qualified in his field, getting work wasn't going to be a problem. I felt confident in my abilities and work ethic, as well. The economy was good. Easily enough, he gained employment with an oilfield company. Looks like we are moving about nine hours away from where we lived. I thought to myself, "Looks like this is happening."

By this time, we had been a common-law couple for about three and a half years. I became the first person on either side of my family to just "live together." It wasn't popular or acceptable at the time—something else that my parents weren't all that pleased about.

I really didn't want to move to a new area without being married. We had been discussing marriage before the pregnancy, so it seemed logical to both of us we would get married before we moved. Because of this decision, it became necessary for him to move before me, to begin work. I would stay behind, continue with my job and we would plan the wedding, via phone.

Exciting Times

We looked at rings together during a private appointment with the jeweler on a Sunday afternoon. There were three that I particularly liked and looked nice on my hand. It would be up to him to choose his favourite, when and if he were to go ahead and propose. I felt this was special for both of us. It wouldn't take away the surprise element of the proposal.

It really did come as a complete surprise when it happened. We were having dinner at home when he asked me to get him another plate. Not understanding why he needed it, I asked him why he couldn't get it himself? After all, I didn't see a piano tied to his butt. He convinced me to get up and get it for him.

I opened the cabinet and there was a box sitting on top of the plates—a small pastry box. Now, anyone who knows me, knows I like my sweets, so I said while laughing, "What's this?" "I bought you a treat." I thanked him for his thoughtfulness and the surprise, and brought the box to the table, setting it aside. We enjoyed our lovely dinner together.

Dessert

Time to open that box to see what delicious delectables it contained. Yummmm . . .You guessed it. Inside the box was another, very tiny ring box. He took it out, opened it, and asked me to marry him. Of course, I said, "Yes."

And there you have it. We became engaged.

Wedding Planning

Before he left, we had agreed upon how we would like to enjoy our special day. It would be up to me to implement our plan. I was excited. It was to be a rather large wedding. He had a large family; mine wasn't as large but a good size, as well.

He would call several times a day to see how everything progressed and profess his undying love and devotion.

Long-distance costs were a dollar or more per minute at the time.

Cinderella, he must love you—a lot!

The date was set. The hall, caterer, and band were booked. My wedding dress was made, along with my bridesmaid's dress. The 500-plus invitations were set for print. (Yes, at that time, they had to be set at the printers!)

My aunt held a large wedding shower for me with neighbours from where I grew up, friends, and family. I received so many lovely gifts! I felt very spoiled, indeed.

Times were busy but I was very enthusiastic about my future. Next task, hand in my resignation letter at work.

Signs

I had a feeling something wasn't right. Did I listen to it? Sort of.

You would think maybe I should have been clued in that there was a problem, when he was so unreasonably upset that I quit my job six weeks before the wedding date? Why the upset? It wasn't as if commuting was an option nine hours away from work!

Ignoring the warning signals, we stayed together as a committed couple. I did, however, postpone the wedding.

Cinderella, maybe the shoe doesn't really fit?
Maybe it never did.

Awkward

Do you know how embarrassing it is to have to let everyone know that you have postponed your wedding after they have given you a spectacular wedding shower with gifts? Of course, the gifts needed to be returned. I kept everything in the boxes. Thankfully, I hadn't used anything.

Time to face the challenge, starting with speaking with my aunt who graciously held the shower for me. Much to my surprise, everyone refused to take back their gifts. I'm sure they felt sorry for me. Oh, the shame and guilt of it all.

Well, I am keenly aware that things much worse can happen, it was quite the ordeal for me. And much worse they became.

Cinderella, that shoe is getting way too tight!

More Signs

Do you recall I mentioned earlier that we stayed together as a couple? One evening, I called my fiancé at work. He often worked late. A man answered and asked if this were, "Sharon?" *Odd,* I thought to myself. I felt a not-so-great feeling in the pit of my stomach.

"No, it's his wife!"

We had lived together for four years by this time and where we came from, were considered legal. "Who is Sharon?" I asked. Silence, then stammering and stuttering, he replied, "Oh, she's a girl that works in the office."

"And she would be calling my husband at this hour, why?" I asked. He mumbled an answer which I don't recall. Something wasn't right.

Betrayal

Remember earlier in I said he was a ladies' man? When he left to make the move, I told him I knew he would likely cheat on me. I thought if I acknowledged that, it would maybe deter him from doing so. At least I think that's what I thought would happen. Or did I?

"Just don't bring her into my hometown," I recall myself saying, more or less joking. Not expecting anything like that to happen. Or did I? People tried to tell me, one of whom was his daughter. Even though she and I were close, I justified my refusal to believe her by accusing her of meddling. What was she trying to tell me?

HE WAS LIVING WITH ANOTHER WOMAN! While he was actively participating in planning a wedding and professing undying love and devotion to me!

One of my favourite sayings is, "listen to the whispers or get . . . the 2x4!" In fact, I wrote a chapter in another book, titled just that, because I have had a few of them. I think I'm an expert on receiving them.

Cinderella, you better duck—the 2x4 is about to smack you, hard!

The Ultimate Betrayal and Then Some

By now, I knew of course, she was right. He made an excuse that he had to work and couldn't come home for Christmas, regardless of the fact that it was my first year without my father. He had passed away after several years of a lengthy and painful cancer journey. Yeah, right,

Christmas came and went. New Year's Eve arrived. I spent it with close friends playing cards. When I got home, shortly after midnight, I decided to call one of my friends to wish her and her husband a Happy New Year.

She asked me what the two of us were doing for New Year's. I said, "I just got home from my friend's house. He didn't come home for Christmas or New Year's." And here it comes . . . my 2x4!

She laughed and said how I was always joking. I said, "No, I'm not." Silence.

"I know something is wrong. Tell me," I said. By this time, she was crying. I froze in place, stone-cold. She told me she had seen him.

"Are you sure it was him?"

"He wished me a Happy New Year at the store, while I was working this evening."

And the icing on the cake . . . *he was with her*!

Cinderella, Prince Charming is a real piece of work!

More Questions Than Answers

Why? How can you be so mean? Why? I was pretty, with long blond hair and blue eyes. I was as slender as he wanted me to be, or so he said. In fact, I was very weight and body conscious, always dieting. He hated it when men whistled at me.

"Don't lose any more weight," he would say. "I don't want you to be skinny." Oh, isn't that nice? He didn't want me to wear too much makeup. "You're gorgeous just as you are. You don't need it," he said. Aww. Isn't that just so sweet? The woman he chose to betray me with was caked in it!

Things Happen For Us, Not To Us

I'm not sure where I first heard this or who first said it, but I have fully come to believe this to be so. When good things happen, it is much easier to understand. When it is the opposite, one wonders. It took me a long time to realize all of these experiences were, difficult as it may be to believe, of benefit to me.

I've learned to listen to the whispers. By learning that, I have been able to share the importance of doing so with others, with the hope that they would not need to go through similar challenges.

I have made the choice to not see him as a horrible man who wronged me in one of the most hurtful ways. True, he wasn't an honest person, but he did have some good qualities. He must have, or I don't think I would been with him in the first place. I have forgiven him. That doesn't mean I condone his behaviour.

For many years, I blamed myself. I wasn't good enough. These were the sorts of things I repeatedly told myself. I took those feelings and built walls so I wouldn't allow myself to be in that position again. By choosing to forgive him, I freed myself.

Cinderella, you are more comfortable in sandals!

Tammy Rader is an emerging speaker. She is a Cancer Mentor and is focused on guiding those with cancer through and beyond their journey. Having been diagnosed just 39 days apart with both breast and rectal cancer, Tammy is now a "Thriver," who finds resilience with the help of humor, practicing mindset, and having gratitude.

Tammy currently lives in Edmonton, Alberta, Canada. She loves the simple little things in life, like going for walks, swimming, the sound of laughter, ladybugs, unicorns, and flip flops.

Linktr.ee: linktr.ee/tammyrader

Chapter 14

Death Is Not An Option

Tammy Rader

In the middle of difficulty
lies opportunity.
~ Albert Einstein

Everything changes and yet everything stays the same. It can be difficult to find motivation and inspiration to get back to living life when our outer reality doesn't match our inner reality. I'm Tammy and I am grateful to be able to share my story with you. In 2021, defining moments changed my life forever, and both times . . . death was not an option!

I was born at 10:38pm in Kitchener, Ontario, Canada, and grew up in the town of Dashwood, Ontario, where you could walk down the street and know everyone, and they knew you. It's true what they say when you live in a small town, it's everyone's business. Dashwood is actually a village and the original name was Friedsburg—that's for another story. Dashwood is located just a few miles from the beautiful shores of Lake Huron and Grand Bend.

I have one brother, Danny, who is three years younger than me. I was his "voice" until he was around three years old. My mom said I loved to talk—and still do—and I did all of his talking for him. He has grown to be a wonderful man, is married to Cheryl, and has three amazing sons. My strict (not as strict when it comes to the grandkids) yet amazing, loving, kind parents, Rose Marie and Richard, celebrated their 50th wedding anniversary in October 2020! Unfortunately, it was during Covid, so we asked people to send "Happy Anniversary" videos, which we compiled for their anniversary gift.

I have one son, Steven, who I call "my little miracle." At 16, I was diagnosed with endometriosis and IBS (Irritable Bowel Syndrome) and was told that I would never have kids. I had several laseroscopies to clear out the endometriosis, as it covered the floor of my pelvis, tubes, ovaries, and bowels (and caused great pain). Between surgeries, I managed to get pregnant. His dad and I married a month before I turned twenty-four.

I gave birth to my beautiful, brown-haired, blue-eyed, little miracle—my son is my whole world! He has grown into a fine young man who I am very proud of. He works hard at his full-time job, working with concrete, and now has his own business in the industry. He also does custom-designed woodworking. He's made some beautiful pieces, but the most precious creation he's made (in my eyes) is the piece he made for me . . . I'll explain later.

Eight years after Steven was born, things didn't work out with his dad and we found ourselves involved in a pretty nasty divorce. It was not amicable and caused a great deal of stress for all of us. (Today, his dad and I are friends.) I became a single parent, and at the time was only making $14 an hour. So, I took on other part-time jobs, including driving for a company in London, Ontario that was a designated driving service.

I would work during the day at my full-time job and then drive 45 minutes to my friend's house in the city. I would get some sleep and then work from 10pm to 4am. Then I would drive back to Exeter, work all day, then drive back to London and do it again every weekend. I did that for ten years! I had to do what I needed to, to show and teach my son that no matter what life deals you, you have to show up and never give up! I worked hard to have a roof over our heads and put food on our table.

For my 40th birthday, I gifted myself a trip out west to Alberta, Canada to see friends and the beautiful mountains in Jasper and Banff. A good friend offered me a job and I ended up working in Alberta, where I met my amazing, handsome boyfriend, David. After two years of flying in and out (rotational shifts), I bought a house in Edmonton. I might add here that those were the two things my mom said NOT to do . . . buy a house and meet a man. Sorry, Mom!

Fast forward to 2021 . . . on a very cold January morning. If you know Edmonton, Alberta, you know how cold it can get (-40° C and below, especially in January) and this particular morning was no exception. I had just stepped out of the shower and had started brushing my long, dark hair, when my hand grazed across my chest . . . something felt different. I looked at myself in the mirror, did a self-exam, and found a rather large lump in my right breast.

Immediately I thought, *What the hell is this?* At times like this, your mind goes "squirrel" and a million thoughts enter your brain. *No one in my family has breast cancer, I'm working too hard. That box I carried the other day was too heavy against my chest. No way, it's not breast cancer, it can't be!* I literally dismissed the possibility and carried on with my day. I couldn't be worrying and losing focus while driving . . . and the lump was nothing anyway . . . right? I had been working extra hours, doing mudding, taping, and painting for the offices upstairs at work. So I just figured I was overusing my right arm, therefore whatever I had felt in my breast was nothing. Was I wrong!

I let things go for a week and the following Monday, after my shower, I checked the area again. Sure enough, the lump was still there. I made the call to my doctor. She got me in for the necessary tests right away: mammogram, ultrasound, and biopsies. I had been telling myself the lump was nothing, but I think deep down I knew.

During work, in the middle of the afternoon on February 18th, 2021, I received a phone call confirming my worst fear and was told those three little words no one ever wants to hear . . . "You have cancer." There were more things said in that conversation, but once I heard those words, nothing else made sense. It sounded like all her words were going through a garbage disposal. Things seemed to move so quickly, yet it felt like I was in slow motion. It was the weirdest feeling ever!

The surgeon called the following week and explained that I had to have a single mastectomy. I cried so hard when he told me. The thoughts that come to mind when you hear that news: *What am I going to look like? Will my boyfriend still love me? What will others think?* . . . and so many more. He explained that I had Stage III (aggressively growing) breast cancer, and with the four biopsies they did, they found that it had already spread to the lymph nodes under my arm.

The next two weeks were filled with phone calls from the doctor, the surgeon, and the absolute worst call I've ever had to make—the call home to my family. That was a very tough phone call, with so many tears, and so many questions I didn't have answers to.

Monday, March 15th, 2021, I had my mastectomy. When I woke from surgery, I had binding on and two tubes coming out of my right side. They had taken my right breast and 17 lymph nodes from my armpit. Just two weeks after the mastectomy, on March 29, 2021, I was told those three devastating little words AGAIN, "You have cancer."

I will back up just a tiny bit. I said earlier that for most of my life I've had IBS and endometriosis. I've also had multiple surgeries on my abdomen, including a hysterectomy and having my appendix removed. I also was in a really bad car accident in 2017, and then rear-ended the next year in 2018 . . . both accidents, not my fault, just to clarify.

In 2019, things just weren't right. I was in a lot of pain. My bathroom visits were getting longer and more painful. I have experienced constipation my whole life, but things were just becoming "different and difficult." The colors that were coming out of me were not colors anyone was supposed to see. I felt things in my body were not right, so I made a doctor's appointment. After discussing things with her, she booked me to see a GI specialist and to have a colonoscopy. You don't usually get appointments like that the next day. The appointment was booked for April of 2020 . . . and we all know what happened to the world in 2020 (eye roll). So, those appointments did not happen; they were pushed back three times. I finally got my appointment on March 29, 2021 . . . only 39 days after I was diagnosed with breast cancer and just 14 days after my mastectomy. I was hit with those three words . . . AGAIN!

Sitting in the GI Specialist's room, waiting for him to wash his hands after giving me an internal exam, the way he looked at me, I just knew what he was going to say! You know that feeling in the pit of your stomach when something is not right? That's what I felt. I asked him not to say the words, I BEGGED him NOT to say the words! David (my boyfriend) was in the room when the doctor said, "I'm sorry, I don't have good news." I said, "NO, please." He went on to say, "You have rectal cancer." I started crying, literally started sobbing. How could this be happening again? David came over and held me, he had tears in his eyes too. I thought, *What the hell am I going to do now?* Most people hear those words once in a lifetime. Some might for a second or even a third time (if the cancer comes back). But to hear those same words SO close together, was an absolute nightmare!

Death. That's one of the first things you think of when you hear those three words: "you have cancer" and immediately it's like, *Oh my God, how much time do I have?* You have no idea, and for me it was like this: Death is NOT an option! I took a few days and tried to process everything, and then decided, "Okay, I'm not going down without a fight!" My perseverance, resilience, my WANT to live and my ATTITUDE—my mom always says, "They broke the mold when they made you." I am stubborn and I am a fighter! My thoughts were *Why Me*? Then I changed them to *Why NOT Me?!*

My oncology team at the Cross Cancer Institute in Edmonton, Alberta had to figure out a new plan for me. With the newest diagnosis, treatments for my breast cancer had to be put on hold, and we started treatments for the rectal cancer first: 36 radiations and three rounds of chemo. When I think of radiation, I used to imagine a "really bad sunburn." Basically, radiation is the worst sunburn you can get and you burn from the inside out. I lost four layers of skin, from my pubic bone to my tailbone and inside my thighs. I also developed a prolapsed bladder after radiation.

Some days, I wondered how David looked at me and what he thought. He was a rock through this! Also, my hair was getting thin and there was a bald spot at the back of my head. Lots of things were happening to my body. It didn't like the chemo but it's part of the process. I'm not sure anybody's body likes chemo, but we have to do what we have to do to survive. After treatments for the rectal cancer were done, and before treatment started for the breast cancer, I received permission from my oncology team and was able to go home and see my family in Ontario, and that's when I made a decision.

You know, it's funny, I was more scared of my hair falling out, and of losing my hair, than of actually having the chemo! People will say "It's just hair, it'll grow back." NO! It's NOT JUST HAIR! (Please don't say this to someone who is going through this, or losing their hair for any other reason!) It's a control thing. Cancer takes SO damn much from you . . . I wanted to take control of this! I NEEDED to! I wanted to be empowered and just let the cancer know that it was not taking this from me!

When I went home, I wasn't planning on shaving my head. I woke up one morning, and asked my son, "Will you help me do something? Will you help me shave my head?" He didn't even hesitate for a second and said, "Yeah, I'll even shave my head right after!" I felt so much love at that moment! My best friend and her daughter were coming that day for brunch. I surprised them and asked if they would be part of this too. They were so happy I asked them!

I put my hair (the hair that I had left) in a ponytail. My son cut my ponytail off and then we each took turns shaving my head! It was such an incredible, empowering, beautiful moment. I still get choked up when I think about it because I took control! I didn't let cancer take that from me and it turns out, I look pretty good bald! I shaved my son's head when we were finished. So many "happy tears" that day, I will never forget the feelings!

I headed back to Alberta and started my treatments for the breast cancer: six rounds of chemo and 20 radiations. My body was not too receptive to the chemo, so after each injection, I ended up in the hospital. The first chemo treatment was the worst and I ended up in the hospital for five days! My neutrophils (white blood cells) dropped so low, I basically had no immune system for 48 hours. It turned out to be the scariest moment of this journey, as I really didn't know if I would be coming home—very scary!

It turned out that they had administered too much chemo. When they mix it up, it's made to fit you, specifically. Your age, height, weight, and type of cancer you have, the stage and grade—all go into the concoction of the chemo treatment. They got it right for the next dose though and I finished my last round of chemo on November 22, 2021. They gave me five weeks to rest and recoup my body before the radiation started.

I finished all of my treatments on February 1, 2022 and got to ring my third and final bell! (When you are finished with a series of treatments, you ring a bell, this signifies this part of the journey is over.) Most people only ring one bell, I rang three! Yeah! Now it's on to healing, recouping and learning to live my best life for the rest of my life!

I've always said I wanted to help people and I never knew what that looked like . . . until now. I want to be able to help people who are newly diagnosed, right in the middle of treatment, or are completely done and are trying to figure out their next steps. I've started my own business: BeYOUtiful Beyond Your Diagnosis (by Tam) featuring programs, courses, one-on-one talks, and eventually, retreats.

I felt alone for most of my journey, for a few reasons. My family lives almost 3,000 miles away from me and when I would call and talk with them they tried, but they just didn't understand some of the things I was saying, or how I was really feeling. The same was true with my boyfriend. Even though he stayed right beside me through this, he still didn't understand some of the things I was dealing with. I don't want anyone else to feel this way! Cancer sucks and is a "lonely disease" but it doesn't have to be!

For me, death was not an option. There are ways to fight, there are things you can do, and keeping a positive attitude gets you so much farther in life! Don't get me wrong, there were many dark days, like the time I ended up in the hospital for five days and didn't know if I was coming home. At night, there were times when I found myself afraid to fall asleep because I didn't know if I was going to wake up in the morning. Having a positive outlook, saying affirmations, drawing up a vision board, and other coping mechanisms really helped me to get through the darkest times. Now I can share all of those tools with others.

I get excited about being able to help others through their journey! Before cancer, I was a parts driver for a company with a fleet of vehicles. Our trucks went to the Northwest Territories, Walmart, and grocery stores, to deliver milk, food, and supplies, so we had to keep working during Covid. We didn't get shut down because we had to stay in service, to supply thousands of people and businesses.

I delivered parts to different companies—everything from tiny pieces to big, heavy drums. Going to work driving a truck and picking up parts didn't fulfill my heart. I know I was doing good work and it needed to be done, however, I now want to keep my cup full. You can't pour from an empty cup!

I am starting a whole new chapter. If you, or someone you know, have just been diagnosed, are going through treatments, or are on the other side of treatments and are not sure what to do or where to turn—reach out and let's chat. Please always remember . . . to smile.

P.S. The piece I was talking about that my son made for me is a large, thick, chunk of wood with live edges. He planed it down and carved a large cancer ribbon in the middle. He filled the ribbon with two colours of epoxy (blue and pink for rectal and breast cancers). In the very middle, at the top of the ribbon, he inserted half of my staples from my mastectomy (my idea—there were 30 total) and placed them in the shape of a heart. He also incorporated lights into the back. It's the most beautiful gift I have ever received! He is my whole world and one of the MANY reasons I fought (and still fight for) my life!

Nancy Lee Bentley is a dynamic Food & Wholistic Health Expert, Speaker, Author, Mentor & Healthy Private Chef, aka "That Gutsy Lady." A Grandmother of the organic movement, co-author of *Dr. Mercola's TOTAL HEALTH Program*, and visionary founder of The Food Circle. She has "done just about everything possible with food," from starting food co-ops and farmer's markets, to organizing the Organic Trade Association, to developing wheat-free recipes for celebrities like Cher, and baking Prince's purple-flowered birthday cake. A visionary champion of sustainability, she has been sowing the seeds of personal and planetary health, food community, and "Remembering Who We Are" for over five colorful decades.

Website: WholeHealthyYouKeys.com
Website: NancyLeeBentley.com
Website: TheFoodCircle.com
Email: ThatGutsyLady@gmail.com

Chapter 15

With Spoon in One Hand, Mouse in the Other...

A Wild 50-year Ride Around The Food Circle

Nancy Lee Bentley

Everything circles in season
and bears fruit in its time.

~ Native American wisdom

You might say I set myself up for overcoming adversity early, right out of the starting gate. In old-school fashion, I was pulled out of the birth canal with forceps, leaving my face crooked and my head misshapen, something they now actually call "banana head."

Yet, I take full responsibility for all that has happened, including this, in my strange and colorful life. If that sounds weird, then you're getting a taste of who I am. I've been called corny, nutty, fruity and flaky. And it's all been about food. Mostly out of the box.

And what a long strange trip it's been. From mud pies in the sandbox, to Madison Avenue food styling on the road to Woodstock, to paving the path of the healthy food revolution. From being chased by the Mob and the police, to surviving COGS and Corporatocracy, *The Men Who Stare at Goats* and TPTB. My motto is "I get knocked down, but I get up again." All of this, and more is why I've earned, and identify with, the title of "That Gutsy Lady."

The French call it "double entendre," literally "double meaning." Word play, puns, playing with your food, all whet my appetite. My penchant for double meaning is reflected in my work and in my wildness—kind of like a mirror of my whole life. And it literally spans the whole nine yards, the whole enchilada, a "full circle perspective" that's been embodied, I realized later, in the printout of my seasoned, and often unsavory life.

I'm a Gemini, represented by "the twins" ~ polar opposites within One Being, striving, trying, dying to bring it all into wholeness, into Oneness. And for me, it's been running two simultaneous tracts: the physical world of food and the spiritual world of nourishment, in tandem, on a long and winding road toward the truth, connection and integration . . . back to the One.

Have I gotten there yet? Well, yes and no. Sure, I've done a lot, seen a lot, learned a lot, and integrated a lot. And clearly, "some cultures take longer than others," another oft-repeated quote out of my opus, evergreen book, *Truly Cultured*, on fermentation, the microbiome, the circle of life. And I'm still not done yet.

Yet, one quite profound thing I *have* realized—it's not about the destination, it's really about the journey.

Some of the things that have happened in my life I never thought I would ever share with anyone. Ever. Yet now, as a seasoned food, nutrition and wholistic health mentor who's committed to the truth, and calling it like it is, I've developed the "guts" to speak, teach and write about at least some of it.

My own journey with food and nourishment started when I was five, playing in the sandbox under the big, shady maple tree behind our farmhouse, right in the center of our circular driveway. It was after a rain, when those drying mud puddles circling the sandbox yielded up some of the most yummy, creamy mud imaginable, just about the consistency of cream cheese.

My Mom had to go into town "for a few minutes to pick up a couple of things," with a "will you be okay?" as she turned the ignition key. Inspired and intrigued by the rich, chocolatey mud drying in those puddles in the driveway, next to my sandbox, I couldn't resist. I just had to jump out of the box to capture some of that superior ingredient, creating the best mud pies I'd ever made.

Spurred on by my spontaneous creativity, I then mused, "Oh WOW! I could make Mommy something really special for when she gets back." Excitedly, I went into the kitchen and managed to get the big, heavy refrigerator door open. Next, I tipped open the lid to the big, heavy flour bin that held 25 lb. bags of flour (made from our own wheat, ground in the mill in town) from which my grandmother made daily loaves of the family bread. From this larder, I created my first recipe: a mix-mash of flour, ketchup, chocolate syrup, pickles, and maraschino cherries.

From then on, I found myself creatively into food in every way I possibly could be. Clipping recipes from magazines, devouring my mother's classic *Betty Crocker* and *Joy of Cooking* cookbooks, I learned to cook by trial and error, trying new recipes every chance I could get. Every day after school, in fact, you'd hear me say, "Mom, what can I make today?"

This was soon followed by helping the ladies at church suppers, and winning a blue ribbon for my first "deviled eggs" cooking demonstration at the 4-H Big Six picnic. And then, getting my first "job" at the ripe age of 13, as an apprentice to one of the top caterers in central New York. I washed dishes because I was too young to legally handle food.

"A girl beyond her age," this prominent food professional effused, in a newspaper article written about my first summer job after high school. This was just before I left town to become assistant to the pastry chef at one of Rochester, New York's most elite country clubs. I was the only woman *and* the only white American in the kitchen.

It was my first experience dealing with male egos in the commercial kitchen. One very hot summer afternoon, the year of the Rochester riots, I found myself helplessly being humped from behind in the walk-in cooler by a brawny, Afro-American kitchen worker; and me, struggling awkwardly with half a case of (2-1/2 dozen) egg flats tucked between my chin to my waist. Uh . . .

I took more abuse, humiliated by the Czechoslovakian head chef. One afternoon when the pastry chef was away, he forced me to "peel" a very large, 80-quart kettle of rhubarb, piece-by-piece, after I had already cut it up. This is a procedure virtually *never* done in commercial kitchens, or home kitchens, for that matter. Fresh rhubarb is routinely "stripped" of its stringy fibers, but never "peeled."

I knew it then, loudly proclaiming "PEEL Rhubarb? Are you kidding? NO ONE ever does that!" And later, I was smiling proudly at my triumph when the rhubarb pies made out of this "kettle of fish" turned out to be a tasteless, pale, and pasty mess. They were just trying to give me a hard time.

I was very blessed as a child; I even had a mentor at the ripe age of 12. She was the Food Editor of the daily newspaper in Syracuse, New York, who lived up the street. She saw my voracious appetite for all things food and learning to cook, and took me under her wing.

In addition to a ton of advice, that affiliation landed me a recommendation to the Director of the Food Demonstration Kitchen at the New York State Fair. And, in high school, I became a student apprentice there: setting up trays and cleaning up, helping the chefs and home economists representing national food companies and commodity groups who were demonstrating recipes promoting their products.

I later "accidentally" ran into Marilyn Jenkins again, not recognizing her, but striking up a conversation with her and her husband, under the Cornell Alumni picnic tent, at my 50th Cornell reunion. What a thrill to inadvertently reconnect with this woman, who had such a profound impact on my budding food pursuits. What an experience, being able to share with her how much I was influenced by, and appreciated the opportunity to work with her, as a young adult. That set the tone for my unusual, pioneering, food communications career. Another of the many "food circles" that have inspired and propelled my food community vision for personal and planetary transformation.

And . . . there are NO accidents.

Once I learned, through my own experience (not just some book) that there were such a things as chefs and "home economists in business," working for large food corporations, their advertising and public relations agencies, and women's magazines, employed in test kitchens and food promotion, developing recipes and doing the "food styling" for the food photography that would eventually become food labels and four-color magazine spreads, there was no stopping me. I was pumped, inspired, and knew what I wanted to do for a living.

But truthfully, it was only through my diligence and perseverance, creative snooping and willingness to go beyond my comfort zone, (rather than just settling for the few mundane dietician, food lab or teacher job options that were available in the late 60s) that I was able to find my own fulfilling "sweet spot" within the world of food, nutrition and health.

I recognize that, over the years, my discomfort has often catalyzed my progress. Lousy grade school cafeteria food, combined with my real zest and talent for writing on the high school newspaper, gelled my move to a Cornell Food, Nutrition and Communications degree, on the way to a professional career in it.

Then, a bevy of leading-edge food/health related jobs in different sectors of the commercial and budding natural foods industry: agriculture, government, education, food service, politics, and media, gave me a huge repertoire of skills and experience.

So, "with spoon in one hand and mouse in the other," I've pretty much stirred and typed my way through a lifelong liturgy of food projects. *From Asparagus to Zucchini* (the still-popular MACSAC book to which I contributed a chapter on organizing regional, seasonal eating); from "Soup-to-Nuts"; and most definitely, "from one extreme to the other."

I've tackled everything from Ozark backwoods farm gardening, food bank and co-op organizing, writing organic certification standards and books on fermented foods, to creating MSG recipes and "Franken food" products for multinational food cartels.

I've gotten flack back from TPTB for going "against the grain" in challenging GMOs and global food rules. And I've garnered praise and adulation for catering elite, gluten-free parties for celebrities like Cher, to feeding people at Woodstock, and making Prince's purple-flowered, wedding-style birthday cake.

This is why I often say, "I've done just about everything you can do with food," and it's how I've earned the moniker of "That Gutsy Lady."

Woodstock was definitely a trip in the "all-you-can-eat buffet" of my life lessons. (And not just a literal one.) It was an indescribable, once-in-an-eon experience that punctuated my then 23-year-old life with an indelible exclamation mark. And yet, some 50+ years later, I'm still somehow writing and talking about it.

In fact, as I've shared in my award-winning essay, "A Wild, Woodstock, 50-year Ride" that I wrote for The

Community Book Project's 2019 *Independence* edition, and reproduced in my own *50th Anniversary, Woodstock Window on Food & Health Activity and Coloring Book*:

"Independence to me, as an old hippie, and a grandmother of the organic movement, is not just about having been at the original Woodstock festival, but about having the guts to share my insights and experiences 50 years later.

"First seeing the posters advertising the Woodstock 'Music & Art Faire,' in April of 1969, I just knew it was going to be "far out!" And I was right. What I didn't know was just how intense it would be, or how it would impact the rest of my entire life.

"With nothing at the White Lake Bethel site, we loaded up my mother's '64 Plymouth station wagon with food, tarps, beer and ice. (Good thing, I ended up feeding a lot of people.) Still, there was no preparation for the shock of close to 500,000 people showing up in an open field: an instant city without infrastructure, food, facilities or shelter. Exposed and repeatedly pelted with rain, we were WET, yet ONE and HIGH together in community. (And not just the media's droning 'Sex, Drugs and Rockin' Rollin' in the Mud' propaganda.)

"Experiencing the most ecstatic joy, peace, and groovy natural-high ever, we were CommUnity with a capital "U" . . . and nourished by something else.

"It was *transformative*. And under the most extreme conditions imaginable, I proved to myself that I could do, and survive, anything.

"So, what did I gain from Woodstock? I achieved my 'independence from need,' and the courage to know that I could make a difference in the world."

Ironically, as I write in my "Recipe for Succeeding Inside Out" chapter in my colleague, David Riklan's *101 Expert* book series, "My most profound insights have come, not from my successes, but from my knockdowns. "

They say, "The tallest trees get the most wind." I was definitely one of those vocal, revolutionary, "beans & grains hippies." After Woodstock, working in social issue advertising and helping to launch the first National Food Day with Robert Redford, I became an all-out passionate activist, heavily involved in food and environment issues.

That included everything from promoting non-toxic, local, whole, organics, "food circle" community, and sustainable agriculture. I also helped create organic certification standards, laying the foundations for the Organic Trade Association. Then I spoke out about the dangers of GMOs and "excitotoxins" like MSG ~ promotion for which, in my earlier food PR days, ended up being my own "guerilla training." Another example of "food circles" in action. What goes around, comes around.

Later, well-launched into championing healthy food issues, after co-authoring *Dr. Mercola's Total Health Program* with Dr. Joseph Mercola, my writing and speaking out against clandestine, global health "grab-for-the-biological-computer" politics landed me in hot water. I even have unbelievable, real life stories of finding my genuine, well-intentioned self personally ensnared in some very hairy and dark "down-the-rabbit hole" intrigue. That will have to be another book.

Then, the carefully planned launch of my own self-published *Truly Cultured Cookbook and Nourishment Guide* was trashed when the books were "mysteriously" mis-bound at the printers. Hmmm . . . This took me out of circulation into a dark, downward spiral, a nearly 10-year plus cycle of working my way back through what most assuredly felt like a total career breaker.

All this diversity forced me to review, face, and take responsibility for creating my own reality. Instead of resisting and recycling the same stuck issues, getting real and diving into the gooey, messy center of myself finally exposed, and helped me to embrace the unsavory buried treasure within. There is where I learned that, "What's *in* the way *is* the way."

Remember the Pearl in the Oyster. It started out as an irritating grain of sand.

In retrospect, my early "jumping outside the sandbox," and going beyond my comfort zone, was strangely symbolic of my life's journey—not just taking, but *creating* the "road less traveled," that has characterized my personal and professional life, this time around.

It hasn't exactly been what you would call *"The Joy of Cooking."* Little did I know, 50 years later I would find myself "stuck in the proverbial mud," bogged down in both my career and the rest of my life. I've bounced back, of course, to organize summits, appear on all the networks, and to be nominated to *Who's Who in America*. But I'll tell you, it's definitely been one rockin', rolling, salty and sour, bitter and sweet, colorful ride.

Studying food, nutrition, and communications as an undergraduate at Cornell (arguably the best in its class) gave me an excellent quantitative, scientific, and journalistic foundation for understanding the importance of food and how the body uses it. This also enabled me to master interpreting science for the layman, teaching, writing, and communicating about our amazing world of food.

I'm grateful that I've been able to download, decipher and discern the significance of food and nourishment on physical, mental, emotional and spiritual levels, how everything is connected and the "Soil-to-Spirit" bridge I know as "The Food Circle."

And yet my real, deep and profound understanding and wisdom about food—the higher, universal spheres of nourishment and the nature of true, whole health—has only come about through my own experience, observation and intuition, deep listening and ultimate mindfulness—remembering who I really am.

And what I've found, without question, is that life is full of ups and downs, circles and cycles. We're spiritual beings having a human experience, here to learn and grow. Our experience depends upon our mindset and what lenses, glasses, or windows we're looking through. And how much we nourish ourselves, how much "we head for the heart." Everything is connected.

Still, no question, it takes GUTS to be healthy and whole. And as the ancient Chinese *I Ching Book of Changes* advises, "Perseverance furthers." Yet ultimately, "Everything circles in season and bears fruit in its time."

Yet, the most important thing I've learned is to REMEMBER: The "secret ingredient" is always LOVE. In Gratitude, I AM, One in the Work.

Marilyn Martino is a semi-retired writer, teacher, and artist. She loves to encourage the exploration of art and writing as a self-care and discovery tool. She currently teaches people how to make and bind their own "Junk Journals" out of mostly recycled materials for self care and healing. She herself uses this artform as a source of focusing on gratitude and joy and is in the process of designing retreats to further share this with others.

She believes there are no mistakes, only lessons. She encourages others to press forward through their hurts and failures in order to thrive, not just survive because surviving is not a place to stay. Marilyn is happy to share her backstory.

Email: MyCreationStation22@gmail.com

Chapter 16

Under the Apple Tree

Marilyn Martino

Identify your problems but give power and energy to solutions.
~ Tony Robbins

For my siblings, and many more, who learned to overcome, under their "Apple Tree."

Just recently, I drove my daughter to the San Francisco International Airport where she boarded a plane for her first trip to Europe. We, of course, used GPS and had a flawless drive to the Bay area, arriving in plenty of time. She happily headed to Amsterdam, where she would be immersed in its culture, food, art, and architecture. Covid had put a huge wedge in her plans to see her many friends there. It was a triumph for her to be able to go. It took a moment to realize that all three of my daughters had now experienced the opportunity to go to Europe. Their own adventures are my joy.

While driving from rural Nevada County into San Francisco, I was awed by how many changes to the city there were. I hadn't been to that part of the Bay area for decades. The bay was still there, but the shoreline appeared much smaller to me. Some of the old buildings hid among much taller ones.

The docks were the same. We had taken a cruise to Alaska from one of those piers once. The triple overpass that had toppled in an epic earthquake years ago looked entirely transformed. It reminded me of change, trauma, and past family history. My daughter was my GPS co-pilot. I refocused on the driving task ahead. It was smooth sailing.

The Wonder Years

When I was a kid I loved being outside playing with my siblings and the neighborhood kids. Summers were the best because we could go visiting throughout the neighborhood and simply come home for dinner. Mom would ring a cowbell to call us in. No texting us back in the day. After dinner, we could go outside again to play games with the neighborhood kids: Red Rover, Kick the Can, Freeze Tag, or just ride our bikes until the sun went down. Streetlights on, time to go in—that was the rule.

We lived an hour's drive from San Francisco, so my dad commuted to the city and did so for 17 years. Our doors were always unlocked because back in the 50s and 60s you never needed to use a key unless you went on vacation. Of course, it's not like that anymore. Now you lock everything in sight.

We had barbeques, Easter egg hunts with the neighbors, and played basketball at the end of our street. The pattern of our life wasn't always this way, though. We were raised with very strict rules and could only go out with permission. That's why summers were so special; we tasted some freedom and autonomy.

School was an oasis. Playing outside at recess was a welcome relief, until bullies and mean girls entered the picture. We weren't taught to be strong and courageous. At one point, visiting neighbors or family became our only hope for a snack or a meal. Those environments offered us a safe place to talk, or just be ourselves—yet, we could never say what went on at home. We didn't know how to put into words what was troubling us. We were children; it was confusing. In our hearts, we knew something wasn't right, yet we trusted the "givers of rules." They knew best. They were in charge. The rules were in place to keep us safe . . . until they didn't.

On the weekends we would drive an hour north up the Bayshore Highway, to see both sets of grandparents, our aunts, uncles, and cousins. There was a two-way stop sign at King Road and 101 to make the left to go north. Car accidents were the norm at that intersection, so we were cautioned to be still and stay quiet during this nail-biting freeway turn, as our lives were on the line. Eventually, it became a four-way stop, then an overpass, and finally, another entirely new freeway was built crossing over the treacherous one. Now there are two overlapping freeways!

What fun we had in those days, visiting and connecting with family. We had the complete freedom to play with our cousins. No training wheels—we could explore backyards on our own. Holidays were the best; everyone was happy, telling stories, eating, and connecting with one another. But when we got home all that changed—back to control.

At home, behind closed doors, was a much different story. Yes, we were fed, clothed, and cared for. But we were taught that "what goes on in this house stays in this house." We didn't know otherwise that this was called "grooming," or that this wasn't normal. That's the beauty of grooming: the abuser gets to present a given scenario, designed to represent themselves as they wish, while they go about their business of lies, deceit, and abuse of those dependent on them.

Obsessive order was the norm in our house: no freedom to have friends over, no talking on the phone, or going outside. An occasional over-the-top discipline blip would occur while we were visiting or out in public. Family saw. Neighbors observed. Friends wondered. No one connected the dots. It was the "frog in the pot" syndrome. We needed to be rescued. It wasn't our community's fault. The veil was designed to keep them in the dark. It worked for a while, then it didn't.

My Swedish grandfather had been a man of many trades. He repaired homes, was a sought-after arborist, and could fix anything! He cultivated and grafted an apple tree that gave us three different kinds of apples each year. Harvesting these apples meant applesauce. Baked apples. Apple pie. Apple Crisp. Apples you could eat off the tree anytime you wanted a snack. We also had peach, pear, and nectarine trees. But the apple tree was my favorite. I'd spend time under its broad branches, shaded by its leaves. I'd watch the apple blossoms grow and drop off revealing tiny apples that grew into juicy ones. We all had such a hard time waiting for them to ripen each year.

Countless bellyaches taught us to be patient taste-testers for harvest time.

One summer, I was yet again harshly spanked—punished for "something." Confused, hurt, and crying, I headed for the familiar apple tree. For fun, I used to read books and bang pots and pans under its shady branches. I would sing along with my pot-banging.

This time I didn't sing. I only pounded out a rhythmic tune to get my emotions out. When I could no longer cry, I quietly uttered a solemn promise to myself that I would be a better mom to my children than what I had received. What child has never promised aloud something such as this? Answer: A child that was hurting and never wanted to hurt others like this, ever! I promised myself to be a determined chain-breaker!

I would wonder later if my mother ever watched, or heard, my distress from the door or window. I'll never know. Did any neighbors hear the cry of my broken heart? Was anyone going to rescue me? Back then spanking was permitted and no one thought of it as abusive. As time went on, lines were crossed, and the definitions became blurred as to what constituted corporal punishment and abuse.

Children know. We learned to behave out of fear of retaliation, not through trust and love. We would learn from our experience what not to do with our future children. Our lesson back then demonstrated that love was conditional, and we performed accordingly. I later learned from the Apostle John this: "There is no fear in love. But perfect love drives out fear because fear has to do with punishment. The one who fears is not made perfect in love." (1 John 4:8, NIV)

Troubles were brewing. It later would remind me of this quote by Eleanor Roosevelt, "A woman is like a tea bag. You may never know how strong it is until it's in hot water." This was what the world saw: a perfect family; four adorable, well-behaved girls. Perfectly dressed. Polished shoes, curled hair, white gloves for church on Sunday. Like *That 70s Show,* we were living the "Wonder Years" family life. Soon alcohol and parties became the priority for our parents. As this happened, food became scarcer, the lights and water were often turned off, and parental discord came to a crescendo, ending in divorce.

No more Wonder Years . . .

The divorce was somewhat of a relief. However, it brought new hardships. As more drinking and carousing crept into our lives, a previously unknown looseness of parenting became the norm. We were on our own, left to fend for ourselves. We became "latchkey children," without the skills to survive. After school, we were often pawned off onto neighbors, who were truly very kind to us.

The rules were in place. The timeline of our lives became all muddled up as to when one way of life ended and the new one began. Certain things do stand out in striking ways. We were not allowed to have friends over, or to talk on the phone. We were not often given permission to participate in school activities like dances, sports, and the like. I think that was when we first began to advocate for ourselves. The divorce forever changed the dynamics of our household. We were all struggling.

Each of us dealt with our traumas differently. Research later in life would tell me how human brains process, cope and protect the psyche from the effects of trauma. None of us actually were protected. We each became easy targets for bullies and predators.

Me? I had to keep the promise I made to myself under the apple tree. I refused to repeat history. I would protect, nurture, treasure, prepare, guide, and mentor my children to be able to defend and care for themselves. I would teach them to be strong and courageous, to develop their own God-given potential, and most importantly: to find joy, love, and fulfillment in this life. Even back then, I had that driving force within me to protect my siblings and rescue them. No one was coming for us. We had to rely on ourselves.

I would do better. Be better. Not be like that. I could never . . . Over time, I thought, *I will get a job and my siblings can live with me! We can have a nice apartment together and take care of each other.* Not that I could even take care of myself.

So I became a keen observer. First, to try to protect myself, and also my siblings, by anticipating potential threats. We had to find people to model our lives after. This became survival. It still wasn't enough. Coping mechanisms worked, the basics helped us along . . . until they didn't.

Treading water

I had failed to rescue my siblings. We were just surviving. An illness caused me to leave college. I was almost done, even though I had changed my major twice. My focus was off. Extreme burnout was on. I had to make money. The conflict of how to provide in the "here-and-now" overshadowed my long-term goals.

At one point I had no mentor and no real support system. I sought out career counseling. They only gave me two tests—nothing deeper—and they left me to make major life choices based on those results. I couldn't decide. My brain was on overload, so I just went through the motions. Get busy. Stay busy. Keep moving forward. You'll make it. I didn't. I came down with walking pneumonia, which required bed rest and antibiotics.

Once I recovered, I got a full-time job in a restaurant and tried to take two classes after work. My momentum had been lost. I dropped the classes and kept working. Eventually, I sunk into depression, alcohol use, and risky behaviors. None of it worked. I couldn't make headway on keeping my "apple tree promise." Finishing college: to be determined; it seemed out of the question, for now.

Up to that point, I was surviving financially. I had a car, a place to live, and could afford to have a little fun. A return to finish college was attempted, but my momentum was diminished. Working to survive took over. When the recession hit, my work hours were cut back and I lost my car, my ability to get to and from work, and eventually had no income at all. Life became very bleak.

I finally reached out to relatives. A dear cousin took me in. My other siblings were doing well. They were all married and had children to raise. I was still single and floundering. I wasn't able to see my singleness as a gift. That year, my dear cousin helped me. She took me to church and shared her faith, and her life, with me. We had many discussions, went on retreats, and attended women's Bible studies and activities. I found my faith in God again, and in people.

During that time of faith-building, I met and married my husband and had three daughters. Before the third one was born, the four of us attended a family party, where our entire family and most of our extended family gathered. On this happy occasion, a conversation ensued, and a sibling blurted out our truth. The story of what we endured tumbled out. Emotions ran rampant which cut the party short. The person of interest was driven home by one of our aunts—a long, difficult drive back home for them, and especially for our beloved Auntie. We were now in uncharted waters. The ripple effect began.

A quote from J.R.R. Tolkien's writing says, "The world is indeed full of peril and in it are many dark places. And though in all lands, love is now mingled with grief, it still grows, perhaps, the greater." This hints at the fact that, when the truth comes out, it can set you free. In the meantime, it can make you miserable. And it certainly did us. None of us actually were protected or prepared for life. We didn't know how to cook a decent meal, clean a house properly, use money wisely, or balance a checkbook.

Other details belong to my siblings. They have their own experiences and perspectives. Those details are theirs to tell or not. I wouldn't even think of taking that from them, with so much already taken. Our perpetrators showed no remorse nor were even saddened by our plight. In fact, they were oblivious to it, which is a sure sign of abusive bullies. They never remember the trauma they've caused, nor the innocence stolen, but we do—for a lifetime. I love what

Tony Robbins says, "Identify your problems but give power and energy to solutions."

The Way Out is Through

When my youngest child became of school age, the school invited Child Safety Puppeteers through Child Advocates in Nevada County (caofnc.org), California to perform in the children's classroom. That actually became part of another layer of my healing. Seeing an entire class full of children enjoying the puppets, and learning what good touch and bad touch were, spoke to my inner child. They were learning through puppetry how to protect themselves from predators and were receiving permission to have a strong voice to say, "No!" But, I was also receiving, while reframing what my inner child needed back then.

The puppets taught the class not only to use words but gave ways to escape and to ask for help. This was priceless to me. This generation would have the needed support and information I never had. It was such a gift, especially since my own child was present and engaged. In part, through Child Advocates of Nevada County, I was able to keep a piece of the promise I made under that apple tree.

A few years back, Dave Lockridge in Merced, California spoke to a pastors' fellowship meeting on ACE Overcomers, (aceovercomers.org—everything you need to overcome the negative effects of childhood trauma and household dysfunction) and cdc.gov (Violence Prevention, Adverse Childhood Experiences; ACES Program). That day my husband attended. He hurried home, bursting through our door excitedly, to share with me what he had learned that morning. Well, that information totally changed my life.

We decided to go through the whirlwind Friday night and all day Saturday facilitator training. Since then, I've realized this is the calling of my life. To be able to teach, reach, and mentor those who are hurting, in order to facilitate healing, is now my focus. I aim to build a team that will assess and make care plans to facilitate healing in the lives of the hurting. As Mike Rowe says, "It's time to 'return the favor.' "

Years of secret-keeping and a divorce separated us from the family that could have, and would have, helped in a heartbeat. One realizes that there has been progress in healing when you've been able to comfort extended family from the guilt they now experience due to the lack of awareness. It's certainly not their fault. It does, though, have a ripple effect. Comforting and assuring them that it's not their fault frees everyone. It allowed us all to feel a bit better and to receive unconditional love from one another, something that was sorely missed by my siblings and me over the years.

It was sad that the needed rescue didn't happen at the time. But the truth caused our tsunami to cease and created an oasis of understanding and support. We remain happy in our faith, comforted and protected by others' prayers and support, with continued hope of overcoming.

I've been overjoyed that all of my siblings are people of faith also. I don't blame people. I don't blame my God. I know where I'm going and where I've been. I know who I am, and I know whose I am. My siblings and I are blessed and finally rescued. We've built solid lives. We've protected and prepared our own children to the best of our abilities. That's not to say that we are without battle scars, triggers, and wounds.

It doesn't, however, needlessly have to take a lifetime for others to begin overcoming, as it did for us. Our wounds no longer define us, they refine us. Our scars are a sign of proof that we have overcome and will continue as forever changed persons. Although we are each in different phases of our healing journey, and have received interventions at different intervals, we are on the journey to process toward continued healing. A counselor at A New Day (anew-day.com) said it best, "You will be surprised by how the right people will appear to assist you at just the right time."

The Truth Sets You Free

The truth is out. The diagnosis is given. The enemy of mankind meant and attempted to kill, maim and destroy. Almost. But not today. That threat was overturned by Love, which covers much and turns lives around. Nothing is ever wasted. Not sorrow, nor disappointment. Not adversity or trials. Without them, we wouldn't know the joy of overcoming or giving back. The promise that we can rise again with strength, to thrive and fly within our God-given potential and calling, is priceless. There is hope. There is healing. It is a process. We know more now. Our awareness and radar are on.

Even though our community missed the mark back then, we are thriving at our best today. We live now as people in process. We live a life of faith, not fear. We live as prepared people, processing and passing on the good to the next generation, and to our communities.

Yes, we bear the scars of trauma and are often plagued by it. But we are continually rescued by God's infinite, miraculous mercy and grace, both in this life and the next, where there are no more tears, no more sorrow, only peace, love, and gratitude. Where we can continually say thank you. We are free and being freed today. May these words help free you today too. May this story perhaps become a part of your own rescue story.

Lorraine H. Tong is an author and former foreign policy advisor to two senators on issues of China, Russia, nuclear arms control, and human rights. For 20 years, at the Library of Congress, she analyzed policy and legislation for Congress on the Supreme Court, appropriations, telework as continuity of operations, and recruitment and retention issues.

Lorraine has mentored hundreds to enhance their professional development. Outreach and strategic planning are her current focus.

A memoir, children's book, and dark comedy are in progress. She has published *Hitler on Trial: Alan Cranston, Mein Kampf, and the Court of World Opinion*

Website: LHTproductions.com
Email: lhtong@alumni.stanford.edu
Book: amazon.com/dp/0999388916
YouTube: youtube.com/watch?v=-5jY0H-Uajc

Chapter 17

Cinderella Becoming Her Own Fairy Godmother

Lorraine H. Tong

The journey of a thousand miles begins with one step.

~ Lao Tzu, Chinese philosopher

Taiwan, November 1960

"You'll never catch me!" I teased over my shoulder. Lagging behind me, Elaine, four years old, and Mimi, three, and I were racing to the rose garden at the park. At five, I had a clear advantage, and seeing my cousins huffing and puffing behind me, I slowed to let them close the gap. The next moment, they ganged up on me and grabbed me. We all tumbled to the grass, giggling.

I woke up with a start. My eyes struggled to adjust to the darkness. I was in a strange windowless room, lying in a strange bed. My view was of the white ceiling because I couldn't turn my head or sit up. In shock, I realized I couldn't move from my neck all the way down to my toes.

Paralyzed.

How long have I been asleep? This is not my room. I couldn't blink away the dried residue in my eyes that was bothering me. Hot, weak, and thirsty, my voice came out a croaked, "Mom?" Then in a panic, "Help!" I listened and waited. And waited. There was only silence in the darkness.

Over the next two days. I drifted in and out of consciousness vaguely aware that people came in and out of the room. My eyes were open, but everything was a blur. I heard my Mom's voice, but I felt too weak to say anything before I fell asleep again. When awake, I was filled with frustration, lying in bed helpless. As an active five-year-old, this was sheer torture. I'd never been a crier, often told that I was more "head" than emotional.

When tears came, it was because the hospital forbade visitors. Elaine and Mimi were not allowed to see me. Twin cousins Liza and Bella, and our older cousins, May Ling and David were kept away. The doctors hadn't been able to diagnose my illness and were being cautious by limiting visitors, to reduce any risk of infection. Only Mom and Grandmother were allowed to visit. Mom came daily after work, and sometimes during lunch, to feed me. Grandmother had studied to be a missionary at the Mid-Pacific Institute in Hawaii. We believed her fervent faith in God and constant prayers kept me alive. Miraculously, on Thanksgiving morning my three-day 104° fever finally broke.

The doctors gave Mom the good news, "Your daughter will live but . . . she may never walk again." Luckily for me, I didn't hear the last part. Doctors and medical students came throughout the days to examine me, talking among themselves as if I didn't exist. It seemed like a non-stop parade for several days. They examined me and poked me with needles to test the feeling on various parts of my body, including the soles of my feet. To them, I was just an object of medical curiosity. I was ill, but there was nothing wrong with my hearing. The doctors discussed possible causes of my condition and various options to treat me. I didn't understand any of the medical terms until one said words I did understand, "Maybe we should cut off her legs." That careless remark horrified and haunted me. Forever.

The diagnosis came days later. *Polio.*

I didn't know what Polio was, I only knew a desperate gratitude that I got to keep my legs, although my whole body lay lifeless under the sheets. I had been stoic until I met small obstacles that made me grunt with anger. When my nose itched, I couldn't scratch it myself. I had to be fed like an infant. My thoughtful and smart Grandmother went to see a glassblower with a sketch of a straw she had designed. The glass straw curved just so, to enable me to sip the chicken broth she had cooked for me, while I was still lying down, as I couldn't turn my head. When I ate, I had to be helped to a sitting position. Helpless as an infant, I could do nothing for myself.

The days were interminable as I waited and lived for Mom's visits. I missed Dad, whom I hadn't seen since I was three. He had gone to America after being accepted to a highly competitive doctoral program at Stanford University. Sometimes when Mom visited me, I could see from her telltale red eyes that she had been crying. I didn't know if it was because she missed Dad or because of me. I think it was me. I kept my tears to myself because that would only distress her more. Ah Nial, my nanny, who was like a second mother to me, had taken care of me since my birth. She, too, was blocked from visiting.

I had no conception of time and the days were endless. I longed for life before polio. Most of all, I missed the ability to skip, run, and play games with my cousins and friends. *I even missed school.* In my entire life, I had never been alone for long stretches of time. We didn't have television yet in Taiwan. I couldn't turn the pages of a picture book. There was no radio. I was bored out of my five-year-old rebellious mind.

The nurse assigned to check on me daily unexpectedly came to see me during her lunch break. Young and kind, she smiled and told me I reminded her of her little sister. Just as she was about to leave, hoping she'd stay a little longer, I asked, "Do you know the story of Cinderella?" She shook her head and that was how I came to tell her my favorite fairy tale, *Cinderella*. Hanging on my every word, her pretty eyes twinkling, she exclaimed, "Oh, I love the part when the Fairy Godmother waved her wand to turn Cinderella's rags into a beautiful ball gown." She waved her hand as if she held the magic wand, then twirled dramatically as if she were wearing a ball gown and not her bland white uniform. We both laughed.

"My favorite part was when she turned her shoes into glass slippers." *If only there was magic. If only I could wave a wand to make me walk again. Will I ever walk? In glass slippers?*

The next day, she came again during break time accompanied by another young nurse. "Please tell us the Cinderella story." In the days that followed, contingents of nurses, who longed for romance and a prince, came in waves asking me to tell them about Cinderella. They returned day after day to hear the story again and again. Their faces, usually serious as they went about their duties, became animated with anticipation. To entice them to return and fill my empty hours, I began to embellish the fairy tale. I was always frustrated about the end of the tale: They lived happily ever after. *Wasn't there more to Cinderella's life? Would I live happily ever after?*

The young nurses brightened my day. Cinderella brightened theirs.

Standing

Paralysis had an upside. The daily jabs of penicillin didn't bother me at all. Water therapy in a giant round pool became part of my treatment. At first, I was afraid I'd fall and slip into the water and drown. Once the therapists gained my trust, I began to enjoy the warmth of the water and its buoyancy. They exercised my arms and legs, giving them a wider range of motion, until I was able to repeat the movements myself. Hope filled me as I struggled and sweated daily to make progress. During my second month in the hospital, my favorite doctor held both of my hands and carefully helped me to a standing position. I was not Cinderella. I felt like Bambi trying out her wobbly legs for the first time. *I can stand!*

Clutching the doctor's arm, I placed one foot a few inches forward, then the other foot. The effort made me break out in a sweat. It was only a few inches, but my spirits soared.

I can walk! With wonder, I repeated the words out loud like a mantra, to convince myself that I wouldn't wake up from this wonderful dream still paralyzed.

The doctors said that my perseverance and patience had contributed to this recovery. At long last, I was well enough to go home. The nurses gathered to say goodbye. Their good wishes and hugs made me feel almost regretful I was leaving them and the hospital. Almost.

They said they would miss me and Cinderella.

Later, I learned that two other hospitals had turned me away because they had no room. Uncle Frank, the father of May Ling and David, had driven Mom and me from one hospital to another because no rooms were available. The third hospital said it had no room but could provide a bed in the hallway. I had faint memories of lying in a bed in the hallway. As the paralysis began to set in, it seemed a swarm of vicious bugs was biting every inch of my body. I remember wanting to scream in agony, but I was too weak. Luckily, the fever caused me to fall asleep. They moved me into a room in the morning because the previous patient had died.

As the weeks turned into months, my gait improved, but stairs terrified me. I would freeze at the top of the steps until someone helped me down. As my legs gained strength, the fear lessened.

America's restricted immigration policy was the reason Mom, and I couldn't go with Dad to America three years before. Mom and Dad had to maintain two households, and overseas calls were prohibitively expensive. They faithfully wrote letters to each other every day. All of Dad's letters were kept in a special box to be read together, when they were old, sitting in matching rocking chairs. Mom and I were always close and grew closer with Dad in America.

The phone rang early one fateful morning. It was Dad! All the necessary papers had been cleared. At long last, we could join him in California. Mom asked him to repeat what he said. Then she burst into a torrent of tears. Mom held the receiver to my ear. Dad laughed with happiness on the other end. Mom couldn't stop crying from relief and joy. Dad said, "Honey, please stop crying. It costs money." My cousins and friends were all happy for me to be reunited with Dad in America. I only cried when the time came to leave my Grandmother and Ah Nial. At the airport, I turned to wave at them not knowing I'd never see my dear Grandmother again.

America 1961

At the San Francisco airport, our reunion was tearful and joyful. Dad proudly took us to the house he had bought. Before we could unpack, Dad held my hand and led me to the backyard. My eyes grew wide at the sight of the swing suspended by two long chains. Dad told me to sit. "The last time I took you to the park, you pulled me to the swing and demanded, 'Higher! Push me higher!'"

He was the best Dad in the world. It was the greatest swing in the world. That night as he tucked me in for the first time in three years, Dad asked me to tell him the truth about my health. I admitted to weakness in one arm and one leg. He told me how much he loved me. When I almost died, Mom didn't call Dad immediately until she knew I would live. Once she told him, he wanted to fly back immediately to be with me, but she assured him I was making progress and that I was getting the best care. "I'm sorry I wasn't there when you needed me most." All I could do was hug him tight. We had a lot of lost time to make up.

After a week, Dad got straight to the point. "I expect you to go to Stanford. Study hard." When a Chinese dad tells you what is expected of you, there is no discussion. You don't question. You do it. Dad wasn't unkind when he said that, as an immigrant, I was already behind. "You have to work twice as hard to be recognized as half as good." I didn't grasp the full meaning of his words, but I later realized, fair or not, he had told me the truth. My spirits lifted when he added, "You can do it. I know you can." Mom also told me she had every confidence in me. My parents' love and support made all the difference in the world to me, especially in this strange new country, where I had no friends and didn't know the language. They had overcome so much in their own lives, surviving World War II in China, the Japanese occupation of China, then fleeing to Taiwan to escape the Communists. Since he was a teenager Dad's goal had been to come to America. He excelled in his field. At Stanford, he became one of a five-man research team that beat the Russians in a scientific Sun project, one of many competitive races after the *Sputnik* success.

Mom, one of two female students at her law school in Nanking University, China, became an assistant to the US. Ambassador's wife after moving to Taiwan. They left everything in China, and sold their small house in Taiwan, to pay for Dad's trip to America. They were achievers and never complained about their sacrifices.

Now, I had to do my part. I was the only Asian student in my elementary school in Palo Alto, California. Most of the students had never even seen a Chinese person. Some would point at me and laugh. Luckily, I didn't even know what they were saying. I did know I was ahead of all of them in math, which was face-saving. They had no English as a second language in those days. As a latchkey kid in first grade, I came home to an empty house to watch *Rawhide* and the classic Tarzan movies of the 1930s. When Dad came home, I proudly proclaimed, "You, Jane. Me, Tarzan." Clint Eastwood and Johnny Weissmuller taught me English.

At age 10, I ran the 50-yard dash, then the 600-yard. At 11, I had an operation on my left leg to correct the way my foot was being pulled to the left side because the muscle on the inside of my foot was atrophied. This time, the hospital stay was only four days with my leg suspended in the air. For three months, I wore a seven-pound cast that reached just below my knee. They replaced the cast with a custom-made, clunky, brown leather shoe with a brace attached to the knee. It creaked when I walked. The ugliest contraption ever created in this world in all of history. I was held hostage in the contraption while other kids played during recess, I sat on a bench and watched. Being sidelined taught me to be more observant. Kids can be cruel. They called me a cripple. I pretended the jeers didn't bother me. The brace was temporary. Their stupidity might well be permanent. And I told myself it didn't matter because I earned the As.

Over the years, Dad's edict about Stanford hovered like the sword of Damocles. Failure to get into Stanford would mean failing my Dad. I would be a failure. He made it clear that it had to be Stanford—not Harvard, not Yale, and not Princeton. I respected and loved Dad so much that the possibility of disappointing him became a driving force.

At Sunnyvale High School, in what is now Silicon Valley, there were more Asian students than I had seen in all the schools I had attended up to that point. Although there still weren't many Asian students, as a ratio to the school's population, Sunnyvale High was diverse. It reflected the uniqueness of California—its diversity. I had different groups of friends, some enjoyed writing, and others were in my speech and debate class.

I studied hard and joined a wide variety of clubs to make my future college application the best it could be. Fortunately, I became a finalist in a contest held by the National Council of Teachers of English, which provided a card for college applications that recommended me for admission. The teachers selected a senior for each subject. I was selected for the English award although history remained my favorite subject.

At a speech and debate tournament, I won an award for an original oratory about President Richard Nixon's trip to China. I had taken French throughout high school and made it to French 5, there were only five students at that level. Together, we wrote and performed a play in French. It was the first time the school had ever recorded a play in any class.

My SAT and ACT scores were decent. My grades were good enough to earn a California State Scholarship based on merit. Aside from school activities, I took a few martial arts classes and fencing lessons, but both proved too strenuous as one leg was still weaker than the other. However, I was able to take classes in belly dancing and archery.

The Stanford essay subject was: If you were to write a book, what would you write about and why? That was easy for me. I had heard so many stories about Mom's father, my grandfather who led an adventurous life. My grandfather, who was a poet and a lawyer, ran away from an arranged marriage to join Dr. Sun Yat-sen's 1911 Revolution that made China into a Republic. Grandfather became Dr. Sun's secretary and helped draft *The Three Principles*. He raised money in California and Hawaii for the revolution. They unjustly accused him of writing a book criticizing Chiang Kai-shek and he became a political prisoner for a decade. The so-called book was never found because he didn't write one. I always wanted to write a book to clear his name. I pounded out the essay and filled out my application to Stanford.

I continued to study hard. I worried more.

Where was my Fairy Godmother? Where was that magic wand?

There was no sign of a Fairy Godmother. I would have to rely on myself.

Stanford 1973

The day arrived. Our mailbox stood at the end of a private road. It was the longest walk ever. I wanted to be alone, to have privacy in case I didn't make the cut. I had done everything I could and yet, I was filled with dread. It was well known that a thick envelope from all colleges, including Stanford, heralded good news of acceptance.

One-page rejection letters made for a thin envelope. With trepidation, I reached into the mailbox. The envelope with the Stanford logo was in my hands. It was thick. I hadn't realized I had been holding my breath until I coughed. Ripping the envelope apart, I scanned its contents. Equal parts of exhilaration and relief filled me.

I'm in!

Walking back to the house, I toyed with the idea of pretending that I didn't get in, but I couldn't suppress the Cheshire grin on my face. Holding the acceptance letter high in the air, I did a little happy dance. Dad became ecstatic. Mom was happy too because she knew, more than Dad, how rejection would crush me. "Let's go celebrate." Mom suggested. She loved going out to eat. Used to having servants all her life, Mom took a crash cooking course just before we came to America. At the restaurant, while we waited for our food, Dad opened up his closed hand and held out a key to me—the key to his white convertible Corvette Stingray. "It's yours. You earned it."

Could the day get better? Hell, no!

It had been a long road from my six-year-old self, to achieve what I desired most, because of what my Dad desired. Laser-focused on my goal, I tamped down the resentment before it could ruin our relationship. When I turned 30 years old, I stated almost casually, "Dad, I got into Stanford for you. But I stayed for myself." Dad wasn't mad, but he seemed surprised. He didn't have to say anything because his genuine smile hinted of respect that I stood up for myself.

Dad was right. I loved Stanford. It turned out to be more than I hoped for. There, I met my best friend for life, Donna. My major was International Relations with a focus on US-China relations. My professors were brilliant, widely respected, and renowned nationally and internationally. A few of the professors gave undergraduate students like me as much attention as those in doctoral programs. They gave us knowledge, insight, and challenged our thinking. They helped me prepare for my future career in the Senate, although I didn't know that was where I was headed after graduation.

To this day, I am particularly grateful to two professors. Professor John Lewis and Professor Harry Harding were outstanding scholars in their fields. I took two courses from Professor Lewis: Political Leadership and Nuclear Arms Control. I remember being only one of two women in the arms control class of over 100 students. Professor Lewis spoke both Russian and Chinese. He was a fantastic teacher who was also approachable to answer questions after class.

Professor Harding was also fluent in Chinese. He and two other professors, all China specialists, led a seminar in which they divided the class into two groups: an American team and a Chinese team, to simulate negotiations to set the terms for normalizing U.S-People's Republic of China (PRC) relations. This was two years before President Jimmy Carter established formal diplomatic relations with the PRC. Professor Harding, also my advisor, was a favorite of the students and won several teaching awards. I felt honored to be invited to his home for dessert with some of my classmates. Little did I know that in less than two years, I'd work on the issues of nuclear arms control, human rights, and US-China-Taiwan relations.

On a whim, I went to the Stanford career advice office, later known as the Hass Center for Public Service. They directed me to a table to look through binders for information on summer internships in Congress. I applied.

From Polio to Policy 1977

My family's love affair with America—the symbol of democracy and freedom for the world—began decades before I was born. Sixteen years after I arrived in this country, it seemed ordained that Congress would be my destination. Upon first sight, the United States Capitol dome, gleaming under the sun like a beacon of endless hope, inspired me for years to come.

What started as a summer internship with Senator Alan Cranston in Washington turned into a permanent job. I was fortunate to have worked for him for eight of his 24 years in the Senate. He was a Senate leader and ran for President to further the cause of nuclear arms control. Decades earlier, in 1939, he warned the world about another threat—Adolf Hitler. He tried to expose Hitler for his evil anti-Semitic ideology and quest for world domination. Only months before the beginning of World War II, he wrote a condensed version of Hitler's *Mein Kampf,* annotating it with a dire warning. Hitler's American publisher sued for copyright infringement. Cranston's publisher was sued for copyright infringement and lost in the U.S. courts.

As his foreign policy aide and advisor, my responsibility was to be on the Senate floor during deliberations of legislation and policies in my areas. That morning, I had changed from my running shoes, now tucked under my desk, to my high heels. As I sat on the couch in the back of the majestic ornate Senate chamber, waiting for my boss, I realized that I loved my running shoes. I had long since traded them for the dream of glass slippers. Seeing Senator Cranston enter the chamber, I stood up and walked towards him.

Denise Varner is an enrolled member of the Muscogee Creek Nation and of European descent. A retired registered nurse and public health nurse, she continues graduate work in the healing arts, is a Reiki level II practitioner and aromatherapist in the realm of energy healing. Writing and speaking about living as an indigenous woman in traditional and postmodern cultures, while healing, is the center of her work.

Email: deniseannbsn@msn.com
Linkedin: linkedin.com/denise-varner-4789ktb

Chapter 18

A Heroine's Journey

Denise Varner

One of the things my parents taught me, and I'll always be grateful for the gift, is to not ever let anybody else define me. ~Wilma Mankiller

Sitting in this moment, as late summer transitions into fall, in this small mountain community, contemplating the transitions of my own life, I find that what has defined my life are ideas centered around themes of timelessness. All is here, present at one time-space in a place that honors the essence of life itself. The fawn and its mother out in the daylight hours searching for nourishment at midday, the family of turkeys feeding closer to the ground, the creek bed below running quietly in the background as the air becomes cooler, less heat-filled.

Those themes were demonstrated through shared family values that extended into school, community, and culture and laid the foundation for many choices in my adult life, including my decision to become a nurse. Today, I often wonder how the education and profession of nursing changed so radically in a departure from its humanitarian origins.

My childhood was focused on the freedom to explore inner and outer landscapes that gave way to limitless possibilities. My mother taught priorities like "clean your room first" before asking a friend over to do homework, practice clarinet or guitar, or play outside. We had a big yard with a hill behind our house to explore, fly kites, or run with our dogs.

School often felt confining except for the library. I felt more freedom there than on the playground where I tried to fit in with select groups of other children who would screen me for acceptance into their groups. At nine years of age, my teacher asked us to write a book report. The book that stood out to me on the library shelf had a dark blue cloth cover with a picture of a schoolgirl dressed in a white uniform with a navy-blue cape and a white cap placed on top of her head. It was a child's biography of Clara Barton, humanitarian, self-taught Civil War battlefield nurse and founder of the American Red Cross.

My grandfather was a traditional Muscogee Healer and a minister in the Methodist church. He and my grandmother gave my younger sister and me children's Bible study material with black and white sketches of the characters, and situations illustrating lessons of the Old and New Testaments. The images that stayed with me were of the sufferings and plagues of the people in those times, as well as the feelings of empathy and compassion. The images touched my entire little being, as they do now.

Grandma and Grandpa always taught us to understand

other people and to respect their differences, because we did not always know what caused them to behave the way they did, even if they were unkind toward us. Mom and Dad would reinforce these teachings at home, even though we were not members of any local churches in those days.

To always be a good friend to others, no matter how harshly they treated us, was a value that wove itself into how we lived at home, as well as guided us on how to behave away from home. Many would refer to this as social propriety or etiquette.

I was fortunate to have a stay-at-home mother, as my father worked five to six days per week at his gas station business and later as a diesel mechanic. Mom provided the structure at home and Dad could fix almost anything mechanical, or of human origin if it involved differences in perspective. They were always in agreement and I never heard or witnessed an argument between them. They were the wisdom teachers I looked up to for how to be in life.

Their partnership could not be sanctioned legally, because of miscegenation laws in the state of California, which were in place until 1978. I would not know this until the day we buried my mother, after her death from devastating brain cancer at the age of sixty. The fact that they chose one another in partnership solidified all of those family values they instilled in me, along with the reasons for extending those values into a world that did not always accept interracial marriages or partnerships.

My younger sister and I had many book collections to choose from. Reading and education were highly valued in our household. The Scholastic Book Club from school got us started with our interests, while our parents invested in family encyclopedia sets, covering topics from the natural world of biology to world history. One book at home drew the focus of my attention. It was a gift, presented to my mother by her auntie upon her sixteenth birthday, entitled *The Family Home Physician* written by the Oklahoma State Medical Society. It was first published in 1883 and featured a sketch of a physician standing beside a horse-drawn carriage with his medical bag in hand, typical of turn-of-the-century doctoring and medical care at that time.

Beyond that title page were color photographic plates of children and adults with common ailments and maladies experienced at the turn of the twentieth century, when community hospitals were not places of healing, but places where one went to die. Home was the place and space to heal, and community physicians were rare and expensive. This book was to guide families until a physician could be contacted for a home visit. Its pages described what to do and how to proceed until a physician could arrive. There were black and white photos throughout the text showing women tending to patients in hospitals, demonstrating the proper methods of care in bandaging wounds, and providing support to those in need of healing.

Those women, in addition to Clara Barton's story, gave me the inspiration to become a nurse. Dressed simply in floor-length skirts with white pinafores, long sleeves, and the same white cap, carefully covering neatly tucked hair, and appearing skilled and confident; this is what I longed to be when I grew up. There were no formally educated nurses on either side of my family. Women were the wisdom keepers who knew folkways of healing and tending until a doctor could be seen. I knew that I was traveling a path known, yet unknown. Inside I knew that this was where I was supposed to be.

Many of us young women, growing up in the path of the Women's Rights Movement of the early 1970s, were abandoning society's traditional women's roles of wife, mother, homemaker, classroom teacher, nurse, or secretary. We all know now that those roles embodied coordination, management, diplomacy, and leadership. Most of my friends were exploring newer territories, not wanting to work in any of those career choices unless their parents were educators.

We took all of the college preparatory classes that would assist in lower division general education credits required for community colleges and universities. Science piqued my interest, explaining what words or a brief demonstration could not, through a process of questions, experimentation, numbers, and results that explained a complete understanding of the world familiar with my mother's indigenous knowledge. As in any field of endeavor, the art, imagination and creativity lie within the structural framework itself. I found that the profession of nursing embodied all of this at that time while honoring the wholeness of my womanhood, in lifelong learning. Public Health would complete my need for whole-person healing in the community.

Choices to add to my bookshelves were centered on holistic herbal and nutritional healing, as well as textbooks on basic nursing care skills. This was in preparation for my approaching decision to declare a pre-nursing major leading to admission into a baccalaureate nursing program that would prepare me for the eventual specialty practice of Public Health Nursing. Taking steps to work as a certified nursing assistant and home health aide in the interim was unfolding.

Since this decision seemed unpopular with many of my friends from high school, I kept this a well-guarded secret to myself, sharing it only with close family members. My father let me know that he could not afford to send me to college and I knew this; it was partly the reason for my working as a CNA/HHA once accepted into a formal course of study. This became the plan.

I followed the plan, including finding a physical chemistry teacher who could teach me the litany of chemistry. Falling in love with organic chemistry, I found myself able to use the language of chemistry to relate to numbers in a new way, beyond pre-calculus math. Not a requirement to get into my chosen nursing school, I pursued pre-calculus math with curiosity, satisfying my need for a logical explanation on how life sciences worked and communicated. Further inquiry established my academic qualifications for grants and scholarships for my first year of schooling.

All of those little girl visions were about to come into full being. The memories I carried of my traditional healer grandfather's knowledge, which he passed down to my mother, provided the opportunity to be who I chose to be in mind, body, and spirit and facilitated optimal well-being along the human life span continuum. Feeling in the flow of my moment of learning felt like I had crossed the threshold of becoming my true inner nature. The program I was about to enter was one of few generalists in the United States nursing curriculum at a time when nursing students were being tracked into specialty areas following the allopathic model of medical treatment. I knew that I did not want to choose a specialty until I had an opportunity to experience the depth of each practice area. Nursing encompassed all walks of life, all cultures and traditions, cradle to grave, and reflected family and community values. Little did I realize that this concept of family care was rapidly deteriorating for an agenda lying outside of well-being even in the midst of the not-for-profit world of health care.

Community and Public Health Nursing were never established as reimbursable services, but rather for basing their understanding on investment in a values structure that reflected the health and well-being of families and communities. This was the structure behind nursing as an investment in maintaining healthy populations. At the time I entered clinical practice as a student nurse, the only hospitals to train in along California's North Coast were Catholic hospitals and two community hospitals. I was placed in the Catholic hospital system where I worked part-time as a nurse's aide in all departments.

The greatest transformative experience I had occurred during my senior year while studying maternal child health. In the hospital, I had the opportunity to work with a local midwife, in sharp contrast to traditional hospital labor and delivery. Midwifery is focused on the care of the pregnant mother and the unborn child developing life inside her womb, including the laboring and birth experience.

One mother received supportive care like warm showers and compresses working with gravity to deliver a healthy baby. The absolute joy at the moment of birth is the healing balm from the often-excruciating pain of the baby traveling through the birth canal. This transition was the only time I shed tears of joy while assisting and witnessing a birth. Compared to the relief experienced by individuals and families transitioning away from their bodies in hospice care, this was an experience of renewal and hope in the future life to be fulfilled with the family.

There was not a specialty area that I preferred in hospital-based care. I viewed each patient, family, and community as part of a greater whole: biologically, psychologically, socially, and culturally. This flexibility enabled my nursing practice to see and interact with each individual in meaningful ways beyond the biomechanical expectations of managed care that came to dominate the American healthcare system.

This integrated way of assessing, caring, and communicating with people was not reflected in the care that my mother received during her illness with a devastating brain cancer diagnosis. It was not given to her except by my father and myself, as we cared for her in her last days of life. Somehow my mother always understood this and did not place much trust in western medicine apart from her father's knowledge of herbs, roots, ceremonies, and prayers that truly healed his community. Through my nursing education, I believed that the best that western medicine had to offer could help her. I was wrong.

Somehow, after graduating from nursing school with

my license and Public Health Certificate in hand, I believed I could change that wrong and make it right. Much of my career had been central to the Indian Health Service and reservation health systems that were open to integrated care, as it is closely aligned with indigenous cultural values of seeing a whole person seeking meaning in their ailments, whatever that may be.

Indigenous epistemology interprets illness as an imbalance with the essence of life force, which takes many forms in nature and in community. It is complex in its understanding but philosophically makes sense when a human life becomes out of balance with his/her true nature, often viewed as a disruption in the relationship with the natural world. I saw this with my mother as she became dependent upon western medicine to treat and heal her; it made her sicker into death. Western medicine does not always know the cause and effect and focuses on disease as a foreign invader with a life unto itself, separate from the person experiencing its effects. Sometimes that is the case but not always.

Working in reservation communities was a homecoming for me after experiencing the illness and death of my mother while I was in school. It created a kind of healing for myself. Many collective traumas of American indigenous people have played themselves out in addiction, and Type 2 Diabetes. I committed to educating tribal members on how to heal with limited healthy food choices and exercise programs, in addition to self-monitoring and medication management. Regardless of milieu, there was nothing more gratifying than witnessing an individual overcome their own ill health through their own determination, and with supportive structures in place. The names are endless.

Many learn to adapt to their losses, not by living in the past, but by embracing what is, such as the amputation of one or more limbs. Some would be the recipient of trans-planted organs, to restore life functioning so those wisdom keepers can continue sharing their gifts with the young ones. For indigenous people, the wise ones are needed to live forward with the strength of community where meaning is held in tradition, honor, and grace. Our elders are our guideposts for how to live life in a good way.

For many living on reservations, the birth of a child had to take place in clinical settings far away from the spirit of family and ancestral influences. Often this resulted in bringing a life into the world that would be forever separated from the spirit of the homelands. As I was exiting from my service to my own people in Oklahoma, I could feel these separations. Our tribe had not yet taken over the administration of local hospitals that tribes were contracted with to deliver our mothers. Only one hospital, begun by the Indian Health Service and taken over by our tribe, was not centrally located and was not always culturally sensitive at the time I served in the community.

In sharp contrast, I left the protective confines of Indian Country for the larger, broader community. Hospice and palliative care seemed like a welcome opportunity to perform basic care away from the cultural traumas I faced daily with my own people. Clinically it was satisfying, but would be the last thing I would ever do in direct-care nursing.

The built-in stressors of the nursing profession can never be underestimated and I always took care to maintain appropriate boundaries between the suffering of others and my own empathic nature. A professional compassionate demeanor is not enough, even when a terminal medical diagnosis is given to an individual and family. Some are accepting and others are not. We live in an American-dominant culture that does not know how to transcend life experiences, often resulting in overpowering grief and a sense of an incomplete life. Hospice and palliative care are the spaces where we are given small windows of time for acceptance, reconciliation, and healthy grieving. Is there such a thing as healthy grieving?

My mother had only a few years to enjoy with my father after my two younger sisters and I each left home to go out into the world on our own. Briefly, we were given an opportunity to have adult relationships with Mom and Dad before they departed on their eternal journeys. Mom was comatose and at home for nine months before she died in the devoted loving care of my father with my assistance. There was no hospice care because she did not qualify, even as a dependent on my father's benefits. He asked me to come home to care for her. I took an educational leave from nursing school to do this, placed my belongings in storage, and remained until she took her final peaceful breath, my father laying by her side, tubes and all.

Working through my grief has always been my coping mechanism of choice, until faced with my own work-related injury that would end my direct caring days in nursing. The grief never fully processed itself out of my brain and body until my own ill health, followed by a catastrophic life altering diagnosis, became my transitioning point.

I experienced the same phenomena as my mother, who never trusted the western medical system. I became part of that system and gained trust in it even though its limitations could not easily be foreseen. One consideration in this is that I did not realize the power of my own human spirit to be the hero/heroine of my own life, as I always had been.

For fifteen years I lived with a diagnosis of chronic myofascial pain and posttraumatic fibromyalgia, caused by a cervical whiplash experienced in a motor vehicle collision. The other driver was talking on her cell phone and driving a Land Rover-type vehicle. She ran a red light and hit the front end of my small economy car, forcing it into oncoming traffic.

This was the beginning of the end of my nursing career as I knew it to be. What was a Northern California native woman doing in San Diego anyway? I was as far away from home as I was from myself and from all of my reasons for becoming a nurse. The journey home to my own safe soul began here.

I didn't ask why or how. I traveled a journey that I assumed would be returned to me in kind for all of the work I had given to the human family in professional care. I found myself caught between two different worlds that did not speak the same language. I sought out the best healers I could find and still it was not enough.

What was not right with me would never be answered by the sophisticated medical science I advocated for twelve years. In fact, its medicinal approaches were making me far sicker and further separated from my own soul. That is the nature of post-modern allopathic medicine, except for a few medical and surgical restorative interventions that I was fortunate to experience through corrective surgeries and recovery efforts.

When I had enough, when every attempt to correct the wrongs in my life had failed, I made the choice to return to Northern California to be among familiar places and spaces of healing. I needed to belong to a group of people who lived similar values and principles. Changing my environment worked for a while. Many changes had happened in the places and spaces I grew up in and around over the many years I had been gone. I found myself in community with people who knew me when I was in high school. Former teachers and childhood friends who recognized me after decades of absence were a welcome presence in my life.

Once relaxed, the overwhelm of unresolved physiological symptoms began to overtake this newfound well-being. Exhaustion, intractable nausea, and flu-like symptoms, without fever, prompted me to once again seek out medical care. Without work and without health insurance I was forced to seek out care from an Indian Health clinic, a one-hour drive away. Ironically, I had trained at this particular clinic as a new graduate nurse, while working in a different reservation health facility after nursing school. I was entering now as a patient, not as a working nurse professional.

After a physical exam, blood tests, and other routine laboratory tests, everything came back within normal limits but I was advised to return if symptoms became unmanageable. Four months later and a change of primary care providers later, I returned with symptoms of recurrent asthma. I asked for inhalers, which I had used when I was first diagnosed fourteen years earlier while living and working in Southern California. Reluctantly, without pulmonary function tests, the physician ordered the inhaler from the pharmacy.

In three weeks, my symptoms became worse and I was unable to breathe using the muscle of my diaphragm. I was inhaling using my abdominal muscles and exhaling using the muscles of my rib cage. I felt exhausted. Barely able to hold my body upright on the exam table, I remember telling my physician in a weakened voice, "I want my life back."

His response, while quickly turning the pages of my medical records was, "Denise, I just want you to have a life." I do not remember driving the 120 miles it took to get there, nor the drive back to where I was staying with friends. I do remember that it would take three months to get in to see the only outpatient pulmonologist who would perform further serum allergen and toxicology studies, as well as pulmonary function tests for further diagnosis. Once consulting with him after these preliminary tests revealed certain specific allergies without toxicities and mild COPD symptoms as the result of urban living in California, I was sent home with a prescription for an additional inhaler and instructions to return in three months. This would go on for three years, until I was finally discharged as fully recovered without the need of inhalers to breathe normally.

In the interim, further neurological symptoms would overtake my body's ability to function normally such as digesting food and fluids, intractable nausea, headaches, and sleeplessness which led to tonic-clonic (similar symptoms of toxic tetanus infection) type seizures of my arms and legs in the middle of the night. One night I awoke in excruciating pain as every muscle in my legs from hip to toe seized and my arms and hands responded much the same. I was falling asleep sitting up during the day only to be awakened by the uncontrolled motion of my thumb and forefinger, as my dominant hand made a strange type of rolling motion. Knowing this was becoming serious I again drove the one hundred plus miles to see my physician who said that I no longer needed an urgent care appointment to see him. When I needed to be seen, "Just come up and I will see you."

My years of nursing prepared me to hear the worst since what I was experiencing could not be reflected in any clinical testing diagnostics. It was my brain, specifically my autonomic nervous system. I asked my physician what would create this imbalance in my autonomic nervous system causing it to shut down the counterbalance of my parasympathetic nervous system? His answer was, "Shy-Drager Syndrome" which is a term no longer used for a diagnosis I would later come to find that ended the lives of two older half-brothers from my mother's first marriage.

There is no treatment, no cause, and no cure, as research dollars are scarce for neurological diseases. I thanked my physician even though he offered nothing in the way of treatment; no prescriptions, no lifestyle adjustment advice, nothing. At least I went home knowing what I was dealing with. The long slow journey to recovery began, as my life as a professional nurse ended.

As my symptoms slowly began to dissipate, and then to disappear, I developed new friendships with academics in the field of social work. They would send the latest research on neurobiology, that I digested like soul food. I became a vipassana meditator and, in addition to traditional prayer, began practicing yoga as my body would allow. I fed myself nutrient-dense, easily digestible organic foods supplementing when needed. In two years, I became strong enough to seek out a local gym membership, where I worked with a personal trainer to retrain my neuromuscular endurance. I did strength and aerobic training. I stretched when it was painful, to recruit every necessary muscle to be able to walk without the use of my cane for balance. I attended water aerobics and swam four days per week for an hour each session. I built myself back to better than I was when I first returned home.

With the help and support of familiar spaces and some new and familiar faces, I called back a part of myself that I was unaware I had lost. I learned to give of my talents and skills acquired through a journey of formal education, forgetting to ask for what I needed to remain balanced.

The caveat of this recovery experience is that the world changed so much, so fast, that by the time I graduated from nursing school and entered the workforce as a professional with skills, gifts and talents to share in facilitating healing the wounds of a wounded world, the nature and shape of those wounds were festering from acute to chronic to incurable. The world I had carefully prepared to enter was falling to pieces and I along with it.

My own healing came from a place and space far greater than my own being. Deep down inside of my own soul's truth I was able to overcome the challenges before me through determination, faith and a collective energy of healing. The journey of the road less traveled, from needing assistance to walk, to regaining balance and strength through physical, spiritual and mental practice—all together, all at one time, is one of returning to wholeness where once fragmented.

As a child I was prepared to live in a world that my elders assured me would be accepting if I became a good human being. School helped me, through grading to get my scholarship and gain the ability to understand systems and their complexities that were for the most part in a constant state of flux, not always aligned with that which sustains being a good human being. Those systems that I was raised to be dependent upon have been crumbling for most of my adult life—including the human caring professions.

Now, in late middle adulthood, I have been given a second chance to live life fully without having to be dependent upon a profession to guide my pathway. Like many I have cared for, in an over thirty-year career as a nurse, I can live my life with meaning and without attachment to an idea of how the world defines my presence in it.

Chris Dyer's calling is investing in people. She is an international best-selling contributing author in *Jumpstart Your Radiant Lifestyle* and has more books and speaking engagements in progress. She is an Innovative Business Strategist and equips business owners with tools to create quantum leaps and results in life and business.

She is the founder and CEO of three new startups: Chris Dyer Consulting, Positively Panache and Embellished Butterfly. Her marketing, entrepreneur and leadership experiences have aided her business into global markets and have helped dozens of entrepreneurs create lives they love while building successful businesses.

Website: ChrisDyerConsulting.com
Email: Chris@ChrisDyerConsulting.com
LinkedIn: linkedin.com/in/chris-dyer-connects/

Chapter 19

Resistance to Resilience

Chris Dyer

Those who bring beauty to the world
cannot keep it from themselves.

~ Chris Dyer

Imagine . . . It's 1973 and you're in sunny Florida, situated alongside the St. Johns River. There's a swimming pool and a little six-year-old girl walks to the deep end of the pool and climbs up the ladder to the diving board. She is standing on the edge of the diving board, contemplating jumping into that deep pool and swimming all the way across to the three-foot end by herself. The six-year-old girl has never taken swimming lessons in her life, yet she has the confidence to know that when she jumps in, she will make it to the other side.

So, the little girl jumps in and she swims, probably just doing the dog paddle—nothing fancy or elaborate. And yet, she knows and trusts her own body to help her tread water, and to dog paddle clear across the pool to the other end. What's interesting to note is, she does this beautifully and without fear.

What happens afterward is this: her mother jumps up. She's holding onto the edge of her seat, watching this child—her child—swim across the entire length of a pool without assistance and make it to the other side.

I am that six-year-old girl, and this is a memory that stayed repressed in my psyche for over 50 years. The moral of this story is: we forget who we are. That little girl had no fear, and yet she had enough trust in herself and in her own body and her own resourcefulness to take a plunge, and swim clearly to safety and comfort—to where she could stand on her own two feet.

There wasn't a lifeguard, but there were other adults, and her mother stood there watching her take this big, brave leap into the pool, and she watched her daughter successfully swim to the other side.

The universe always has our back . . . and yet, we forget to trust in ourselves. There are people standing on the sidelines watching us, cheering for us to succeed and to reach our goal. But what's interesting (in the mind of a child), is that my child-self remembered—and believed—that my mother saw something to be frightened of.

This little girl (me) had an amazing lack of fear and fully trusted in herself. She also had a wild imagination, and a desire to self-express. Yet, as is often the case when a mother has no control over her own life or circumstances, that lack of confidence is handed off to the child in the form of suppression, repression, and even oppression of who they are truly meant to be.

Children are meant to be curious and to experiment. When parents see this as a possible threat to the child, or possibly even feel that they as the parent, have lost control over the child, then what do they do?

They place those fears and insecurities on their children, and that is the story of the six-year-old girl who went through life not being able to trust herself. She was told that her feelings and emotions were inappropriate, and she learned to repress and hide her dearest thoughts inside her heart. And due to this, she suffered a true loss of intimacy—first with her mother and worst of all, with herself.

So, fast-forward a few years: she's a teenager. She has grown weary of being controlled, manipulated, and not being seen, heard, or validated. When she's eighteen years old, she's ready to fly the coop. It doesn't matter how she lands or where she lands, she's just done . . . ready to make her own decisions and fly by the seat of her pants. She wants to figure out her life without looking back. There was no looking back.

So, that is a success story that came about with plenty of tribulations and growing pains. And yet, she still found a way to stand on her own two feet, take care of herself and her young family.

She did all the right things and lived up to all the expectations that were given to her. You're going to grow up. You're going to go to college. You're going to get married. You're going to have kids.

And then what happens after you achieve all those goals? Living the "American Dream" thirty, forty, or fifty years ago . . . the American Dream that was impressed upon me. What happens to women when they've done all that, when they're showing up and being the perfect wife, and the perfect mother?

They're doing all the right things, and being all the things to people, because they're expected to. Those women soon feel a deep discomfort within themselves, knowing that there's more—there has to be more. Otherwise, they are suffocating, living a life they truly weren't intended for. Wherever there are questions, there are opportunities.

Fast-forward ten more years in this young woman's life. She was, on the surface, content with having gone to school, beginning her career, raising her family, being the dutiful wife, being the dutiful daughter, being the dutiful volunteer in her community. But, she knew there had to be more. She wanted more for herself. Then, there came an opportunity for her to bust out of the old paradigm.

She took it upon herself to leave her comfortable job in order to experience a whole new world. She took an outside sales position and began working in a male-dominated industry, in a male-dominated territory. She didn't do this for herself; she did it for her family. She certainly did find out about the amount of emotional resilience required when you truly step out of your comfort zone, as her then-husband wasn't willing to take the extra steps to move forward.

She allowed herself to expand, grow, and change that paradigm of what the dynamic is "supposed" to be for a woman in charge of running her household and family.

I was working in a male-dominated industry in a male-dominated territory. I was green. All I had was the belief that I could do it and it took me a good three years to really establish myself.

It was like I was up against the "800-pound gorilla." I was this young mother, tapping into this brand-new territory. A woman had never worked in this territory before, but I didn't let fear stop me.

Most of the men were nice enough and gave me an opportunity. I was still up against a major competitor: the guys who had been their business partners, with their "good old boy" mentality, right in western North Carolina. That old mindset where women should be seen and not heard and needed to "know their place." "You should be in the home taking care of your family."

But eventually, people saw me as being consistent and persistent, having integrity, and not afraid to step out of my comfort zone. It was like the tortoise and the hare. I was the tortoise—persistent, consistent, methodical and intentional. I kept showing up, kept doing the work, and eventually they all respected me and counted on me.

I learned the basic principles of sales such as:

- No, today doesn't mean six months from now.
- Continue to be persistent and consistent and show up.
- Deliver—even if somebody gives you the smallest of tasks or the slightest opportunity.
- Deliver on what you promise, and with a can-do attitude.
- It's the willingness to roll up your sleeves and do whatever it takes and doing the tasks graciously that sets you up for future success.

I think that's what a lot of our younger generations are struggling with. They think, "I'm going to make six figures in six months and they don't realize the twenty and thirty years of work that others have already put in to get to where we are today. We didn't consider ourselves "too good" to do some of the jobs that we're asked to do. It is being willing to be a team player and willing to follow until you're given the opportunity to lead. A good leader is also a good follower and takes direction. There are many layers, I'm just barely touching the tip of the iceberg. I could really go into a lot of depth, but that's another book.

Fast-forward another five years. She finally realizes that it's time to wake up from the dream. She realizes that how she has been living has not been authentic, or in integrity. It wasn't serving her at her best, and certainly wasn't setting her up to live her best life. To serve her greater purpose, she made the decision to change her family dynamics. After 13 years of marriage, she decided to end it—to continue raising her two children, but to take her marriage in a different direction. She stood up for herself for the very first time.

Her mother was not pleased with her. Her mother basically abandoned and disowned her for about 18 months, when she was going through this transition of leaving the traditional life. That left her feeling very vulnerable and being very much alone, but she still did it—on her own.

You know, this young girl never knew her father as she was growing up. She wasn't really allowed to have friends, wasn't allowed social connections with other girls, or to play, or go do the things that young girls typically like to do. And so there was a lot of loneliness and isolation as she was growing up.

Fast forward again . . . Thirty years later she (I) realized that everyone's definition of success is different. So for this little girl (and me) success means having true intimate connections and relationships with people. It doesn't have anything to do with money.

Growing up lonely and isolated was my poverty, even though my mother did the very best she could to provide a roof over my head. I had clothes; I had food. We had basic necessities, but the loss of intimacy and having a true connection—that was my poverty. My mother was a nurse, which is the irony because she was a wonderful nurse. She was very nurturing to her own patients.

Now, my purpose is to ensure that the people in my space are included, so they know they're not alone. I show them ways to connect with other people, and to be a better human every day.

All of those basic tenants and concepts have carried through my adult career path, to this day, as an entrepreneur. You know, we talk about marketing and branding ourselves—what makes us different from everyone else. I have a love of health, the human body, science and physical science and that's what differentiates me as a coach, guide and a mentor. I have that that skillset to add to the mix.

I love to go back to the basics. What was it in school that really lit me up? It was music and science. Chemistry was my favorite subject in high school, as well as biology and any of the physical sciences. My chemistry teacher was the one who actually saw me, at a time where I felt like I was invisible and not seen.

I was not a popular kid—kids picked on me. I mean, that's an entire other layer of being isolated, not feeling like I belonged to any group of people. That girl learned to belong to herself through all the different resistances that were thrown at her. She had to go back and love that little girl inside that was her and bring her through the rest of her life. And so now we have the ego of the little girl, integrated into the ego of the adult woman and being committed for life, as if in marriage. And that's truly the story and the evolution of a self-love journey.

I'm a very high-nurture individual, and also high knowledge. I'm creating a persona on how I show up on my social media, and how I show up when I speak to audiences. I am *The Connection Chemist.*

Authenticity is a collection of choices that we have to make every day. It's about the choice to show up and be real. The choice to be honest. The choice to let our true selves be seen.

~ Brene Brown

Melissa Bollea Rowe is the owner of Rhyme Partners Music Publishing in Nashville, Tennessee. She's a successful songwriter, author, entrepreneur and public speaker. She's had songs cut by artists all over the world.

As an author, she's celebrated two #1 best-sellers to date. *God, Gratitude & Giving*, an inspirational book detailing the impact and power of these three words for her life. She is also the creator, co-publisher, and co-author of *The Musical Imprint*," along with Neuropsychologist, Dr. Sarah Allen. *The Musical Imprint* is an anthology of 24 compelling stories and pivotal moments connected to a song.

Melissa thrives on creativity and inspiring others to chase their dreams. She's always at the threshold of something exciting and new.

Website: MelissaBolleaRowe.com

Chapter 20

We Were Twelve

Melissa Bollea Rowe

"Day by day, night by night we were together.
All else has been forgotten by me."

~ Walt Whitman

From the time we're little girls, until we become young women, we dream of our prince—the one they sell us in fairy tales. But most often, our lives don't look like that of the true Cinderella story. Instead, we learn to become the princess of our own story. By some modern-day standards, we don't need a man; we're taught that we're tough, we're independent and we can do things on our own. And while that's true, I found my prince at a young age, lost him, then found him again. I am one of the lucky ones.

It was early October of 1980. I was a shy brown-eyed, brown-haired girl with braces walking the crowded halls of Franklin Middle School in Tampa Florida. I was shorter than all the other kids, but I remember looking up and seeing the most handsome boy coming toward me. He was very tall, very thin, with blue eyes and brown, wavy hair. I noticed him talking to a friend of mine who I had a class with, so I asked her if she would introduce us. Later that day after class, I stood frozen in the hallway as she approached him at his locker and pointed in my direction. When he looked up, I managed a smile and then bashfully took off in the other direction.

He says he fell in love with my smile right then and there and begged my friend to tell him where the classroom I had just run off to was. After that class, he approached me as I was walking amongst all the other kids and said, "Are you that girl? Missy?" I remember being so nervous, and excited, and saying "Yes" without hesitation. While it seemed like he had just bumped into me, he had actually made an effort to find me before the next bell. We didn't have long to talk, and being at such an awkward age we didn't really say much. I remember giving him my phone number right away. I couldn't wait for him to call me.

Although I had never had a boy call me, I wasn't shy about giving him my number. I guess I thought it would be okay. You see, I lived with my aunt and uncle because two years earlier, at the tender age of ten, my mother was senselessly killed by her jealous boyfriend. My father lived in another state with a new wife and was battling a drug addiction. Needless to say, my heart was heavy. It was all I could do to find a reason to smile. He certainly gave me a reason to smile that day.

Little did we know that from that moment on, we set in motion what would be a lifetime of love and friendship. Every morning Sean waited for me by the steps near the school auditorium, closest to where I got off the school bus. Those five to ten minutes before school were sacred to us, two young kids experiencing butterflies for the first time.

Franklin Middle School was a seventh-grade center at the time and oddly enough, we did not have a single class together. So mornings, and passing notes in between classes, became highly anticipated for us. Once we even agreed to meet in the hallway, going up the stairs to the second floor, for our very first kiss. I distinctly remember standing a few steps above him so I could reach him. I felt absolutely nervous and clueless as to what would happen after our lips met. And once again, I ran off saying, "I think the bell is about to ring." I guess I was always more of a barker than a biter, so the kiss never happened.

It would not be until the next summer, at our mutual friend Linda's house, that we would have our first innocent kiss. I still remember every detail of it, which I find so strange because I could not tell you who else was at her house that day, or the details of what it looked like. I could not tell you what day it was, or even if I spent the night with her. Although she recalls that I did and that the whole meetup between Sean and I was planned. But what I can tell you is exactly what that kiss was like. I recall Sean pressing his lips to mine and his tongue touching mine ever so slightly. And after that, I proudly claimed I had my first "French kiss."

By that time he and I were now thirteen years old, with summer in full swing. Sean and I talked on the phone as much as possible and every time our calls ended with, "you hang up, no you hang up, no you hang up . . ." Eventually, my uncle or his mom would holler at us to get off the phone.

But, it's a tough thing when you are thirteen and don't get to see each other more than maybe once or twice all summer. We were children doing what children do in uncontrollable circumstances, so we began drifting away from one another.

As life would have it, over the next several years I would move and change schools often. This meant I didn't follow most of my friends to the same junior high or high school that many of them would go to, including Sean. It's hard to recall the details of just why I moved as much as I did, or maybe I have blocked a lot of it out. But the bottom line was, I had to move often between aunts and uncles and grandparents. I think after a while my extended family found it difficult to raise three kids (me, my brother, and my sister) together, so we ended up being split between different family members. I felt sad a lot because of it and starting new schools wasn't easy.

A few years later, the school I was attending took us on a field trip to Tampa Stadium. There were other schools there as well, and as fate would have it, I sat only a few rows down from Sean. I remember we caught each another's eye; time seemed to stand still. I remember thinking to myself, *He's right there behind me,* as I sat down, but I didn't turn around and I didn't wave. There was no opportunity for us to talk afterward.

I cannot tell you what we went to see that day. I cannot tell you anything about the field trip other than that moment and that memory, which I find so strange—

similar to the day at Linda's where I only remember the details about Sean and me.

Later, Sean told me that the entire time he had wanted to talk to me, he just didn't know how. He sat with a group of boys and felt a kind of peer pressure to be cool. He says he wished he had said or done something. Looking back, it seems to be normal teenage behavior. Those are awkward years where you don't have enough life experience to know that you may not get the chance again, or even what to say, honestly. Teenagers aren't articulate at expressing their feelings. We were truly right out of a scene from The Wonder Years. We both wanted to talk to each other, but the moment slipped away from us.

Sean tried to call and keep track of me over the years. On occasion, we would hear things from mutual friends about each other. Once, for a brief week, I even ended up back at a high school with him. But at that time he was dating a girl he'd met and I was kind of dating a boy I'd met. I remember seeing Sean on a sidewalk outside the school between classes. We both paused, not sure what to say, other than to exchange some small talk. Then just like that, I moved to another school.

Over the years we lost track of each other. With both of us becoming young adults and moving on in life, the phone numbers we had for one another were no longer valid. Back in those days, if you didn't know someone's phone number, or couldn't find them in the phone book, you didn't have much of a chance of locating them. There were no mobile phones and we had only just begun to see the use of pagers, and we certainly had no social media yet.

My teenage years were no different; they were very hard. I barely made it through high school. I felt so alone. I felt extremely lost in terms of who I was and what I would do with my life. As I mentioned earlier, I lost my parents young: my mom, when I was ten years old, to a jealous boyfriend who took her life, and later, my father to suicide. Growing up the way I did left me feeling isolated in my mind most of the time. I spent a lot of time just wondering where I would live or where I was going to sleep.

One day, I was getting a few dollars worth of gas when I randomly looked up as I walked out of the local general store. I had just gone in to pay for the gas, when who was holding the door open but Sean. He and his best friend Phil had stopped by the 7-Eleven and the timing was impeccable. It all happened so fast; it took us both by surprise. He paused as if to talk to me, but I quickly put my head down and kept right on walking.

To this day, I don't know why I did that except I had so much on my mind and heart I could not manage a conversation. Maybe I felt embarrassed. I literally could not look him in the eye as that moment came and went so quickly. Sean says he was shocked to bump into me; it all happened so fast. I definitely gave the impression I didn't want to talk, but he wishes he had chased me to my car and attempted to anyway. Again, things that happened in the moment would later become memories tied to the regret for what we wished we'd done. I suppose much of life is that way.

As time moved on, I met a nice guy named Chad at the local skating rink, we had mutual friends and began dating. By 1988 we were married, and shortly after, I had my first and only child, my son Chad. He became my whole world. Being a mom was the happiest time of my life, but being a wife was tougher. You see, I realized early on in my marriage that we did not have a whole lot in common. We were a young married couple with a child. My new husband worked a lot to take care of us and was out of town most weeks. As a writer, I learned early on that as far as my personal relationships would go, I craved connection and communication. Chad was quiet and didn't really have too much to say when he was home. It felt a lot more like we were friends than life partners, but divorce was not something I wanted to consider at that time. I just thought I needed to tough it out, or maybe things would change.

One day I came across the phone number of Sean's best friend, Phil, as I was going through some of my things. I called the number and I got Phil's father and said that I was looking for Sean. I left my number with him. He was kind enough to give the message to Phil, who gave the message to Sean, and a few days later I got a phone call from him. We talked for a while and caught up.

Sean married a woman he met while working at a restaurant and she had a daughter, who he was raising as his own. We enjoyed talking and decided to meet up at a nearby park. By that time we were both around twenty-two years old and had not seen each other since the day I bumped into him at the gas station, without so much as a hello.

Sean was working on his bachelor's degree and doing photography on the side, so he ended up bringing his camera with him and took several photos of me and Chad that I still have to this day. We enjoyed getting caught up on one another's life and, for the next few months to a year, we stayed in touch. Occasionally, Sean would watch Chad for me because back then, I would go out to try and win a singing contest for grocery money, or to pay a light bill.

Our friendship seemed as effortless as it always had been. I viewed Sean as my dearest friend. One afternoon, several months later, he came to me to tell me he was getting a divorce. He had realized he still loved me and felt it was unfair to his marriage. I honestly didn't know what to say or do. At that time, all I could think of was that I was married and had a young son. I was afraid of imagining any other scenario, and so I told him I did not have the same feelings for him. I told him I saw him as my dearest friend in the whole world but nothing more. It was a hard conversation for both of us. There he was professing his love for me, getting a divorce, and I could not see any way to do the same. Shortly after, he took a job opportunity and moved away. It became a tough time for us.

After a few more years of wishing my marriage could be more, I made the hardest decision of my life—to get a divorce. It wasn't something I took lightly; it truly broke my heart. I became very unhappy. Little did I know there was an entire world out there waiting for me.

Over the next several years, I embarked on being a single mom and working in a nail salon, while also working on my songwriting career. It never crossed my mind when Sean moved a few hours away that we would lose touch again, but that is exactly what happened . . . life.

Sean met another woman who also had a daughter and much like his first wife, he raised her as his own along with his first stepdaughter.

When he moved away, we spoke on the phone a few times, but eventually came to the realization that he still had strong feelings for me that I wasn't able to return. He realized it was not fair to anyone and the phone calls stopped. He began his new life and the last communication I sent him was a card in the mail. On the front of the card was a picture of Winnie the Pooh and Piglet, and on the inside I wrote, "Dear Sean, sometimes I wonder, how are you?" Sean tells me now that when he got that card he became very emotional. He wanted to reach back to me but decided he couldn't for many reasons. He had an eight-hour drive that day and said he was sad the entire time. It's hard, knowing that now.

And so, I never heard back from him, but in my heart, I knew why. And I was okay with it . . . I had to be. You see, I loved Sean. I wanted him to be happy and if our friendship got in the way of his happiness, then I felt okay with his choice. But I had no idea it would be over twenty years—twenty long years—before I would see or hear from him again.

My life was anything but easy. I ultimately moved to Nashville, Tennessee to pursue my music career. Before and after, I dated men who I struggled to feel safe with, commit to, or see a future with. Much like the early years of my life, I experienced heartache, more struggle, and a life of uncertainty. Though I traveled the path to living out my life's purpose of becoming a songwriter, I was the furthest I could possibly be from my happy ending, from my love story.

It seemed that by the time I reached my mid-thirties, the men I met were ready to settle down and start a family. My son Chad was my family. Because I was young when he was born, I wasn't interested in starting over again in my mid-30s. I would end any serious relationship because I could not see myself in a new marriage or family, and I was hyper-focused on my career. Dating became zero fun. So, for many years I remained single. I felt fine with my decision, but in the back of my mind loomed the question, *Where is my person?*

One day, I remember feeling like it had been a very long time since I'd heard from Sean. So I sat down and Googled his name. I found it odd that by this time, with Facebook and other social media sites available, I could find no trace of Sean. It scared me. I thought for sure that if he didn't have any social media presence, it meant something had happened to him. I remember the sinking feeling, wondering what if he had died? What if my dearest friend in the whole world had died, and I didn't know it? It had been over twenty years and suddenly I felt sad, very sad. In fact, I tried looking even harder online and struggled to recall the last place I had known he was living and working.

I finally found a number on the internet and I called, thinking, *Melissa that's crazy. He's probably not working at the same place he worked at twenty years ago.* I hung up the phone and didn't leave a message. I distinctly remember tears falling down my face, and I felt an emptiness inside of me that I could not explain. Nor did I question it. For the next few months, I would go in and out of depression, trying not to think about Sean because it hurt. Why suddenly, all of these years later, did I feel a kind of desperation to speak to him when I hadn't in so long?

Little did I know that halfway across America, in northern California, Sean was suffering a loss. And what I had been feeling was that loss. Let me explain.

Not long after those tear-filled days and months spent thinking of Sean, on my 47th birthday, I woke up to an email that exploded my heart with joy. An email that simply said, "Dear Missy, sometimes I wonder how are you?" Exactly what I had written to him in a card over twenty years earlier. I instantly cried tears of relief—he was alive and not just alive, but in my inbox on my birthday! He went on to wish me a happy birthday and tell me that he was traveling and gave me his phone number saying if I had time to give him a call.

I was rushing out the door for an appointment when I opened the email, but I had to reply and let him know that he'd made my day and that I would call him as soon as I got out of my appointment a few hours later. And that's exactly what I did.

Within moments of reconnecting later that day by phone, it felt as if no time had passed. Affinity happens in a single moment and that moment happened for us when we were twelve years old. Though life took us on many ups and downs, we found our way back to that moment all those years later.

You see, Sean lost his wife suddenly, months before reaching out to me. During those months when he was suffering, I was suffering. When I thought maybe he had died and I couldn't understand my sudden urgency to see him, it was because he suffered, and I felt his pain. I only wish I knew it then and could have been a source of comfort to him. But then again, I suppose he needed to mourn the loss of Julie and reach out to me when he felt ready. Because from that day on, we have never been apart again, and we were married nine months later on October 8, 2015.

Life can be bittersweet. Love is a mystery, and for as much as the greatest poets in the world have tried to capture and put it into words, it remains a mystery. I could have beat myself up for not running into Sean's arms back in our early twenties when he professed his love for me and we had a chance to build a family together, but I know now we each had our own journeys to go on.

I never understood the scripture that reads, in part: "love suffers long" in First Corinthians, Chapter 13. I always wondered why love would suffer. Now I understand. Neither of us likes to think about all the years we didn't see, or speak to one another. Nor about the suffering that each of us went through to get to where we are today. But we are eternally grateful to have been given a second chance to spend the rest of our lives together. We now have a condo in Nashville, a beautiful home in Florida, and a vacation home in California with some of our favorite pictures on the wall from when "We Were Twelve."

Be strong, be fearless, be beautiful.
And believe that anything is possible
when you have the right people
there to support you.

~ Misty Copeland

Dr. Ann K Schafer is a Professor Emerita at Sacramento City College, a California Community College. She has published *Ask Dr Ann . . . About Basic Skills and Learning*, a compilation of her articles from the National Literacy Coalition column, "Ask Dr Ann."

She is a licensed clinical psychologist and holds a certification in Neuropsychology from UC Berkeley. She has worked in 3 colleges and for 7 hospitals. Her current book, *The SoulGrowth Solutions*, examines the healing path to wholeness created by an individual's unmet childhood needs. This bio-psycho-social healing program was originally developed by the Italian physician, Dr Roberto Assagioli, under the name Psychosynthesis.

Email: askdranns@yahoo.com
Website: askdoctorann.com

Chapter 21

An Immigrant's Daughter

Dr. Ann K. Schafer

Do the best you can until you know better.
When you know better, do better.

~ Maya Angelou

It took "Little Ann" a long time to figure out why the room went silent when being of German descent was discussed. It wasn't so much the silence, but the essence and energy of the room that changed, almost as if a switch had dimmed, both the lights and the sound. Much later, a more educated and somewhat older, wiser Ann became aware that Germans were apparently not so popular when she was younger and small. And, oh yes! The war came that captured her dad, the war that everyone talked about, and the daddy that was absent at the dinner table.

Following Daddy

During and after World War II, Little Ann was Mommie's good luck charm, her playmate, her daughter, her security blanket, and simply all hers, which included her "parent-in-training" lessons. Daddy was getting ready to go to Germany (what?!) and fight with guns, against the very people he was born to? American soldiers were all very young and barely knew what a gun was, let alone how to fight, other than at home with siblings, or at school with classmates, or on sports teams.

Little Ann curiously found herself in Louisiana with Mom, following Daddy. Little Ann learned a little Cajun ("Ma-Ma! I got a bo-bo.") A very large and sturdy Granny adopted "Toddler Ann," putting orange soda pop in her milk bottle, much to her mom's dismay. Boot camp ended, and Daddy left to fight the Germans. So Toddler Ann went back to Idaho with Mom.

Home to Idaho and Grandma Schafer

It wasn't long before bitter tears fell, as the telegram came reporting that Daddy was MIA (Missing in Action). This frequent message came to many a home and family during World War II. What was worse was the fact that Daddy's brother, Fritz, was also reported MIA and they say that's when Grandma lost her hearing. Mother almost lost her mind and her very soul as she clung to "Little Ann" with an ever-tighter hold. Now, Mother was no stranger to the death of a loved one. Her own mother, Anna Elizabeth, Little Ann's namesake, died quite young, leaving young 11-year-old Bette (Mom) at a most tender age. Mom was one of three girls who all suddenly lost their intelligent, lovely, Swedish beauty of a mother. She died of pneumonia, a condition which today would be treated very simply with penicillin.

As it turned out, Little Ann's father had been captured and imprisoned in a German camp and then released towards the end of the war, thus enabling his return to the family. Little Ann first remembers Daddy in uniform, overjoyed to see his now 3-year-old "Little Ann," whose baby shoe he had carried throughout the war to remind him of his destiny to return.

After the Homecoming

In those days, there was almost no treatment for the rampant Post Traumatic Stress Disorder experienced by returning soldiers. (They called it "shell-shock" in those days.) Little Ann witnessed her grandfather, Ernst, and her father, Conrad, proudly building a tiny bungalow from cinder blocks and mortar. Grandpa, a German mason, knew just what to do. As it turned out, building a house proved easier than finding a job. Again, Grandpa saved the day by opening a Mobil gas station and a small town car repair shop, which then gave his two sons jobs after their return from fighting the war. (Yes, Fritz survived after being captured and released from a prison camp on the island of Guam.) With both of Grandma's boys safely home, only happiness seemed to drive the family engine. There were many good times in Grandma's backyard with her boys, Bette, and Little Ann.

Scholastic Excellence

Little Ann blossomed when she entered Eastside Elementary School. She became the teacher's helper. She could already read, and new words became her best friends and playmates. She was "teacher's pet," a pattern that repeated itself throughout her academic career, which to this day is an ongoing saga. More and more, Little Ann became competent scholastically, and with ease. Her anxiety pattern only emerged from "nervous" habits like nail biting.

Little Ann was again called to take on a parental role after her daddy became, now MIA on the home front. The phone rang in the middle of the night. It seemed Daddy had been drinking, and out of town, when he lost control of his vehicle. At a time prior to seat belts, he was thrown from the car and his pelvis crushed. They took him to the very hospital where his own mother reigned as "Head Nurse"—the same hospital where both Little Ann and her mother were born.

You'll Be Okay

Looking back, how could 5-year-old Little Ann handle being left alone with only a Bible to hold and a promise that the neighbor would watch over her from next door? Not at all well! When Mom left for the hospital, only minutes passed while Little Ann tried to understand what was happening, but that didn't work. So she high-tailed it to the neighbor's back door, trying to keep the proverbial stiff upper lip. (German people do that very well.)

Keeping a "Stiff Upper Lip"

"Keeping a stiff upper lip" became the theme throughout both Little Ann and Bigger Ann's life experiences. Ann sailed through classwork in elementary school. Reading, spelling, writing, and simple math were readily mastered. Ann was, in fact, an only child, with no siblings at home.

When others went home from neighborhood play, they had a family. Ann had a mom, and not much of a dad. Family memories included trips to watch Daddy pitch in softball league games. The tournaments were a "big deal." Mom spent much of her time at the PTA as President, participating in anything having to do with Ann's success at school. This pattern certainly gave Academic Ann the idea that school was important.

Music, in the form of piano lessons, became a pleasant childhood activity and no one ever had to remind Ann to practice her piano. Piano recitals were rigorous and lots of fun, and auditions to review her skills were another "big deal." In between music recitals, Ann learned to roller skate competitively, complete with fancy costumes which her mom happily sewed and ironed perfectly. Earlier in Ann's childhood, Mother made sure Little Ann had performance experience. This came in the form of ballet, tap lessons, and recitals. Mom thought church socials and potlucks were fun for Little Ann. (In spite of the fact that Little Ann really didn't like ice cream.) What Ann liked and craved were the people and the playtime with other kids.

The New Baby

The happiest day of Ann's life was when her mother brought home a little baby sister for the family to play with. This baby turned out to be the sweetest part of being 10 years old! For two years, Ann thought she had the most playful live baby doll ever. She sang to her little sister, played piano for her, and helped her laugh and giggle as much as possible. Finally, Little Ann had a playmate. Then came a fatal moment of darkness to their little homemade bungalow in Idaho. It was as if the world stopped in its tracks, and the sun forgot to shine.

Dark Days Ahead

The dark days began when Little Ann came home from school to find both parents in tears and frozen in shock. Daddy didn't stop staring out of the picture window for days. Mother's eyes were red and puffy as a blowfish. Mother learned that Daddy had been unfaithful. Then our worst nightmare began.

Mother had only learned to drive a car at age 30. Now she needed to get a job away from her children and move us "across the tracks" to the worst part of town. Grandma, always "Head Nurse" somewhere, helped Mother get a job as a switchboard telephone operator at the health facility where Grandma worked. Since Mother had been a telephone operator as a young adult after high school, she remembered how to say, "Number please," in between crying and blowing her nose.

Ann, in so many ways, became the "parentified" kid. From that time on, Pre-Teen Ann took care of her baby sister, in spite of the fact that there was always also a hired babysitter present. However, the babysitters were sometimes truly unattentive. Little Pre-Teen Ann had responsibilities far beyond the levels expected for a 6th or 7th grader. Her mother cried a lot.

Ann worked on memorizing the "stiff upper lip" role. Someone had to be an adult. Mom was an adult, albeit a depressed one. Fear was not helpful or appropriate, so someone needed to be brave. Brave became Ann's job. Ann mentally said, "It's okay; I'm here." Ann cooked, did the dishes, took care of the two-year-old, and never cried or whined about it. Ann learned not to cry when she knew it wouldn't matter if she did. She tried to keep her mom from being so sad, which proved an impossible task, understandably so. Ann's understanding self was precocious. Daddy had left now. This different kind of war took him away. Something happens when the male energy of a daddy leaves the family.

From Grandma Schafer to Grandpa Madding

The next big crisis came when they moved from Idaho to California. They had stayed with Grandpa when Daddy had gone missing in action during World War II. But now Daddy was missing in action, only this time, he wasn't captured by Germans, but by an affair with another woman—who wasn't his wife!

Daddy left for Oregon, and Mom, Ann, and sister Patti left for California. Ann was in the 7th grade when she entered school in the multi-grade Northern California country schoolhouse. She figured out that she was about one scholastic year ahead of her classmates in this country school setting. She became valedictorian of her 8th-grade class but since, in Ann's mind, there was no real competition, it felt like a bit of an empty award.

Life in the Orchard

Living at Grandpa's included an education in fruit tree identification, living in the middle of a large fruit corporation, complete with pear, plum, and peach orchards and fruit packing sheds. This is where "Teen Ann" got her first real job at age 14. Grandpa was the corporate bookkeeper, and that might have influenced the hiring of staff. Ya think?

After the summer job in the packing shed, Ann started high school. She was still babysitting her sister after school, and Mother managed to find the very best switchboard job she could, at a local hotel. Ann cooked for Grandpa, for herself, and for her sister, and she made sure the Mickey Mouse Club played every day for entertainment. It turned out to be the highlight of her day because her sister stayed glued to the TV.

High school was a new world: taking the school bus to town, where the country school gave way to a small-town larger high school, complete with football games, dances, and feeder schools bringing a bigger selection of academic peers. Ann's entertainment centered around classes, books, teachers, interesting classmates, football games, dances, and new friends.

Meanwhile, Mother met a new male companion at her hotel job, and she soon introduced him to the children. He and Mom married and moved the family to town, away from the orchards and Grandpa. Problems began when the stepdad's drinking and smoking became a very toxic environment for Ann. Still, Ann maintained the "stiff upper lip" role. No, she hadn't forgotten how to play that role, and she added the "one foot in front of the other" role to her arsenal. If "stiff upper lip" didn't work, then "one foot in front of the other" usually did . . . with almost anything.

Teen Ann learned that hard work and grit would win in the end, and she simply didn't entertain collapsing into despair and depression. She had seen her mother do that very well. Though Mom's new husband did seem to want to take care of the family, the drinking habit usually got in the way.

Ann didn't fully realize that it was dangerous to ride in a pickup truck with a drunk driver. She didn't fully understand that most kids didn't stop at bars to play bumper pool while their stepdad drank and visited with cronies along each stop on the way home.

When Ann turned 16, she'd had enough of this ugly environment (the stepdad's drinking, smoking, and speaking to Mom in angry tones), so she moved out on her own, even though still in high school. Mom cried. Her stepdad said, "Let her go." Little did Ann know that her sister would feel abandoned.

Steps to Freedom

Her first step to freedom was to rent a room above an elderly lady's garage. She worked at an A&W burger stand, where the trays had to be delivered while wearing roller skates and a short skirt. Her roller-skating competitions paid off because she never dropped a tray, and she got to buy sandwiches at half price. While doing all of this, she kept her grades high enough to be in the California Scholarship Federation.

Teen Ann, a senior, ready to graduate, discovered she was scholarship material. Too bad no one connected the dots to help her do the paperwork needed to fill out college and scholarship applications. No one talked about going to college, except Ann knew the community college was nearby, and she would continue school there. And she did!

Learning Continues

Adult Ann also met a man, got married, and had children, and that's a whole separate story. Through all these new experiences, Ann always knew that learning was her most satisfying life path. Long ago, she knew that leaning over the back fence in the neighborhood to discuss detergent choices was just not enough for her. At all corners turned, education proved to be the saving grace and lifesaving action taken. And yes, Ann kept putting one foot in front of the other. She kept a stiff upper lip. And she also managed to fill her happy cup with music, theater, and the proverbial search for life in a castle with Prince Charming.

Ann did, in fact, achieve a life moving from poverty to living in a castle or two, a ranch, an inn, and a retreat center. She also discovered that the most important daily actions would be to stay curious, to keep learning, and to transform what appears to be negatives into what works best at the moment. She learned that the Cinderella story could only be realized by participating fully in her own successes, and by gathering wisdom from many mentors and wisdom-keepers. She learned that decency, respect, and civility are among the most honorable, non-negotiable, and transformational traits.

Ann put one foot in front of the other long enough to get her Bachelor of Arts degree at UC Davis, her Master of Education at UC Davis, her Ph.D. at Rosebridge Graduate

School of Integrative Psychology, and her Certificate in Neuropsychology at UC Berkeley. She was fortunate to have served as a teacher and a college professor, as well as to have worked in seven hospitals as a clinical psychologist.

She has written over forty articles and three books and is busy with her fourth book and creating an online course. By the way, Dr. Ann has encountered many princes who are quite charming, and some are still attending charm school. Dr. Ann promises to reveal much more complete details in her upcoming memoir, a must-read. Then you will know, as Paul Harvey said, "the rest of the story."

Jessie Haver Butler grew up in Pueblo, Colorado on her father's cattle ranch. She attended Smilth College in New England and was on the front lines of the suffrage movement in Washington D.C. with Carrie Chapman Catt and Alice Paul as the first woman lobbyist in Washington D.C. Before that, she helped set the first minumum wage for women in the U.S. from $4.00 a week to $8.00, and worked tirelessly to stop child labor. In 1911, she helped organize the Pulitzer School of Journalism at Columbia University. She later spoke several times alongside George Bernard Shaw, Eleanor Roosevelt, Gloria Steinem and Marlo Thomas.

You can read more about her in her memoir, *From Cowgirl to Congress - Journey of a Suffragist on the Front Lines*, available on Amazon. She is also featured in the book, *From Parlor to Prison,* and is the author of *Time to Speak Up.*

Website: milajohansen.com/jessie

Chapter 22

The Rest of the Story

From Cowgirl to Congress

Jessie Haver Butler

We do not have to become heroes overnight.
Just a step at a time.

~ Eleanor Roosevelt

Being the first child in our family, born in 1886, there was no one there but my father to help with the process. In that valley of the Arkansas River, near Pueblo, Colorado, the farm area where my father started his ranch, there wasn't a single family whose mother brought up the children. They all died early. There were no midwives, no sinks in the kitchens and no bathrooms. My own mother died when I was ten years old.

My mother, Clara, an educated woman, read everything she could get her hands on. She had strong views on health and believed that no one should eat supper. My brother, Fred, and I, starving by nightfall, took to stealing vegetables from nearby gardens to feed not only ourselves, but our little sister, Emily, and the six ranch hands as well.

In the fourth grade, I invited all the girls in my class to come out one Saturday for a picnic. I persuaded them to take off their clothes and swim naked in the nearby river—just like the boys did. Soon, the willow trees were covered with a rainbow of dresses and petticoats.

All of a sudden, one by one, they felt ashamed and put their clothes back on and hurried home. The following Monday, I found myself treated with noticeable stiffness by all my girl classmates, who, no doubt told their mothers what had happened. Thus, I suffered early in life for trying to reform the members of my sex.

When I related the incident to my mother, she smiled to herself but pointed out that I had taken a serious risk. The river was full of quicksand and deep water holds into which one of us might have fallen. Yet, there lingered more a feeling of satisfaction over having persuaded those girls to dare to do something against their upbringing. Somehow, I knew I had given them an experience they would never forget.

I remember with vivid clarity when the campaign for women's suffrage circled throughout Colorado, how my mother climbed into the spring wagon. Clara toured that valley to urge the men to vote for women's rights. And that wasn't something that a good little housewife, even in Colorado, in those days was supposed to do.

She proved to be a staunch feminist way back then. Of course, it was the same time when the great women's suffrage leader, Susan B. Anthony, spoke all over the state for months. Clara helped women secure the victory for voting rights in 1893. The western women were "wild with joy" when Colorado became the first state to enfranchise women through popular referendum, and it happened over a quarter of a century before the achievement of national women's suffrage in 1920.

My mother possessed an exceptionally good mind. She must have longed for intellectual stimulation. But she soon found herself overwhelmed with the demanding round of household duties, along with the near-constant cycle of pregnancy and childbirth.

With four children to care for, my mother cropped her hair short to her head to make life easier and to keep it out of the way. Much to my dismay, and with many tears, she cut short my beautiful head of hair at the same time. Mother carried on her heavy work without complaint, but I often found her in despair.

Mother must have been exhausted most of the time, but she never stopped working. How could she? Too much depended upon her.

Like most housewives, Clara did the cooking, baking, and churning; washing and ironing; sewing and darning. She scrubbed floors, cared for four young children, and fed six hired hands—all in a house lit by kerosene lamps, heated by stoves, and without running water. Every drop of water had to be pumped from the well or carried in from the irrigation ditch. In addition to all this, she raised chickens and sold eggs to earn spending money for the house.

She must have been very lonely for the companionship of women her own age. There were no cars, no telephones, and no radios to break the monotony of those long days. Mother made me her confidante. I know now that she must have felt trapped, with the ever-present threat of pregnancy and the never-ending workload.

But the real trap became psychological in nature. Her frustration caused by her inability to continue her intellectual interests fueled the bitterness she felt and explained her almost fanatical determination that I should be spared "her fate," as she called it. She planned for me to have an education, which would fit me for something "better than the kitchen of some man's house." As I grew older, she used to talk to me about this more and more.

I didn't believe the doctor when he told me my mother was gone. My father said she had taken carbolic acid, mistaking it for peppermint oil. But I never heard her go downstairs to the cupboard where it was kept and became suspicious that my father lied about her death. I heard a terrible argument between them earlier that night. My mother and I returned late in the day after hearing Susan B. Anthony speak from the back of a wagon in Pueblo, and my father was upset.

I remember that day so well, because as I looked up into the face of Susan B. Anthony, I made a silent declaration. I wanted to grow up and help women gain the same rights as men and inspire them to live their dreams. My own mother, Clara, climbed into the Spring wagon and traveled around the countryside persuading the men to vote for women's rights. Colorado gave women the right to vote in 1893. The 2nd state to do so, with Wyoming being the first in 1869.

I became afraid of my father and feeling frightened and confused, I ran away. I followed the railroad tracks until I found a hobo man heating up a can of beans over an open fire. With a friendly face, he offered to share his meager meal with me. Being famished, I accepted. After many questions, he insisted I return home and he accompanied me. My father met us at the front door pointing a rifle at the man and told him if he ever returned, he would shoot and bury him.

The man did return some months later, on his way back through Pueblo, to check on how I was doing. When I went into the kitchen to get him some food, he and my father disappeared. Later, Father said the man was in a hurry to meet the train and had rushed off. A pit in my stomach told me that again, my father could be lying.

From then on, I avoided being alone with my father as much as possible. He remarried and they birthed a son. But, as it happened to many women on the prairie, my new mother became mentally disturbed, locking herself and my little brother in the upstairs bedroom, leaving me and my sister, Emily, with all the cooking and cleaning.

Then in high school, a teacher came along who helped me get into Smith College in New England. Just before I was to leave by train for the East Coast, my stepmother committed suicide. My father wanted me to stay home to keep house and feed the ranch hands, but Miss Mumford insisted that if I stayed, I would be dead within the year from the extensive workload.

I attended Smith College, in 1906 for two years, where I got plenty to eat and wore pretty clothes. I reveled in the fact that I no longer had to do any cooking or housework. I did, however, feel twinges of guilt for my good fortune as I passed the silk stocking factory next door. I suffered as I watched the women and children walking to work on those icy mornings in their tattered sweaters and holey shoes.

I found my first job after Smith College working for the Macmillan Publishing House in New York City, but I couldn't leave well enough alone and spoke out against the long hours and low pay for the women working there and lost my position.

For my next job in 1911, I helped put together the new Pulitzer School of Journalism with Professor John Cunnliffe, which proved to be a much better paying situation. But when the program opened and was taken over by Talcott Williams, a hardened newspaperman, I again found myself complaining about long hours late into the night. Mr. Williams conceded, and it turned out that I lasted longer than any other secretary who ever worked for him.

I soon found myself hired by the Minimum Wage Commission in Boston. I was sent to the same hosiery factory next door to Smith College to inspect the wages and working conditions. We changed the minimum wage from $4.00 a week to $8.00 and worked hard to get child laborers out of the factories.

Another opportunity took me to Washington D.C. where I joined the women's suffrage movement. I became the first women lobbyist at the capitol when hired to work for the Washington D.C. Minimum Wage Commission and set the same minimum wage for women across the entire country. I took on senators who told me I should be home keeping house and having babies.

Finally, a model Minimum Wage Bill for the District (providing mandatory penalties for offenders) was introduced and referred to the District committees of both the Senate and the House.

The chairman of the District Committee of the House, Congressman Ben Johnson of Kentucky, was known to be a stubborn old gentleman where women were concerned. He used to badger the women lobbying for suffrage by shouting to them to go back to their homes where they belonged.

He remained the bane of the citizens of Washington, for he seemed to delight in killing anything new or progressive or humane. If he opposed some legislation, it was as good as dead.

"What are you going to do about Ben Johnson?" Josephine Goldmark asked one day. "You know he has to be seen. In his position, he can easily kill the bill. He will be delighted to do just that because the bill would help women who work in laundries and stores to get a decent living wage. He thinks they should all be at home taking care of their families!" I relied on implicit faith that Congress would help us once I pointed out the need.

Finally, the day arrived when Congressman Johnson had to be interviewed. The day came, hot and sultry, when I arrived at his office, clad in a bright red-and-white checked gingham dress, freshly starched with a frilled ruffle down the front.

No one occupied the outer office, but the door to the inner office stood wide open. So, in I sailed, with chills rippling down my back in spite of the heat. There he sat at his desk looking like an old bear as he glanced up and scowled at me.

"Good morning, Congressman," I said in a sweet and respectful voice.

"What do you want?" he roared.

A powerfully built gentleman, he stood six feet, two inches in height, with a handsome large head and a great mane of graying curly hair.

Prior to this visit, I had spent hours in the gallery of the House watching him in action. A man of force and character, who, when he believed in a bill, he could fight for it with such oratorical skill and wire-pulling as few men possessed.

Timidly I replied, "I just came to see you about the Minimum Wage Bill for the District, which has been referred to your committee." I shook, scared to death.

"What are you doing here?" he bellowed at me. "Why aren't you home having babies, where you belong?"

A heavy silence permeated the room. The fate of our bill hung on my reply. That I knew.

"Well, you see, Congressman, it's very awkward," I heard myself saying as if I were someone else talking. "It is customary to have a husband to have babies."

"Well, why don't you get a husband?" he asked.

"All the best men are married! What am I to do?"

At that he threw back his head and roared with laughter.

"That's tough," he said. "I'll have to help you."

"Yes, I need help."

"Now what is it you want me to do?"

Taking a deep breath, I began to speak: "We need you to set a date for a public hearing on this Minimum Wage Bill so that women in laundries and stores can receive a decent living wage. The District Consumers League wants you to help us get this bill through Congress."

I told him that Mr. Filene, who would speak at the hearing, had won glory for Massachusetts by being the first store owner to pay his employees a minimum wage of eight dollars a week instead of four.

"There will be a lot of front-page publicity for you too, if you'll help us on this bill. There is a great deal of interest in this subject among employers of women in the District." I hurried on to get in all the important points while I had his ear.

"Who's against it?"

"No one so far. If Mr. Filene speaks, I doubt there will be any opposition because he has such a high standing among employers. He founded the National and International Chambers of Commerce too, so businessmen respect him and his ideas."

"What do you do to have fun?" he asked suddenly.

Here was another moment weighted with heavy potential for my cause!

"I go swimming and canoeing all the time I can get," I replied.

His eyes lit up with pleasure. Then he proceeded to spend nearly thirty minutes telling me of his swimming experiences in his home state when he was a boy. He proved human after all and seemed glad to turn from the complicated problems, which must have weighed heavily on his mind. He stopped his reminiscing and asked, "When do you want the hearing on this bill?"

I suggested a date, which he put on his calendar. Then I departed, after thanking him for his interest and cooperation.

The bill passed the House in less than six months, with little opposition. The next day, I ran into Congressman Johnson in the hall and thanked him personally for what he had done.

"That's all right," he said. "It was a real pleasure to work for the Minimum Wage Bill. Just call on me any time you want something done. You know, I have a lot of influence around here."

I began going to Alice Paul's place. She and I were born in the same year—1886. Alice, a Quaker from a prominent family, had a PhD from the London School of Economics, where she learned her militant methods from Emmeline Pankhurst. Alice became the leader of the National Woman's Party. She had been given a lot of money by Mrs. O. H. P. Belmont and organized a lovely house as her headquarters right on the edge of Lafayette Park, across from the White House. There was a big dining room, and I took a great many of my luncheons there, even while I was working in the U.S. Bureau of Labor Statistics, and that's where I met all those women. They were my intimate friends.

One of the leading pickets, Mrs. Harvey Wiley, later became one of the women who attended my first class in public speaking when I returned to Washington after eight years in London.

I dined daily with Alice Paul and shared the lecture podium with Carrie Chapman Catt who invited me along on a cross country speaking tour. We waged a hard fight to win the right to vote on August 18, 1920. President Wilson finally came to our side in 1918 after Alice Paul burned his speeches on the White House lawn, but the amendment lost by two votes and we waited another two years for it to pass. Alice Paul tried to get me to join her militant group, but instead I chose Mrs. Catt who believed in parliamentary procedure. I believe that without both women fighting, each in their own way, women may have not got the right to vote in 1920. England didn't give women the right to vote until 1928 and believe it or not, in Switzerland, not until 1971.

Most people do not realize women received the right to vote in 16 states before 1920—including black women, who were allowed to vote in many of the Western and Northern states.

I began attending the hearings held in the Capitol on the Meatpackers Association who commanded a monopoly on meat sales. I knew, firsthand, what these ruthless thugs were doing because a few years prior, my own father was run out of the cattle business by them. He loaded his cattle into train cars that would take the beef from Pueblo, Colorado to the killing yards in Kansas. My father was promised a fair market price, but when the cattle arrived, the cattle barons dropped the price so low that he wouldn't make a profit. He had no choice because the price to return the cattle was extremely prohibitive. The next year, the entire herd wandered into quicksand in the Arkansas River and perished. My father went into selling real estate.

No major newspaper would report this injustice due to the huge ads the meatpackers paid for and took out each day. So I hurried down to the Christian Science Monitor office where a friend worked and gave her the reports I had written each day, in the perfect journalistic form taught at Columbia.

The news soon got out and President Wilson passed a bill against the monopoly. I am certain if the Chicago meatpackers knew who had gotten the information out to the public, my life would have been in great danger.

During the suffrage struggle, I met my future husband, Hugh Butler, who I assumed was just a platonic friend. Together, we started a new phenomenon due to the housing shortage during World War I. We put together the first coed housing in the city, which raised plenty of eyebrows. We hired a cook and housekeeper and dined together each evening vigorously discussing politics. On the weekends, we all canoed up the Potomac River.

The suffrage struggle stalled and met with impossible odds, but all of us women persisted with the bravery of men marching off to war. In the end, the final decision hinged on one man's vote—young Harry Burn, a member of the Tennessee legislature. He broke the tie by voting "for" instead of "against" as the other legislators expected him to do. Men rushed up to him, thumped him on the back and told him he had made a mistake. Whereupon he pulled out of his pocket a letter from his mother who told him to "Vote for suffrage!" And that's what he did. In the end, it was a humble woman living in the mountains of Tennessee who gave seventeen million women the right to vote.

Back in D.C., I arranged with Poli's theatre for Carrie Chapman Catt and the other women to speak. Flowers poured in and the theater filled for the long-awaited celebration! One sad note that day—Mrs. Catt respectfully refused to share the podium with her adversary, Alice Paul. The militants were left out of the celebration and that I did not agree with. But, because they were left out, they held their own meeting in Alice Paul's place across the street from the White House. They sat up late into the night and created The Equal Rights Amendment that we all know of today.

The only problem, after this great success, was Hugh's mother, a famous Christian Science practitioner from Chicago. She became afraid that I would interfere with her plans for her son never to marry. She expected Hugh to live with her the rest of his life. One day, I returned from a canoeing trip to find her installed in one of the bedrooms of our coed home. All the other boarders vacated upon her arrival, leaving Hugh and me to deal with the intruder. I left too. Hugh soon became frantic and asked me to accompany him to his new job at the American Embassy in London . . . as his wife. His mother fully expected him to invite her to go with him. In one last desperate attempt to keep her son tethered to her, Mrs. Butler confessed to me that Hugh had been immaculately conceived. I laughed. Hugh and I were secretly married and on our way to England on the celebrated Christmas ship, The Aquitania.

We lived in England for eight years. We attended the Fabian Summer School and met George Bernard Shaw. A confirmed teetotaler and a vegetarian, he invited me to share the podium with him several times on the subject of prohibition. He named my lecture "Alcohol is Just Like Murder."

I met my lifetime friend, Lady Astor, an American from Virginia, who became the first woman to sit in Parliament, a position she held for 28 years. She spoke out for women, children and laborers. When I finally returned to the U.S. we wrote back and forth, across the pond, for two decades. Nancy Astor wrote the foreword to my book, *Time to Speak Up*.

Hugh and I were presented at the Court of St James's in 1928 and met Queen Mary at the following Garden Party where I influenced her, and an article, in the London Times, came out two days later on the subject.

We had our two children, Rosemary and Richard, while living in London. Hugh's mother came for a visit and again tried to take over our household by faking a sickness and remaining in bed, refusing to leave. We finally found a way to send her packing back to Chicago . . . for good.

I attended four important funerals while in London: Mrs. H.G. Wells alongside Bernard Shaw and her husband, Emmeline Pankhurst, Isadora Duncan and Dame Alice Ellen Terry.

After eight years, we returned to Washington D.C. Jobs were scarce right before the 2nd World War, but Hugh finally received a commission in 1935, from Franklin D. Roosevelt, to head up the new Social Security Program. I began teaching public speaking classes to women, which Eleanor Roosevelt endorsed by speaking at the opening of each session. She often invited me and my students to rehearse speeches at the White House.

I attended Georgetown University and received a degree in Public Speaking, which led to my book, *Time to Speak Up*. Because of my book, I was invited to speak and teach all over the country to auditoriums filled with 200 to 2,000 attendees. My book sold like hotcakes.

I continued my speaking career into my early nineties when I was invited several times to share the podium with Gloria Steinem and Marlo Thomas as the elder suffragist.

So, a badly dressed, drab young girl, with a tragic childhood, made her escape from the dusty fields of Colorado to experience the front lines of many of the historic events that shaped the future of women in America and subsequently, the world. *Women voting anywhere promotes women voting everywhere.*

Made in United States
Orlando, FL
12 November 2022

24444581R10214